PRAISE FOR *BECOMING DR. Q*

"This is a spellbinding story of a champion who harnessed the power of passion and dogged determination to triumph over adversity. Be prepared to laugh, cry, and come away enlightened not just about the human brain and its miraculous capacities but also about the human heart."

Venus Williams, author of *Come to Win*

"Ever since I first heard Dr. Q's story, my main question was: how does a migrant farm worker with no money and no English overcome the odds and pursue his aspirations at the highest levels of the medical field? Wow—not only is it the stuff of which fairy tales and Hollywood movies are made, but it's also a much-needed prescription for the soul."

Chris Gardner, author of *The Pursuit of Happyness*

"The life of Dr. Q is a testament to the power of poverty to motivate social ascent, the power of intellectual prowess to scale academia's heights, and the power of altruism to give back, through the most highly developed medical treatment and the creation of new knowledge, through mentoring the next generation, and through his own unique family."

Joe L. Martinez Jr., professor of neurobiology, University of California at Berkeley

"Quite simply, Dr. Q is a hero to many people in the Hispanic community. He went from the farm fields in California to the most advanced operating rooms in the country. He earned $3.35 an hour cultivating tomatoes and chili peppers in the San Joaquin Valley. What makes his journey unique is that the same hands that picked vegetables are now touching the brains of his patients and saving lives. I can't think of a better example of what an immigrant with ambition and dedication can do in this great country of opportunities. He is, no doubt, a real hero."

Jorge Ramos, senior news anchor, *Univision News*

"I used to think that Superman was an American who went by the name Clark Kent. Now I know that he is a Mexican American who goes by the name Dr. Q. Read this book to believe it."

Katrina Firlik, MD, author of *Another Day in the Frontal Lobe: A Brain Surgeon Exposes Life on the Inside*

"This is a poignant and timely story that needs to be told. Dr. Q is a heroic and resilient man, whose odyssey should make it more difficult for pundits and others to demonize immigrants from Mexico and Central America."

Paul R. Linde, MD, author of *Danger to Self: On the Front Line with an ER Psychiatrist*

"Even as a little kid, Dr. Q dreamed really big dreams, and no matter what the obstacles, he never gave up. I know firsthand that if you don't dream it, you can't become it. Now as a man, not only has he become it, but even more important, he is helping others to realize their dreams. Young people around the world will identify with and be motivated by Dr. Q's story. This book is a slam dunk! Rock on, Dr. Q!"

Jason McElwain, author of *The Game of My Life*

Becoming Dr. Q

 A NAOMI SCHNEIDER BOOK

Highlighting the lives and experiences of marginalized communities, the select titles of this imprint draw from sociology, anthropology, law, and history, as well as from the traditions of journalism and advocacy, to reassess mainstream history and promote unconventional thinking about contemporary social and political issues. Their authors share the passion, commitment, and creativity of Executive Editor Naomi Schneider.

Becoming Dr. Q

MY JOURNEY FROM MIGRANT
FARM WORKER TO BRAIN SURGEON

ALFREDO QUIÑONES-HINOJOSA, MD
With Mim Eichler Rivas

UNIVERSITY OF CALIFORNIA PRESS
Berkeley   Los Angeles

University of California Press, one of the most distinguished
university presses in the United States, enriches lives around the
world by advancing scholarship in the humanities, social sciences,
and natural sciences. Its activities are supported by the UC Press
Foundation and by philanthropic contributions from individuals
and institutions. For more information, visit www.ucpress.edu.

University of California Press
Berkeley and Los Angeles, California

© 2011 by Alfredo Quiñones-Hinojosa

Library of Congress Cataloging-in-Publication Data

Quiñones-Hinojosa, Alfredo.
    Becoming Dr. Q : my journey from migrant farm worker to brain
surgeon / Alfredo Quiñones-Hinojosa ; with Mim Eichler Rivas.
    p. ; cm.
    ISBN 978-0-520-27118-0 (cloth : alk. paper)
    1. Quiñones-Hinojosa, Alfredo.   2. Neurosurgeons—Mexico—
Biography.   3. Mexican Americans—Mexico—Biography.
4. Transients and Migrants—Mexico—Biography.   I. Rivas, Mim
Eichler.   II. Title.
    [DNLM: 1. Quiñones-Hinojosa, Alfredo.   2. Neurosurgery—
Mexico—Autobiography.   3. Neurosurgery—United States—
Autobiography.   4. Mexican Americans—Mexico—Autobiography.
5. Mexican Americans—United States—Autobiography.   6. Transients
and Migrants—Mexico—Autobiography.   7. Transients and
Migrants—United States—Autobiography. WZ 100]
    RD592.9.Q46A3   2011
    617.092—dc22
    [B]   2011011531

Manufactured in the United States of America

20   19   18   17   16   15   14   13   12   11
10   9   8   7   6   5   4   3   2

The paper used in this publication meets the minimum requirements
of ANSI/NISO Z39.48–1992 (R 1997) (Permanence of Paper).

In loving memory of my sister Maricela

Contents

Prologue

"Is this the neurosurgeon on call?"

The urgent words set my heart racing as I picked up the line from the San Francisco General Hospital emergency room at the beginning of a night shift in June 1999.

"Yes, this is Dr. Quiñones-Hinojosa," I replied formally. Then I quickly amended my answer, offering the nickname given to me in medical school. "This is Dr. Q. How can I help?"

"An ambulance will be arriving any second, bringing in a patient with a gunshot wound to the head who needs immediate attention!"

"On my way!" Springing into motion, I sped down the hallway of the hospital—still new territory to me since I'd arrived only a few days earlier, fresh from Harvard Medical School, to begin an internship and residency in neurosurgery at the University of California, San Francisco. For my first night as the on-call neurosurgery intern, I was green enough to wonder if someone had made a mistake in assigning this crisis to me. A gunshot wound to the head?

Though I'd been given a preview of the demands placed on residents at SFGH—the only Level I trauma hospital in the Bay Area and one of the busiest in the nation—little in my academic training had prepared me for the war zone atmosphere of trauma services. Fear gripped me as I ran down the stairs and then through the corridor leading to the emergency room.

Alfredo, get hold of yourself, I thought. But there was nothing of myself to hold on to! The faster I tried to fly down the hall, the more my breathing accelerated, the slower my footsteps fell. My head felt disembodied, as though floating in the air above me. Sweating heavily, my heart pumping wildly, I struggled for balance, certain that I was about to collapse on the floor—right here in the hallways of this magnificent building and institution.

From outside the hospital on that gloomy summer night came the sounds of police sirens, honking horns, and distant voices echoing down dark streets. No music, no order—only chaos. A feeling of powerlessness washed over me as I approached the emergency room. Who was I attempting to fool? Why not admit my fear, turn around, and dash off in a different direction? Other questions countered these thoughts. Was I ready to give up? Was I going to let terror of the unknown win this battle without a fight? Or could I accept my fear as a familiar foe—as I had for most of my thirty-one years—and struggle even harder to find a way back onto solid ground?

The answer was clear. I composed myself, pushed through the staff door into the emergency room, and strode to Trauma Zone I, Bay 2, where the members of the trauma team were finishing up their evaluation of the patient. As I moved toward the partitioned space where the patient lay with feet toward me, I saw that he was a young African-American man, in his late teens or early twenties. On further approach, I observed that the yellow transport table underneath him—used by paramedics to bring in highly injured patients—was drenched with blood and gray matter.

A wave of nausea and dread hit me hard. The room began to spin. But I moved closer to assess the damage, fighting the feeling that I was descending into quicksand. When I reached his immobile body on the transport table, I slowly knelt down next to his head—where I could see that part of his skull was missing. Peering more closely, I was jolted by an unforgettable and shocking sight: a tunnel through his head with a bright white light glaring at the end of it.

My God, I thought, *how can this be?* Then my answer came. The light was from the X-ray box secured on the counter on the other side of the patient! The light at the end of the tunnel was no metaphor for a patient whose life hangs in the balance, but in fact this patient's real condition—defined by an actual tunnel in his head through which a bright white light blazed from a source outside of him.

Rocked off balance again, my knees buckling, I felt for the floor to steady myself, seeking a semblance of terra firma. But to my surprise, I found my grounding force not in the physical support under me but in an arsenal of memories that suddenly surfaced. A memory I had once tried to forget overshadowed the rest: an image of me at the bottom of a dark abyss, battling death, holding fast to the sight of my own light at the end of a tunnel, in need of a miracle.

That image arrested my freefall, and in a surge of faith, I recalled the years of my education and the life lessons that had prepared me to face other crises. Memories arose to remind me of the courageous doctors and caregivers who had inspired me to choose medicine. Courage, I remembered, was not an absence of fear but a refusal to give up, especially in the face of great fear. Within seconds, I found my footing and my voice. With the past guiding me, I was able to take command of the situation and provide direction to the members of the trauma team so that we could fight for our patient—whose life was steadily bleeding from him on the table in front of us.

More than a decade has passed since my first night on call at San Francisco General Hospital, although I frequently think back to that profound experience and reflect on what it taught me about the power of memory. The simple awareness that came to me then, and which I carry with me every day, is that I have been that patient myself, on the same yellow table, literally and figuratively.

And if not for those who refused to give up on me, I wouldn't be alive today. That's why I can never give up on any patient without engaging in the same kind of battle that saved my life. It's also why I never forget how blessed I am to be here and why, whenever I prepare to step foot in the operating room, I pause to remember other times and places when I've stood on the threshold of uncertainty. My ritual, as I lather my hands and vigorously scrub up and down my arms, is to use the time to super-charge myself with the extra volt of energy needed to benefit a patient; to concentrate, meditate, and appreciate the gift that is life. In order to walk toward the operating table with certitude that I will make the best possible decisions in this life-or-death setting, I need the confidence that comes from everything I've learned about our miraculous human capac-ity to defy the worst odds.

Yet, as I regularly tell my students, there's a fine line between confi-dence and arrogance! When walking that line in the OR, it's also impor-tant to place my feet on solid ground, firm in the knowledge that I can't control everything, and in the reality that I am only human. This was another lesson I learned on that night in June 1999, staring at the light at the end of the tunnel through the brain of a critically injured patient at San Francisco General Hospital.

In the final hours of his life, my patient was a reminder of the uni-versal lesson that we human beings are more alike and more connected to one another than we tend to acknowledge. Take away the boundar-ies of language, culture, ethnicity, and background, go below different skin colors, and you'll find that under the bone casing of our skulls, we each have a brain that is fundamentally the same as the brain of every other human being in the world. The most beautiful organ in the human body, our brain is the storehouse of our individual identities, our unique thoughts and feelings—yet its gray matter shines the same in everyone. Peel away the dura, the velvet-smooth covering of the brain, and we discover that we all have similar treasure chests of memories, similar capacities to stargaze at the night sky, and similar human aspirations to "live well and prosper"—as the great *Star Trek* saying goes.

My dying patient—I still recall the stark beauty of his emerald green eyes against his dark brown skin—would never be able to tell me about his life's journey, but I tried to imagine what his hopes and dreams had been. Somewhere outside the hospital, I knew, he had family, friends, and loved ones who were waiting desperately for news, fearing the worst.

In those days, we didn't refer to unidentified patients as John Doe or Jane Doe; instead, we assigned them the first name "Trauma" and the last name of whatever letter of the alphabet was available. My patient that night was assigned the name "Trauma Zulu." Though I never learned anything else about him, I've always felt a connection to Trauma Zulu. His memory gives me courage every time an emergency call comes in, and his story, which will for the most part remain untold, is one of the reasons I chose to write this book—as a means of paying tribute to him and to all my patients, who are not only among my best teachers and true heroes but who have given my story its purpose.

In early 2005, I placed a rose on the grave of one of the people I was never able to thank for saving my life and helping me make my way to terra firma. On that occasion, I made a promise to myself that whenever I told my story, I would pay homage to him. I could never have become Dr. Q without co-workers like him and without my family members, friends, colleagues, staff, mentors, students, patients, and loved ones. Each one of them is woven into the fabric of who I am. And this story wouldn't be worth telling if not for my wife, Anna, and my three children, Gabriella, David, and Olivia—who have inspired me to take this journey of hope and imagination with you now.

PART ONE Stargazing

A bright white light, circular in shape, looms high above me at the top of what appears to be a tall, dark tunnel. My mind races, trying to backtrack and remember how I came to be lying at the bottom of this railway tanker, gasping for want of oxygen, fighting to stay conscious, staring at the light high above me.

Facts present themselves first. I know that I'm twenty-one years old, the first-born son of Sostenes and Flavia Quiñones. I know that ten minutes earlier—on an otherwise typical Friday morning at the remote industrial site where I am employed by California Railcar Repair as a welder, painter, and driver—I was at the top of this tunnel, looking down.

The accident happened without warning, as I went about my business of supervising the removal of the heavy round lids from the huge pressurized tankers. With my number two man, Pablo, I headed up the crew responsible not only for removing the lids but then operating the equipment needed to get them into the hanger area for restoration and repair. Earlier on this day, like any other day, just before our lunch break I had approached one of the railway cars with Pablo following behind me and climbed speedily up the exterior ladder to the top of the tanker. Despite the weight of my Red Wing steel-toed boots and the tools in the pockets of my coveralls, I strode briskly along the narrow walkway to the mid-point where the pressurized lid was bolted tightly to the massive tank—which had last carried thirty-five thousand gallons of liquefied petroleum gas. Though the tank was supposed to be empty, we knew from removing hundreds of these lids to expect residual fumes once we undid the safety valves. Since we wore no protective masks, we were also accustomed to the smell—reminiscent of a gas leak from a stove.

Pablo, in his midforties, moved behind me at a slower pace. When he reached my side, the two of us began methodically undoing the valves and then loosening and removing a series of nuts and bolts so that we could finally lift and slide the hefty lid away from the one-and-a-half-foot-diameter hole it covered. With Pablo's unruffled manner and my youthful energy, we made an efficient team. Not a big guy, Pablo was still in excellent shape, although I was the muscle man when it came to lifting the lids. My family joked that this was my "Rambo period." Well, between my own workout regimen and conditioning on the job, I was at an optimal level of fitness—a lean and mean 138 pounds. Actually, at times this led me to underestimate certain physical challenges.

Such was the case on this day. After moving the lid to the side, still holding a wrench in one hand, I started to gather up the valves, nuts, and bolts we had just removed—each a valuable piece to be restored—when one of the metal nuts fell into the hole and tumbled to the bottom of the tank. Why it fell, I didn't stop to think, but I wasted no time deciding to use a rope to shimmy down and retrieve it. A quick fix, I thought.

Pablo watched me tie the rope to a railing beside us and grab onto it as I prepared to squeeze into the hole and shimmy down the eighteen-foot drop to the bottom of the tanker.

"No, Freddy," Pablo said abruptly, looking worried. "It's too dangerous."

"No problem, it will just take me a second." I gripped the rope and took the plunge.

Almost halfway down, the petroleum fumes hit me like a sledgehammer—stirring up nausea, dizziness, and disorientation. It hadn't yet dawned on me that I was headed for no-man's-land. But as I dropped to the bottom and grabbed the fallen nut, feeling victorious for a split second, and then started to climb back up the rope, I realized with a sinking sick feeling that there was no oxygen down here.

This was where I was—just before briefly losing consciousness—when I first glanced up and saw the bright white light at the end of the tunnel.

This is where I am now, conscious once more, straining not to black out again, opening my eyes wide as I connect to that light and to the shadowy shape at the center of it, which I now discern is Pablo's face peering down at me. I suddenly realize with blazing clarity that if I wait for help, I'll die; the only way out is to climb back up on my own. Wasting no time, I grab the rope with both hands and with supreme effort, pull myself up, feeling like I'm lifting a derailed freight train, rising only a foot from the bottom.

"Pablo!" I shout as loudly as possible but hear my voice only as a distant whisper, as in a nightmare. Afraid of what my loss of hearing might mean, I climb harder and faster. But without oxygen, I am like a man underwater: the faster the seconds pass, the heavier my body becomes, and the slower time moves in this well of absolute silence—a deafening sound, both terrifying and mesmerizing.

With gravity pulling me down toward the void, I battle back harder, climb another foot, and intensify my focus upward on the light and on Pablo's face.

"HELP!" I hear him shout as though he is at a great distance but with fierce urgency and in English, a language he barely knows, signaling the peril I'm in and jolting me into climbing even faster.

Everything is chaos. The harder I push and the higher I climb, the heavier and heavier my body feels, weighted impossibly by my gear. Fear sends shockwaves to my brain: if I let go, I die. The voice of logic taunts me: "You can't get out of here alive. Nobody could!"

But another inner voice pushes me on, forcing my muscles to keep climbing, my senses to stay alert.

Halfway up the rope, I see Pablo with his mouth open screaming "HELP!" a second time.

To my horror, I can no longer hear him. Like a dreamer observing himself within a dream, I understand that losing my ability to hear is the beginning of the end, a descent into permanent sleep. Unwilling to give in to that possibility, I keep going, holding on fiercely to the belief that I can make it. Taunts of "you can't" and "who do you think you are?" have never stopped me before, so why should they now?

As I climb, hand over hand, inch by inch, I have only one reality: If I'm going to die in this tank, I will not go without a fight, not without giving it everything in me.

And yet, more exhausted than I've ever been in my life, I fight an overwhelming temptation to rest — if only for a moment. My mind plays tricks on me, lulling me into a false sense of security that lets me think I'm out of danger and can take a break. But I battle back and dig into previously untapped energy reserves, climbing as though swimming up the side of a tidal wave.

With only five or six feet to go, I watch Pablo call "HELP!" for a third time. Again, I can only see him dimly and I still can't hear him, even at close range. A disastrous sign. If my hearing is gone and my vision's about to go too, what's next? Will my lungs give out and my heart stop beating? Have I given my all and come up short? Am I done?

From the depths of my most primitive self, a place of last resort, a survival mechanism kicks in, giving me just enough energy to scale the final few feet of rope. Everything is now slow motion, every move a gargantuan effort. The view in front of me starts to slow into separate images, like still shots in a movie being run frame by frame. Pictures of past, present, and future — people, places, dreams, and fears — unfold in front of my eyes and then begin to fade.

Very close to the top, I watch with strange detachment as the last images disappear, thinking only how ironic it is that the story of my life will end here today. So many possibilities, no longer in sight. How sad that all my efforts will come to nothing. What a heartbreak for my parents, after all their sacrifices, to lose another child — this time their firstborn.

With only three feet more to go, through blurred vision and literally at the end of my rope, I recognize Pablo's hand, outstretched toward mine.

Unbeknownst to me, when Pablo's three calls for help rang out, they had alerted my father, Sostenes Quiñones Ponce, who was employed as a janitor in the shop where we did our restoration work. Also unbeknownst to me is that earlier this morning, Papá hadn't been able to shake a dark premonition that something wasn't right and that it somehow involved me.

This is why the instant my father heard Pablo calling from the tracks, he knew that I was in trouble and came running at lightning speed. Not waiting to find out what has happened, Papá now sprints up the ladder to the top of the tanker *in the same moment that I'm reaching for Pablo's hand. Others, responding to the commotion, follow close behind as my father—screaming and crying my name—flies toward Pablo. One of my co-workers sinks to his knees beside the tracks and begins praying loudly to God to spare my life.*

None of this enters my awareness, which has narrowed to a singular focus: Pablo's outstretched hand. Time has slowed almost to a standstill, and fractions of seconds feel like eons coming to a close, life winding down to its final heartbeats. And as I'm about to clasp the hand of my co-worker, I feel the presence of my grandparents, no longer living, waiting to welcome me, as always.

So relieved, so happy, I summon a final molecule of energy and grab Pablo's hand—with an intensity he'll later describe as having the force of ten men. The hardest part comes next—to accept that the only path through the darkness is to surrender, to know that I've done all that is within my power. I surrender to faith, putting my life in the hands of others. I let go all effort, all resistance, releasing my grip from the rope and from Pablo's hand, giving in to the pull of gravity and relinquishing consciousness.

Pablo later told me that when I took his hand in mine, he thought first that I was going to crush it and then that I seemed to be shaking it good-bye. On my face, he noted a "tender" smile that he would never forget—like the smile of a child who has just drifted off to sleep.

But at this moment my father is rushing with superhuman powers to the top of the tanker, knowing that Pablo can't hold me much longer. He's three steps away when the dead weight becomes too much for Pablo and I slip out of his grasp.

Deep in my psyche, I register a feeling of falling slowly, everything encased in darkness. Falling, falling, falling.

Outside, where the bright white light at the end of the tunnel was, Papá has taken his last two strides, arriving at Pablo's side in time to hear the loud thud of my seemingly lifeless body landing at the bottom of the tank.

ONE Starry Nights

During the many minutes when I lay at the bottom of the tank without oxygen, struggling on the battlefield between life and death, there was something about the image of being on my back, enclosed in darkness and staring up at the light, that connected me powerfully to my childhood years. Indeed, whenever I travel back along memory's narrow pathways that lead to the furthest past, the familiar, starry night sky is the first image that rises to welcome me home.

There in the outskirts of the tiny village of Palaco where I was raised, in the northern part of Mexico's Baja peninsula, I spent many of the hotter nights of the year up on the roof of our little house. I would often lie awake for hours studying the infinite expanse of blackest outer space—everything lit by a glowing moon and millions of bright, sparkling, dancing stars. It was there, underneath the panoramic dome, that many of life's most pressing questions were first planted in my imagination—and where my high level of curiosity and hunger for adventure were cultivated. Under the stars, I could also find relief from the weight of daily concerns and from other worries whenever sadness or sudden misfortune struck.

Such was the nature of my earliest, clearest memory, which was of an event that took place when I was three years old. The trauma had to do with one of my siblings, my baby sister Maricela, whom I would always remember for her big brown laughing eyes and her round, chubby, smiling face. Suddenly, when I came home from playing one morning, she was nowhere to be found.

At the time, we lived in the two back rooms of my father's gas station. When I walked into the kitchen area of our living quarters that morning, I felt terrible sadness in the air. The day was gloomy, humid, and uncharacteristically cold. Unfamiliar yellow vinyl chairs had been arranged in the kitchen, where my mother, Flavia, was seated. A pretty, petite woman who was usually joyful, Mamá was sobbing as she cradled Maricela's twin, five-month-old Rosa, to breastfeed her. At her side was my little brother, two-year-old Gabriel. Gazing around with his large, thoughtful eyes, Gabriel sucked his thumb quietly as he leaned against our weeping mother. In front of the yellow chairs sat a tiny rectangular wooden box—a casket, I later learned—covered by a colorful handwoven blanket. Family members and neighbors filed into the room, many of them softly crying.

When I asked my aunt why Mamá was so sad, she explained that this was the funeral of my baby sister Maricela.

"Where is Maricela?" I whispered, unable to connect my happy, chubby baby sister with the casket.

"Maricela went to heaven," my mother said solemnly, wiping her tears.

Why was everyone so sad? After all, I had been told that heaven was a wonderful place where people could go to be with the angels. Shouldn't we feel good that she had gone to such a nice place?

Years later, I learned the tragic circumstances of Maricela's death—acute diarrhea and the accompanying dehydration, a common and curable condition, if the right medical resources are available. Initially, she wasn't taken to the hospital because we lived in the middle of nowhere with no accessible facilities nearby. The difficulty in obtaining medical attention was a function of the relative poverty in this rural area outside of Palaco, a small village of about five hundred families, some thirty miles from Mexicali—the border town that is split by a fence and is known as Calexico on the U.S. side. In our village and environs, we had no private doctors who made house calls, nor were there clinics close by. Many everyday medical needs were met in the *boticas* housed in local pharmacies. When Maricela's symptoms first appeared, my mother took her to the *botica*, and the pharmacist gave Mamá medicine to ease the baby's stomach problems and the pain later diagnosed as colitis.

That evening, when my father came home from work, Maricela began to laugh when he picked her up in his arms. Papá took her smiles as a sign that the medicine was working. But in the middle of the night, as her screams worsened from what was clearly horrible pain, my parents rushed Maricela over to my grandmother, Nana Maria, my father's mother, a *curandera* who specialized as a midwife and herbalist. My grandmother had delivered hundreds of babies through the years and was revered for her ability to know when a case required special attention. Nana knew at once that Maricela needed to be taken the hour's drive to the *seguro social*—the public hospital—without delay. My parents understood the gravity of the situation and raced to get there.

At the hospital, one of the physicians on duty knew my grandmother and heeded her concern, admitting my little sister immediately while reassuring my parents that she would improve by morning. With their hopes raised, Mamá and Papá then suffered the anguish of watching Maricela's convulsions increase over the next two days, and in the end, losing her. Though they did everything they could, their efforts weren't enough to combat her colitis, which had quickly reached an advanced state, nor to make up for the fact that the small, poor hospital didn't have the medicine or other forms of treatment that could have saved her. Tragically, in developing countries such as ours, diarrhea and resulting dehydration are still the main cause of death of little ones. But I know that my parents continued to ask themselves *Why?* and the question hung over the household for years.

My father and mother were not strangers to loss. My father had been one of eleven children, one of whom had died at the age of ten before my father was born and whose death left a lasting shadow in that household. My mother had been virtually orphaned at the age of six when her beloved mother had died in childbirth, essentially leaving her to raise the younger children, slaving under the abuses of her paternal aunts and trying to hold the family together while her father, my grandfather Jesus, struggled to find his footing after his wife's death.

Though my parents never spoke openly of their sorrow, it was a presence in our lives, an undercurrent of sadness that affected each of us differently. I suspect my sister's death had something to do with the added sense of responsibility I felt as the oldest of five children in our household, and with the recurring childhood nightmares in which I would find myself in the midst of disaster—fire, flood, or avalanche—and know that it was up to me to save my mother and siblings. In each of these dreams, part of the story was that I'd been given superpowers—able to walk through fire without being burned or swim through tidal waves without drowning (in reality I couldn't swim and would never be at ease in the water). The notion of having special powers must have come from my ambition in those years to follow in the footsteps of Kaliman, a Mexican comic-book superhero who could fight off the attacks of multiple demons in one move: the gravity-defying Kaliman maneuver that I was determined one day to master. In my waking hours, I was convinced that I could really do this. But in my nightmares, to my despair, before I could put my superpowers to work and save my loved ones, the dream would end and I would fail in my mission. Every time, I'd wake up crying in bewildered frustration.

The death of Maricela, my repeating nightmares, and the considerable amount of responsibility I felt from an early age may help explain why my most primal struggle was to understand and make sense of life and death. These experiences may also have planted the seed for my later interest in medicine. In the meantime, the idea that my sister had gone to a better place was comforting. It fueled my already active imagination and my curiosity to know more of the world beyond what I could see and observe in the everyday comings and goings in the outskirts of Palaco. Long before medicine was a remote possibility for me, I dreamed of a life of travel and adventure!

Then again, as I recall my nights of stargazing in the period when I was six and a half, almost seven years old, I was ready to settle for being an astronaut. I announced my plan one stiflingly hot night in the autumn of 1974 to my mother, my five-year-old brother Gabriel, and my three-year-old sister Rosa.

Everyone laughed. I was definitely the family dreamer!

There were many nights like this one when the suffocating heat made sleep impossible inside our two-bedroom house, where we had moved a year earlier. Just across the canal from the gas station, the adobe-style house—built of cinder blocks in one part and mud in the other—lacked air-conditioning and was like an oven, baking everything inside it! When the heat was unbearable, as on this night, the four of us opted to climb up to the rooftop, first spreading blankets over the scratchy tar-paper surface, then settling into position. Rosa curled up on one side of Mamá, while I was on the other, in between her and Gabriel. Our flight to the roof was to escape not only from the heat but also from the ever-present threat of earthquakes known to collapse houses and create mudslides in this part of the Baja, where the San Andreas Fault trails down from the west coast of the United States. Up on the roof, you were more likely to survive by avoiding having the house fall on you—as had happened recently in the area, killing hundreds. Yet those worries seemed to vanish under the stars—where all was safe and peaceful and fun!

Clasping my hands underneath my head, I made a pillow for myself, and with my legs crossed, I was at ease—happily engaged and ready to savor the show playing out in the sky above us and in our surroundings.

For a while, we were quiet. None of us said a word as our senses awakened to the sights, sounds, and smells of the night. I could hear the chirping of crickets and the buzzing of other insects, along with the loud croaking of the toads as they sang with a bravado that reminded me of the strolling mariachis who frequented the restaurants of Mexicali.

In these years, we were fortunate to be dining in restaurants every now and then, and to be part of the lower middle class in our village, slowly rising out of poverty—thanks to the modest earnings from my father's gas station. While our status was more precarious than we knew, I recognized that the steps up the ladder were many. I was aware too that not every family could afford to eat some meat once a week as we did and that none of our good fortune would have been possible if not for the family work ethic. I had been taught this fundamental lesson starting from the age of five, when I went to work at the gas station every day after school and on weekends, pumping gas, learning to fix cars and trucks, even driving them in and out of our mechanic's garage with the help of many cushions. I saw nothing unusual about being a five-year-old who could drive or climb up on hydraulic lifts to look under the hoods of cars and trucks to assess what needed repairing—all part of the job.

My family imparted the importance of hard work directly and by example. My father started his day at dawn at the gas station and didn't close down until nightfall, when he would go out to spend some of the day's earnings for food and other necessities for the family. For that reason, he wasn't usually up on the roof when we went up there to sleep. But I knew that when he returned home later, he would probably have something for all of us to eat in the morning—often my favorite, a loaf of *pan dulce*, sweet bread.

Up on the roof on this night in my memory, I imagined with pleasure what breakfast would bring even as I inhaled the green, wet, earthen smells of the night, savoring it all. Everything was fresh, present, and alive—like the smell of newly picked watermelon lifted from the wet soil, ripe and ready to be eaten. How well I knew these smells from recent outings to work in Palaco's cotton fields. Though our efforts weren't needed for the money at this point, my parents believed that we would use lessons from the fields in other ways. Papá also wanted to show me that working at the gas station was a much better job than standing out under the blazing sun all day and picking cotton, my bare hands bleeding.

Out in the field, there was no use complaining. So I made the best of the situation by watching the process unfold—as we walked up and down the rows, picking the light fluffy pieces of cotton and putting them into long burlap sacks, and then watching how the filled-up sacks were weighed so that we could be paid by the kilogram. There was no shame in being a field worker. This was opportunity. Besides, I felt proud of what I could accomplish with my bare hands. And the moral of the story was twofold: first, every job in the entire operation counted—no job was meaningless; second, no matter how small and fluffy that piece of cotton felt, if we kept pushing ahead, all those bits of fluff would accumulate and have real weight—as much as twenty or thirty kilos that were worth their weight in pesos!

Such was the value of honest, rigorous work—bringing with it the pride of a job well done, some form of compensation, and sometimes opportunities to advance in the world. This was how I came to purchase the used bicycle I desperately wanted. Gabriel—a much more obedient child than I, who also had more common sense—was unimpressed when I brought home the bike. "How can you ride it?" he laughed, pointing out that it had no pedals or brakes. To prove him wrong, I learned to ride it sideways and basically roll wherever the bicycle wanted to go.

However, Gabriel was considerably more enthusiastic when the two of us found a used black-and-white RCA television in a secondhand store and convinced our father to buy it—though he was careful to point out that we had only one line of power to the house and it was needed for the refrigerator and the two light bulbs that lit our home. Unfazed, we managed to build a makeshift outlet that gave us enough juice. Once we replaced the picture tube, magically the picture came on, thrilling us—at least during the few hours that Mexican television aired the two stations available.

Since the TV image was very grainy, we covered the windows with blankets to darken the rooms. With temperatures as high as 120 degrees outside, the insulation only made the interior more ovenlike. But we didn't care! The TV was a luxury item that connected us not just to the rest of the world but also to the fantastic possibilities of space travel to strange new worlds. We were hooked on the afternoon reruns of *Star Trek,* raptly following every move of Dr. Spock and Captain Kirk as they explored the galaxies—facing dangers, fighting battles, dodging asteroids, and venturing into unknown realms.

There was one huge problem. After being so industrious and using our ingenuity to fix the television set, I could seldom watch it because I had to work at the gas station after my father picked us up from school at midday. Sadly, that meant I could see *Star Trek* only on a catch-as-catch-can basis. I remember being desperate to watch an episode that was to air at four-thirty on a Thursday afternoon. When Papá picked me up at school and I asked if he could make an exception for this day, he firmly replied, "No, Alfredo, you have to work," and left it at that.

I was devastated. But I didn't cry. Instead, when we arrived at the gas station, I hopped out of the car, set my jaw, and went about my duties with greater purpose, hoping to forget all about the *Star Trek* episode I was doomed to miss. By the time four-thirty rolled around, I had almost succeeded in pushing it to the back of my mind. Papá then called me over and gestured toward home, telling me, "OK, son, you can go to the house," and before he could add "and watch your show," I was out of there as fast as my speeding little legs could carry me.

When I flew in the door, Gabriel informed me that I had missed only the opening credits, and we were able to watch in wonder together as the USS *Enterprise* journeyed into the unknown. The episode was everything that I'd anticipated and more! And on that hot autumn night in 1974, up on the rooftop with Gabriel, Mamá, and Rosa, I knew that I could land on a hostile planet some day, just like Captain Kirk did during that episode, and use my skills of diplomacy to keep the peace. Energized by the sounds of the wind in the brush of the foothills to the north of us, I basked in the main event already under way: the *real* star show. I loved the speedy stars—the ones that may have been the smallest but looked to me as if they were on a special mission, moving with purpose and power. Amazing! For the would-be astronaut in my six-year-old self, millions of stories and possibilities presented themselves on the giant blackboard above us.

In the second grade, I was beginning to have a sense of geography. I had heard that Palaco—which stood for Pacific Land Company— had been founded by a long-gone American company that had come in around the 1930s to cultivate the various crops in the valley. I also knew that we were a satellite village like many others in the vicinity of Mexicali, and that there were other, much bigger cities far from us in the huge country of Mexico, of which I was a citizen. We had been taught about countries and continents, and their geographical differences. Whereas a few years earlier I had believed that the world was flat and that if I reached the end, I would fall off the edge, I now understood from school and from *Star Trek* that the earth was round—and was stationed much like a star in the universe. Aside from those basics, I had only questions: What was beyond the stars? What was between the stars and the blackness that separated them one from the other? Who created them? My mind couldn't conceive of where this expanse began or where it ended or how it could be measured relative to me, such a small being in the vast picture.

The only other person who seemed to be considering such mysteries was my paternal grandfather, Tata Juan. In fact, he helped plant the seeds of these big questions in my mind, urging me on to ever-greater heights. "If you shoot high and aim for a star, you might just hit one," he would say.

Once, when I was about five years old, I took his advice literally. I took my slingshot and a handful of stones up to the roof one night and did exactly as he had recommended—shooting each one forcefully as far into the sky as I could muster. Although I didn't hit a star that night, I was certain that one day I would.

.   .   .

According to family accounts, from the moment of my birth on January 2, 1968, I kept everyone on their toes. First off, an unusual bump on my head raised concerns, interestingly enough, that I might have been born with a brain tumor. Today I understand that I had a cephalohematoma—nothing serious. But at the time, family members wondered how I managed to survive the fist-sized protrusion rising from my skull—composed of burst blood vessels—which looked like a second tiny head trying to push its way through the skin.

Relieved when they learned that the bump would disappear on its own, family members turned their attention to my hyperactive nature, worrying that I would hurt myself. Even before I could walk well, my parents were shocked at how fast I could toddle off. I also learned to speak expressively by my first birthday and soon thereafter taught myself to tie my shoelaces. Now the real trouble began. My vanishing acts usually required the entire extended family to go out and search for me—like the time when I was about three years old and everyone was afraid that I'd fallen into the reservoir. They eventually found me selling the tiny shrimp I'd discovered in the irrigation holes out in the fields. My many uncles thought these antics were hilarious, but my numerous aunts disagreed. They soon labeled me a hellion in need of better discipline. My parents did their best, but little worked. Nana Maria predicted that if they didn't set some kind of boundaries for me, I would be a danger to myself. The job then fell to Tata Juan, who took me under his wing and became my first true mentor.

Tall and lanky, with chiseled features and an eagle's beak for a nose, Tata was a towering figure for all of us. A self-made man who had never been to school, he nonetheless learned to read and write music while teaching himself to play multiple instruments. Tata also managed to make a few wise investments during his years toiling in agriculture (as we used to describe working in the fields), and throughout his life, he carried himself with such a regal bearing that he could have been mistaken for an aristocrat. A gentleman as well, he was never without his hat—a sign of dignity, I believed—and he never forgot to remove it in the presence of ladies.

"How are you today, my ladies?" he would say with great courtesy, sweeping off his hat and bowing whenever he passed a group of women of any age. I mimicked this mannerism as a child, even though I didn't have a hat. I enjoyed the reaction whenever I bowed and said in my most proper five-year-old pronunciation, "How are you today, my ladies?" The move worked so well, I've done it ever since!

My fondest memories of my grandfather come from our trips to a cabin in the Rumorosa Mountains. Everything about the region—from the giant, rocky mountain peaks to the mysterious series of caves with prehistoric wall paintings left by ancient human hands—filled me with wonder. Along the hiking trails that led up the mountains, Tata defied his age and ran like a gazelle. On purpose, he would sometimes sprint off into the woods and I would have to think fast and follow him into the brush. There were times when he would disappear, and just before I started to panic, Tata would reappear and we would continue up the steep mountain together, far from the main path.

On one occasion, he put the lesson of our hikes into words. Placing his hand on my shoulder as we climbed, he said, "Alfredo, whenever you have the choice, don't just follow where the path leads. Go instead where there is no path and then leave a trail." I don't know whether Tata had ever heard the similar quote by Ralph Waldo Emerson. But I wouldn't be surprised if he had.

Not until we reached the rocky peak would Tata Juan finally sit down to rest. Then he would watch in delight as I continued to run wildly, calling him at the top of my lungs, "Tataaaahhhh! Tataaaahhhh!" and loving the sound as it echoed down the mountainside.

Though my parents never said anything, they must have been relieved when the two of us returned from the outings in one piece. I know they were also pleased that we were so close. But not everybody shared their feelings. One of my father's sisters famously complained that out of his fifty-two grandchildren, some of whom were senior to me, Tata seemed to spend more time with me than with anyone else. Papá probably suggested that it was helpful to have someone in the family who could control me!

My mother often enlisted Tata to act as an intermediary when she had to explain to me why I had to accept the consequences of disobeying the rules. I would argue against the punishment, whether it was to sit in the corner or to give up television, telling Mamá she was too strict. Whatever my transgressions were—whether I skipped my chores or got into a fight—Tata would ask me to tell him the whole story and then pass judgment. That's what happened one day when my mother was upset with me for playing on the railroad tracks behind our house. (Coincidentally, these tracks were part of the line that carried freight trains and railway tankers from Northern California. The train cars that passed through my backyard were the same tankers that I would one day clean and refurbish—and put my life in jeopardy in the process.)

As a child, I used to volunteer to help the switching guards and the engineers since they couldn't move as fast as me. My job was to wait by the side of the tracks until the last minute to identify whether the locomotive needed to have the track switched and, if so, leap over the track while flagging the guards and the engineers to pull the appropriate levers at the right moment. In my opinion, this was educational and excellent training in my quest to become either an astronaut or a super-hero like Kaliman. My mother begged to differ.

On the day in question, Tata asked me to explain a particular incident and tell him why my job helping the switching guards required me to climb up on a tanker car that had only stopped temporarily—forcing me to jump when it suddenly got going again. After hearing me defend myself along with a few other details, he spoke slowly and sternly, "Your mother is absolutely correct, Alfredo. You could have been killed. You set a bad example for the other children. I think you should consider this as you go and sit in the corner." He had just repeated what my mother had already said—almost word for word! But when the words came from him, I agreed completely. The punishment was no longer unreasonable. In fact, I thought it was an honor to face my consequences at his request.

One reason I respected Tata was his ability to overcome the obstacles he had faced throughout his life. When he was growing up in Sonora, where he was born in 1907, his father was murdered by a band of *pisto-leros*—lawless, thieving gangs who terrorized the countryside during the Mexican Revolution. His mother spiraled down into mental illness afterward—making life even tougher for my grandfather, who more or less raised himself.

Nana Maria had overcome much adversity too. Though I wasn't as close to her as I was to Tata, I was in awe of her role as a healer and pillar of the community. Through her work as a *curandera,* she taught me the most important lesson I would learn about the treatment and care of patients: in all matters, the life and the well-being of the patient must come first. Nana had a gift for connecting with her patients in an immediate, tactile way—looking into their eyes, studying their small-est symptoms, putting her hands on their shoulders to be encourag-ing and to share her powerful healing energy. No one ever died in her care because she was so thorough that if she had any concern about whether someone required more than she could offer, she would refer the patient to a hospital or facility that could provide necessary services. Nana Maria never charged a single peso for her services. Her reward was being able to teach women how to take care of their reproductive health and their babies, and as a midwife, she considered it an honor to save lives and to lend a hand to new life coming into the world. That, to her, made for a richly rewarding existence. On call morning, noon, and night, she would remain awake and alert throughout protracted periods of labor and challenging deliveries, standing and working through the cold nights in the small unheated adobe homes of our area or through the stifling hot nights when everyone else fled to their roofs for relief.

After one very long delivery, when I was around six years old, on a blazing hot summer morning, I caught sight of Nana Maria on her front porch as I was playing outside my grandparents' house. Nana looked surprisingly fresh and renewed after a sleepless night as a midwife, though she was resting her legs and feet. She walked with a limp that my father said was caused by a deformity or illness like polio that had caused one foot to be much smaller than the other. Even in the days when she and Tata worked the fields, my grandmother never complained. Nana did believe, however, that too many of us took for granted the marvelous ability endowed to us through the power of our own two feet. And she never held back from admiring the beautiful gait of someone else or from expressing a wistful desire to have two normal feet and even to dance as others could. Perhaps this sense of her otherness made her all the more compassionate toward those in pain and in struggle. But that morning as I played with my cousin Cesar—a master at rock throwing who was helping me improve my technique—I noticed something magical about Nana Maria. Instead of appearing worn out, she was smiling and talking to Tata, as though invigorated. To have so much energy after going so long without eating or sleeping was incredible, and to achieve this while caring for others was a most noble act.

Just then, right on cue, a young couple walked down the road toward my grandparents' house. The young woman carried her newborn baby under a blanket while her husband cradled a live chicken in his arms. I was struck by the gratitude on the faces of the young mother and father as they offered my grandmother the chicken, the most valuable gift that they could find to express their thanks. Nana Maria was gracious, assuring them that their thoughtfulness would not go unappreciated in her humble home. Yet perhaps the gift she most valued was the chance to peek under the blanket and see the healthy tiny baby, knowing that she had done her job and done it well.

The story had a twist that makes it stand out in my memory for another reason. After the young couple left and Nana went into the house, I decided to practice my new skills. The first rock left my hands with excellent speed. Unfortunately, my aim was terrible and I broke a window of my grandparents' house. Holy guacamole! But not giving up, I threw the next rock, carefully avoiding the house. Unfortunately, this time I wasn't careful enough to avoid hitting Cesar's head, causing a gash that bled profusely as his screams brought my grandparents running.

Nana pointed out that I had once again shown that I needed to be more mindful of my actions. Tata was greatly displeased. Of course, I felt terrible about my cousin and the window. But most of all, I didn't want my grandparents to be mad at me. And, in truth, they weren't, although they did worry. My grandmother spoke to my parents, I later learned, telling them I would go far in life only if appropriate boundaries were set. Tata Juan warned Papá, "Alfredo is unusually bright. But you must watch him. Otherwise, he will miss out on many opportunities." My parents were in full agreement. Their solution, rather than being overly critical, was to make sure that through education and the discipline of the classroom, I would settle down. The need for me and my siblings to go to school, work hard in the classroom and on homework, and make the most of our education was all the more important to my parents because neither of them had much formal schooling.

Before my maternal grandmother had died, she had taught my mother to read and write at home. In fact, one of the only memories my mother retained from this time was seeing my grandmother's loving smile of approval as they read together. But after being orphaned and made into a servant by her aunts, my mother had no option but to teach herself. Considering these limitations, Mamá did very well and was able to apply the basics in qualifying for a training program to become a nurse, her dream. Sadly, her father, my grandfather Jesus, refused to help her pay for nursing school. Still, Mamá continued to educate herself, developing skills she put to use when she later went into business, buying used items that she would refurbish and then sell.

My father was thirteen when his family moved close enough to a school for him to attend for the first time. But as the oldest student in the classroom, already with facial hair, he felt like a swarthy giant sitting there. Though he managed to learn enough to later teach himself to read and write, he lasted only three months in class before quitting. No one was more disappointed than he was. Later, expressing regret that he hadn't been able to accomplish everything he wanted in life, Papá would tell us, "If you want to grow up and be like me, don't go to school."

After my parents married in 1967, they had considered continuing their education in some form, but with babies to feed and a gas station to run, they never had time. My father had taken on the business in his late teens when Tata Juan came to him and said, "Sostenes, I have been thinking about buying the Garcia Gas Station that is for sale. Would you like to be my partner?" Then, as a wedding present, Tata took my father aside and announced, "The gas station has always been yours, son. I knew that you would need it when you started your family."

Papá wanted nothing more than to make his father proud—to prove himself worthy. That task turned out to be more challenging than he expected. But in keeping with Tata's expectations, my father devoted himself to making the business a monumental success, soon transforming the ordinary gas station into a colorful, eye-catching enterprise. With his fondness for vibrant colors, he painted it a fluorescent mustard yellow with bright lime green trim. You couldn't miss it!

My father bequeathed his love of color to me. But his most important legacy was his oft-repeated phrase, which he would deliver either with a smile or with tears in his eyes: "Every man is the architect of his own destiny."

．　．　．

Tata Juan was of the strong opinion that charm and charisma could carry a person a very long way, and if you added hard work, honesty, and a good heart, you would go "a long way *and back*." He also believed that out of small efforts, great results could come. To prove it, he gave me my first marble, explaining, "If you use this well, in time you will have more marbles than you can count." How right Tata was. I soon became the king of marbles, setting up tournaments that I managed to oversee while working at the gas station. Thus began my training in multitasking—an indispensable skill for the future clinician, surgeon, and scientist in me. Soon, untold numbers of jars filled with marbles of every color lined the nooks and crannies of our little house.

At the age of six, however, my ambition to win all the marbles—a competitive streak that would get me into trouble later—worked against me when I was lured into a contest with a nine-year-old challenger. While he let me win, his older sidekick snuck into the entrance of the station and stole fifty pesos! Faced with such cold-blooded dishonesty, I had to avenge myself. But having tried before and gotten my ass kicked by bigger kids, I concluded that it was time to cultivate an entourage—a lasting tradition. My team was made up of former bullies I had befriended. They brought the muscle; I brought the brain.

I did not stand back from the fight, however. After all, I was still in training as Kaliman, still certain that I could perfect the maneuver he used to fight off several adversaries at once. Studying the comic book version carefully, I analyzed the components of the maneuver and understood that to pull it off successfully I would need to embody the green-eyed, pantherlike agility of Kaliman by jumping five feet into the air while extending my arms and legs. The goal was to knock out four foes—two by punching them with my fists and the other two by kicking my feet. With lightning speed, I would not only disarm them but then land back on my feet—again, like a panther. It was also important, I decided, to make sure that my eyes blazed with defiance—just as Kaliman's eyes turned a more intense shade of green whenever he fought off demons.

As I explained to Gabriel and three of my cousins, "I am going to practice the Kaliman maneuver and I need your help. Do exactly as I say and you won't be hurt too much."

Seeing some concern in their faces, I reminded them about the problem we had been having with local bullies who were roaming the area and shooting their BB guns at us. We had to practice the maneuver ahead of time in case of attack.

We all took our places, bracing for the blows to come. I focused, inhaled deeply, bent my knees, and leapt into the air, rising two feet at the most. At the same time, I extended my arms and legs to simultaneously punch and kick but managed instead to miss my targets entirely and land face down in the dirt—knocking the air out of my chest. Talk about eating dust! When I sat up on my haunches, the four of them stared at me in horror and shame that I had failed so miserably. Then they began to laugh uproariously.

My conclusion? Clearly, the comic book had exaggerated Kaliman's powers! From then on, as the tougher kids continued to make trouble for the rest of us, I looked for other ways to disarm the bullies.

Incredibly, even as an alleged hellion, I managed to survive childhood with only one visit to a doctor. On this occasion, the pain and infection in my bicep became so acute that I had to confess that I had fallen on one of the drumsticks I'd made to go along with the drum setup I'd put together. The wooden point of the drumstick, as sharp as an arrowhead, had pierced my arm, breaking off in the right bicep. It was amazing to me that the doctor could examine my infected injury and, like a wizard, remove the piece of wood from my bicep and give me the correct medicine to make it all better. Magic!

Although it crossed my mind that being a doctor would be a noble undertaking, my first true role model was Mexico's beloved Benito Pablo Juárez García. After starting kindergarten, I was introduced to his story when my teacher learned that I already knew how to read and selected me to recite a poem about him in front of a gathering of hundreds of students. This was my first public-speaking opportunity, and I was terrified! I had to stand up on a chair to speak, and the microphone had to be lowered and turned sideways so that I could reach it. From my perch, I could see a quote by Benito Juárez high above me on the stone wall: "Among individuals, as among nations, when there is respect, there is peace." This got me going, and when I started to speak, I forgot about the crowd and poured my passion into paying homage to Juárez—a poor young man of native heritage who grew up to become the president of Mexico. He embodied real-life heroism, fighting on behalf of everyday people.

From the beginning, as my parents hoped, school offered me structure with defined boundaries, in which I could excel. At home, I could break the rules with my experiments and explorations, giving free rein to my curiosity. School was a different kind of fun, with challenges and excitement. There I learned how to be still and focused, thus becoming the most obedient, disciplined student.

My father loved telling about the day he came to pick me up from kindergarten, and my teacher told him, "I think that Alfredo is ready for elementary school. You should go see my sister, and then see what she says."

Lucky for me that her sister, Señorita Jauregui, my teacher for first and second grades, not only decided that I was ready for elementary school but took me under her wing at the start of my academic experience. She had faith that I could go far in my education and in the world. Soon, I became the teacher's pet—a mantle that stayed with me and was alternately an honor and an invitation for other kids to beat me up on the playground and after school. Being younger and smaller than the other students in my grade was bad enough. On top of that, I was from outside of town—a country bumpkin in the eyes of the city dwellers who lived in Palaco. If not for my street-smart best friend, Niki, my large sidekick, I would have been in real trouble. Soon my would-be attackers figured out that if they messed with me, they'd have to mess with him or some of the other, tougher kids I befriended. But despite my defenders, I continued to think of myself as the underdog and to identify with others who got picked on—especially the ones who couldn't defend themselves.

There was an instance that caused me to become particularly upset one day when a little boy in my second-grade class, also named Alfredo, raised his hand to ask to go to the bathroom. The teacher asked him to wait until class was over. Unfortunately, he wasn't able to contain himself and pooped in his pants. Alfredo was mortified. I felt so bad for him and was mortified for his sake when the rest of the kids started to tease him. As soon as we got out to the schoolyard, I decided to tease those kids for their various shortcomings, hurling sharp-tongued remarks that came easily to me. Championing his cause wasn't going to solve everything for the other Alfredo, but at least I hoped it would cheer him up.

I also would never forget a young girl in the area who was born with a disfiguring cleft palate that made her appear to have two faces—like a little monster, some said. A few family members, being very poor, charged admission for others to come and stare at her, even to shriek over her deformities and taunt her. There was no way I could stand by and allow such cruelty—even if it meant a fight with kids who were bigger than I was. Most of the time, I didn't win those fights. But I hoped that somehow the little girl knew that someone was sticking up for her.

·   ·   ·

Some of my happiest memories of childhood exist not in story form but in scattered images or recollections of smells and tastes. For instance, I can vividly recall waking up to the smell of my mother's tamales on Christmas mornings. Just the memory floods me with warmth and contentment, along with the happiness I felt on one Christmas in particular when I received a surprise gift. It was a racing car set that my mother had refurbished after buying it on one of her excursions across the border. In those days, it was possible to obtain an official identification card that allowed Mexican citizens to travel to the United States as tourists to shop or visit friends and relatives. My entrepreneurial mother would go over the border to Calexico on such shopping trips, usually with my father, and after rummaging through garage sales and picking up discarded items, would return and fix them up for sale. I knew that the racing set would have sold for a tidy sum of money. But instead she had decided that I was to be the lucky recipient. Just as I recall my own joy in receiving the gift, I can still see the smile on my mother's face as she watched my delighted reaction.

I have similarly happy memories of time spent with my father and my brother Gabriel, particularly our periodic trips to the Sea of Cortez. Even though Papá traveled there to set up his stand and sell refurbished items—frequently trading them for food—to me these exciting expeditions felt like vacations. The drive down to San Felipe required us to journey south and through the desert. Our three-hour trek through the desert was made not just in any automobile; it was in my father's one-of-a-kind, custom-painted, custom-built flatbed truck.

To visualize the shade of green that my father had painted this truck, you might want to imagine a neon green parrot. An ugly green. The always-colorful Sostenes Quiñones, of course, would have disagreed. He was equally proud of the multicolored spiraling stripes he had painted on the truck bed—twenty colors in the pattern of a barbershop pole. A true work of art! If the exterior was outrageous, the interior was like-wise laughable. The springs poked out of the seats and made for a sore behind for all occupants. The floorboard was apparently added as an afterthought, leaving cracks over the engine. The stick shift and the knob atop it would come out of place if we shifted too forcefully, causing the truck to slide around the road in between gears as the driver held a knobless stick in his hand while trying to deal with the jammed axle. Plus, the truck wouldn't go much faster than thirty miles an hour. The drive was always a journey—a fantastic, unforgettable adventure.

The road was full of dips and dives, winding over crests and around curves, so the only thing we could see as we made our way around the side of a hill and approached the town of San Felipe was desert. But all at once, we would come over a rise and see a spectacular panoramic view of the Sea of Cortez. In the morning sun, the shade of blue was deep and pure, incomparable, like an ocean of shining, rippling sapphires.

It felt as if we might drop right down into the sea itself. I loved the vantage point from the top of the hill that let me look down on the hori-zon rather than view it at sea level. It seemed to open up to infinite possibilities in the world beyond, somehow bringing me closer to the stars. Each time we headed off to the Sea of Cortez, I would anticipate this sight, becoming more excited with every mile. And the image would stay with me long after the excursion was over—symbolizing hope for my future and firing me up with the spirit of navigation that applied as much to the sea as it did to outer space.

One of our more memorable trips took place in 1977, when Mexico's economic downturn was starting to send tremors across the country before becoming a full-blown earthquake and forcing the catastrophic devaluation of the peso. On this trip, as soon as Papá parked the truck, he sent me and Gabriel off to play for many hours on our own. On a weekend day like this, we were usually at work at the gas station, so this truly was a holiday. We spent most of the morning building an elaborate sandcastle—a fortress fit for a king—until it was time to comb the beach for the small shiny rocks and shells that we determined were gold and pearls.

Then it was time for our feast! My father had exchanged goods for so much fresh fish that he had enough to cook us dinner before we made the journey back home. He cut the fish open, cleaned them of bones before stuffing them with vegetables and spices, and then baked them in tin foil over a fire that he made on the beach. The smell of the baked fish when my father first peeled back the foil was so intoxicatingly fragrant that I could almost taste it with my nose. The lens of memory captured it all: the red embers of the wood heating the package of tin foil, the seductive peeling back of the foil, and the vapor rising from the fish, just caught by local fishermen, waiting to be eaten. A feast to be remembered, savored again and again, and always appreciated.

Upon our return from the Sea of Cortez, even as leaner times began to seriously encroach on our lives, I refused to be robbed of childhood and constantly sought creative ways to hold on to the magic of life. The prime opportunity to challenge darker days occurred whenever it rained and a lake would form outside and then flood the lower part of our house, where everything was already made of mud. To my mother, this was a housekeeping nightmare: a messy, salty, sticky, disgusting ordeal that would take weeks to clean up after the rains were over and we were no longer wading through water up to our knees. But to me, it was our very own Sea of Cortez—inside our house! By a wonderful stroke of luck, my father had purchased a wreck of an old fishing boat, basically a wooden board with sides that he insisted on keeping in the yard. Obviously, it was a pirate ship begging to be put to use!

You should have seen the surprised faces of the adults when I created a contest to determine who could command the old boat in the waters filling up the lower part of the front yard. Of course, I didn't wait for the sea to form. The minute the rain began to fall, it was rock 'n' roll time! Gabriel and I would rally our younger cousins, I'd assign roles, and then we'd let the games begin.

No matter how hungry, wet, or sticky with mud we might have been, we didn't care. We were having fun, and it didn't cost a peso. We could create the magic with the superpower of our beautiful brains! How much did I learn from my trips to the Sea of Cortez and from my other research in the laboratory of childhood about how to use mental resources to withstand the tests to come? Everything.

TWO Faraway

Misfortune seeped into my family's existence very slowly at first, almost imperceptibly. Then, toward the end of 1977, when I was nine years old and in the fifth grade, tough times seemed to descend on our household all at once, like a drastic shift in the weather. Even through the foggy lens of memory, I can recall the moment when I understood that we had left behind the simpler, more secure days and were treading upon shaky ground.

The moment of realization arrived when I found my father behind our house, alone, crying desperately. Something was very wrong. My first reaction was to ask Papá why he was crying. But I was too shocked to ask. Here was my father—the strong, stubborn head of our family, highly intelligent though not educated, hardworking, honest, and kindhearted, the colorful, passionate, larger-than-life man who was my hero—crying his eyes out.

For some time, there had been clues that business at the gas station was going poorly, but not until I found him crying did I understand the magnitude of the crisis. Without being told exactly, I figured out that the worst-case scenario for our family—losing the gas station, our primary livelihood and means of putting food on the table—had occurred. The station was our family's identity—not just where I'd worked since the age of five but a place of business that gave us stature in the community. Even at nine years old, I understood why this loss was such a blow to my father's sense of self, not the least because his father, Tata Juan, had chosen him to be his partner and then given him this endowment that was to have secured our future well-being.

In the year that followed, I came to better understand the circumstances that had led to this predicament. One factor was the financial downturn in Mexico, which would continue for several years and become a widespread economic depression. Before, we had steadily worked our way up and into the lower middle class. But without the gas station, we tumbled so far from that rung that we had to struggle to obtain the bare necessities—including the money needed to feed a growing family.

This descent was a shock to our system, as it was for much of the country, which had been enjoying relative prosperity and improvement since the 1930s, when American companies and other foreign investors had come in to develop rural areas and outposts like Palaco. The influx of outside investment created jobs and helped lift many families out of poverty. But in many cases when the companies left (or were forced to do so when the laws in Mexico changed to limit foreign-owned business), so did jobs and family security. The middle class sank to lower levels, and the poor became the really poor.

The other factor that contributed to the loss of the gas station only came to light after my father had to sell it for next to no profit. To do so, he had to first turn it over to his brother, my uncle Jesus, in whose name the government had originally issued the PEMEX (Petroleos Mexicanos) permit and who had wisely renewed it over the years—to his credit, since few such permits were available anymore. When Uncle Jesus tried to turn the gas station over to new management, a survey of the property revealed a startling fact. All those years, unbeknownst to Papá, there had been holes in the gas tanks and they had been steadily leaking their contents into the ground. So much gas from the underground tanks had seeped out that everyone's first reaction was to thank God that no stray lit match or mechanical explosion had ignited an inferno that would surely have swallowed all of us up. During all the years in which we had lived in the apartment at the back of the gas station, we had been unaware that such a horrific event—of a type that was all too common in our area—could have occurred and ended our lives.

Why had it taken so long to realize we were paying more for the gasoline than we were selling at the pumps? It should have been more obvious that the profits were literally leaking away into the earth under our feet.

Papá may have had distractions that kept him from noticing our sinking bottom line. And he was young and inexperienced, never having had the chance to explore the world before settling down, instead going from marriage at the age of twenty to becoming the father of six children within ten years. My father might have been fighting depression, which became more evident as our financial status worsened and as alcohol became a more frequent means of escape, a way to self-medicate.

Looking back, as I try to understand what my father went through, I truly believe that he was destined for great things, as my grandfather had foreseen. But Papá wasn't on steady ground when sudden misfortune capsized him, so finding his way to terra firma became that much harder. Losing the gas station also represented a decline in our standing in the Quiñones family and in the community—even though my aunts and uncles, as well as my paternal grandparents, maintained a policy of denial about how much trouble we were in. Still, despite our attempts to keep up appearances, they must have known of our struggles.

But within our household, the reality couldn't be ignored. It is hard to be in denial when your stomach is empty. One scene is burned into my memory: my mother standing over the stove making tortillas, just flour and water and a touch of oil in the pan to feed us children—me at ten years old, Gabriel at almost nine, seven-year-old Rosa, Jorge at about four years old, and baby Jaqueline not yet six months, then asleep for her nap. There we sat at the table, hands folded, waiting quietly to split the tortillas as they came from the pan. Decades later, I can still conjure the smell that told us how delicious every morsel was going to taste.

Remembering that near silence in the kitchen, I can still hear the music of the tortilla sizzling in the oil—the most hopeful sound in the world at that time. To this day, the mere mention of the word "hunger" summons that scene to my mind.

That was dinner—flour tortillas with homemade salsa. Gone were the days of eating meat once a week. Gone were the nights of imagining that my father was out somewhere picking up bread or something hearty for our breakfast. Gone were Christmas mornings waking to the smell of my mother's tamales. Now, as I lay on the roof, instead of looking up at the sky and dreaming of traveling beyond the stars, I dreamt of more practical desires—a piece of *pan dulce* and a time when we would have beans and potatoes at our table again.

Every now and then, I dreamt of things that I'd like to do or own for myself that weren't food or family related—like the time I became very focused on owning a pair of Ray-Ban sunglasses. Back then, they were the essence of living *la vida loca!*

Strangely, it was in this darker period that the nightmares that had plagued me for most of childhood suddenly ceased. Now actual threats to our security occupied my waking thoughts. But instead of feeling helpless, as I sat up on the roof late into the night, I was emboldened by thinking of ways to help. Surely real problems could be met with real solutions.

I was also convinced, as I told Mamá, that the many hours spent in church, as an altar boy and in confession, could be better spent working to help the family. Besides, sitting in church was boring and my attention span was not my strong suit. My mother thought for a moment and then pronounced her decision. "Alfredo, if you continue as you are until your First Communion, after that, it will be up to you to choose whether or not to attend church anymore."

She had only two conditions: first, I must remain observant and good during Easter week every year; and second, before taking First Communion, I would have to go on my knees from outside of the church into the sanctuary, confessing my sins as I crawled all the way to the altar.

Now I had a tough decision to make. Easter was actually a dark, somber holiday in my estimation. The rituals were strange to me, unlike those of my favorite celebration, Día de los Muertos—the Day of the

Dead—when we ate candy, danced, and dressed up in skeleton costumes and skull masks, giving death its respect but mocking its finality. Still, if these gestures meant that much to my mother and I only had to go to church one day a year, this wasn't a bad deal. The real challenge would be coming clean, in public, about my many misdeeds.

And yet, at ten years old, that's just what I did. On that long crawl, as I shuffled on my knees up the steps and down the aisle on the cold, hard, marble floor, I asked to be forgiven not just for the past but for future wrongdoing as well. These sins of mine were not generic or abstract; they weren't extreme, but they weren't inconsequential. They included the little pyrotechnic experiments I had conducted in the fields with my investigative team in tow, as we created geysers of flame high in the air. As I had admitted to our priest in previous confession, I also had a habit of not telling the truth, the whole truth, and nothing but the truth when interrogated by my elders. Though I didn't lie outright, I had found a way of avoiding the truth by saying nothing—like the time when I was seven or eight years old and my father questioned me about a particular boast that I had made to the older boys out in the schoolyard.

Rather than asking me if it was true that I had bragged that I was so fast I could run around and pull up girls' dresses without their realizing it, my father asked, "Are you behaving yourself at school?"

I was outraged. "Of course!" This was true when discussing my behavior in the classroom, where I was an angel. Out in the yard, a little devil got the better of me.

"Tell me the truth, Alfredo, were you trying to look up girls' dresses?"

"What?" I put on a disgusted, shocked look. Very convincing, I thought. "Who said I did that?"

"Never mind. I'm asking if you did or didn't. Well?"

"And I'm saying that is a terrible accusation, and whoever made it must not have known what they were talking about!"

We could go on like this for hours. As long as I wasn't caught in the act, I figured, I couldn't be convicted. But I knew deep down that my action counted as a sin by omission and confessed to the priest soon afterward. The priest seemed more upset that I had looked up girls' dresses than that I had lied. Clearly, I wasn't living up to the moral standards of the church or showing the kind of character that honored my family and my parents' values.

While crawling on my knees from outside the church, I expressed true remorse again for that episode. And there was more. Besides having a sharp tongue and sometimes lashing out with sarcastic comebacks, I had been known to tell a dirty joke or two. Or three.

For these sins and more, I asked forgiveness all the way to the altar. Even though I had no reason to feel responsible for the loss of the gas station, just in case, I begged for forgiveness if anything that I had done or not done had contributed to our misfortune. More important, I also asked to be given the responsibility and the strength to help relieve the problems, along with the understanding to make sense of what was happening to us.

Thus ended my relationship with organized religion. From then on, though I attended church occasionally, I communed with God wherever and whenever I chose: at night under the stars or on my walk to and from school or to various jobs. There were times when my one-on-ones with God led to some heated questioning: why was there so much suffering, how could a merciful Supreme Being allow poverty, illness, injustice, and misfortune to exist, and what had my innocent baby sister Maricela done to be taken from the world? The explanations were rather hazy, although my faith that I would one day come to understand these mysteries was not.

In the meantime, my source of inspiration in coping with our earthly difficulties was my mother. Unafraid, without complaint, Mamá made up her mind that she was going to hold her family together, in spite of the already strained relationship between my parents and even with our ongoing challenges that had no easy remedy.

Already resourceful, Flavia now expanded her activities. In addition to buying and finding used goods to refurbish and sell, she soon set up a little secondhand shop in a market area outside Palaco. Forty miles south of the border fence that ran between Mexicali on the Mexican side and Calexico on the U.S. side, her shop attracted both local customers and tourists who wanted to venture into the country but not too far. When Mamá had raised a bit of capital, she bought an old sewing machine with a foot pedal and began doing piecework at home at night for a costume company—sewing, of all things, sexy outfits for hookers at the local brothel!

Word of this particular work spread in the neighborhood, and I was not amused when the taunts started. Too bad for the kid who sneered at me one day, "What's it like to be the son of a woman who makes clothes for prostitutes?"

Putting my sharp tongue to use, I responded, "What's it like to be the son of the woman she's making the clothes for?"

After getting my butt kicked badly for that remark, I resolved to fight less and to find a better way to harness my outgoing personality. With help from my Uncle Abel, one of my mother's brothers—and money from trading in all the marbles I'd been amassing for years—I went into the hot dog business. Who could resist a child with a big voice, standing up on a stool and hawking hot dogs? No one, I thought! Unfortunately, few could afford my wares. I then started selling roasted corn, but as the national economy worsened, I didn't fare any better.

Desperation set in. Just when things became really bleak, my mother's oldest brother, Uncle Jose, began to make periodic deliveries from the United States, where he worked and lived part-time—bringing food staples and sometimes money that meant we could eat for the next few months. The sight of his pickup truck heading our way and kicking up dust on the road—loaded with burlap bags of beans, rice, and potatoes— was like witnessing the arrival of the cavalry in old Western movies. Just in the nick of time!

I didn't know the extent of Uncle Jose's generosity at the time—he had few resources himself—but I did know that he cared enough to help. Interestingly, no one ever told Uncle Jose how bad things had gotten for us. Somehow he figured it out.

No one else did, including my mother's brother, Fausto, who came down from the United States to visit us every Christmas, bringing my cousins, Fausto Jr. and Oscar, with him. Uncle Fausto had gone to California as a migrant worker in the 1950s through seasonal passports provided by the Bracero Program. Thanks to his tenacity and ability, he had found permanent work as a top foreman at a huge ranch in the town of Mendota in the San Joaquin Valley, where he was raising his two sons as a divorced father.

A plainspoken man, Uncle Fausto would have said something about our deteriorating circumstances if he had picked up on them. Instead, my mother had to raise the issue and ask him about the possibility of going to the United States for a summer of migrant work. When Mamá first brought up the idea to my father, he didn't protest, although I imagine he wasn't happy about the prospect of having to go across the border to America and pick cotton and tomatoes. But since he didn't have any better ideas, my mother decided to talk to Uncle Fausto during his annual Christmas visit.

This decision came after months of tension at our house. Nobody said anything about it to us children, but the look on my mother's face when my father came home in the middle of the night spoke volumes. Papá never laid a hand on Mamá, but he had a bellowing voice, and when the two of them began arguing, the sound of his unhappiness filled our house, making me feel that I couldn't breathe, much less stop their arguing. One day, when Gabriel and I were in the background during a heated exchange, Rosa got caught in the crossfire. She stood between my parents, crying and begging them to stop yelling at each other, to little avail.

Mamá knew that we couldn't go on as we were. But when she spoke to Uncle Fausto, her tone was casual, as she reminded him that we all had the required paperwork to travel back and forth across the border for tourism, so we wouldn't need any new or special documentation. The plan, my mother suggested, was that she and my father could work, and we children could enjoy a summer holiday.

"Let me see what I can do," Uncle Fausto replied with a shrug.

Not too much later, we learned that everything was in place for the summer and that when school let out, we were going to Mendota for two months. Road trip!

I couldn't wait. My American adventure was about to begin.

.   .   .

Mendota, California, bills itself as the cantaloupe capital of the world—a distinction that made me feel right at home, since I came from melon country. But something else also lent familiarity to our journey, literally providing a link to my backyard at home. Mendota had been founded by the Southern Pacific Railroad in the late 1800s as a switching station and storage area for repairing and housing railroad cars, and most of the products of California agriculture were unloaded and reloaded here. What were the odds? The tracks that passed by Mendota originated at the Port of Stockton (where I would eventually work)—where the ships docked to unload their cargo onto railcars at the water's edge. After Mendota, destinations could be switched eastward or westward, or the trains would continue south to the end of the line in, yes, Palaco!

None of the dots had yet connected for me back in 1979 when I was eleven years old. But I had a feeling of destiny about that summer. As my first exposure to the United States, Mendota was as close to paradise as I could imagine—a Garden of Eden about forty miles west of Fresno in the middle of the fertile San Joaquin Valley that stretches for miles from Stockton down through the middle of the state, almost to Bakersfield.

As much as a quarter of the produce grown in America comes from California, and most of it is grown in the San Joaquin Valley. As soon as we arrived at the ranch where Uncle Fausto was a foreman, I reveled in the freedom of the first real vacation I could remember. And we could eat for free! I looked out upon field after field, as far as I could see, rich with abundant growth and produce of every variety. All around me were rolling hills, wooded glens, irrigation canals, and winding dirt paths, all begging to be explored. Plus, my cousins Fausto and Oscar were always ready to join me and my siblings in the fun.

Every morning, after the adults left for the fields, the main goal for the day was to figure out how to get to a magical place we called "Faraway." You would only know you had arrived there when you got there! If I needed a break from our escapades, I hung out at the garage where tractors and farm equipment were serviced, offering my mechanical know-how and skill in maneuvering large vehicles. I also started a business cleaning workers' rooms at a nearby barracks. Because my rates were lower than the competition's, I was in demand.

Unfortunately, the competition, a fifteen-year-old, came after me with his posse. One of the guys pinned me down and twisted my arm so painfully that I couldn't use it to clean. Clearly, the time had come to learn some real Kaliman maneuvers for self-defense.

Thus, when we returned home to Mexico, my first thought was to take boxing lessons at a gym in Mexicali. But after sadly saying good-bye to the paradise of Faraway/Mendota, our family was soon stretched as thin as ever, and I accepted that I would have to create my own self-improvement program. So I came up with a bold plan to turn the out-of-doors into an obstacle course for my self-designed training regimen. Aha! On my way to school or work, I'd race against my previous pace, pushing myself faster each day, sometimes inventing athletic moves that called for leaping over creeks, catapulting over fences—anything to squeeze out another ounce of energy.

Such was the Kaliman approach. According to the comic-book hero's history, his DNA was not superhuman. He had simply pushed his human abilities to their optimal levels, training himself to be as strong as fifty men, to levitate and practice telepathy and ESP, and to fight evil and injustice without ever taking a life. Except for his occasional use of sedative darts to temporarily paralyze evildoers and a dagger employed only as a tool, he needed no weapons to overcome an adversary. Kaliman would even risk his own life to avoid causing the death of another human being. Dressed all in white except for the jewel-encrusted letter "K" on his turban, he was also a scientist, often spouting interesting facts about nature and the cosmos while embracing the attainment of knowledge with such philosophies as "He who masters the mind masters everything."

Fortunately, school still provided a positive place for me to work on mental mastery, even though being the youngest student and the teacher's pet brought problems. These concerns intensified when I changed schools and no longer had my circle of protectors. Worse, there were some seriously scary kids at the school. One of them, Mauricio, a mountain of muscle, did back flips and propelled off walls like a circus acrobat, and the ground shook whenever he walked by. The only person who wasn't afraid of him was his sidekick—known as El Gallo because he crowed like a rooster when he was triumphing over anyone who made the mistake of tangling with him. The Rooster was one of the tallest thirteen-year-olds I had ever seen, with long, sinewy arms designed for landing jabs and uppercuts. Of all the kids I was determined to avoid as part of my survival, these two were at the top of the list. Guess what? Just my luck, Mauricio was in my natural science class, sitting right behind me and peering over my shoulder to copy off my tests.

I saw only one solution and that was to offer him and his fellow bad boys my tutoring services. We settled on a fee, in addition to a promise that they would provide protection from any of the bigger bullies. As I explained, they were on my payroll.

The tutoring sessions were not as transformational for my pupils as I had hoped. Their understanding of the fundamentals improved, but I soon concluded that the more expedient (and profitable) path was to let them copy my answers on my tests. Of course, I knew that this solution was wrong, and I didn't pretend otherwise. But on an up note, the school saw a downturn in troublemaking during this time.

With tutoring and restaurant work, I could contribute to our family's welfare without falling behind in my studies. However, I soon began to lament that I couldn't pursue much of a social life outside of school. At fourteen, I had experienced my share of flirtations with girls in my class, but I had not had the money or time to explore romance. No dates, no dances, no strolls down the sidewalk holding hands. Did I feel sorry for myself? No, I couldn't allow that. But working every waking hour outside of school, day in and day out, was definitely getting old.

I finally confessed these feelings to my mother, trying to explain for the millionth time why, at the age of fourteen, I believed that the time had come for me to return to Mendota for the summer, on my own. If I could work there for two months, I could help the family so much more than if I stayed in Mexico. Moreover, I could put money away so that I wouldn't have to work full-time during the school year.

This would also allow me to move more rapidly in completing the special training program I'd recently begun that was the equivalent of a college curriculum for those studying to become teachers. Mamá and Papá agreed that becoming an educator was an excellent choice for me: not only was it a respected profession, but it would enable me to start earning a living in a shorter amount of time than, say, studying to become a lawyer or a doctor. And, in the best of all worlds, if I became a teacher, I could afford to continue my education toward those other professions if I desired.

Although I didn't have a work permit for my summer plans, that hurdle could be overcome with the passports that let us go back and forth across the border. Nothing anyone could say was going to convince me that this survival strategy was not a good idea; it was the only idea. Mamá finally gave in and went to the phone booth to call Uncle Fausto.

"Absolutely not," was his firm response when she asked if I could return to Mendota and work the fields for the summer. However, he quickly added that he would love for me to come for a vacation.

Grateful for his offer, I was determined to change his mind. During the entire ride up to Central California, as I sat quietly in the passenger seat of a car driven by a relative who was heading that way, I pondered how to convince Uncle Fausto to give me a shot at proving myself. When I was finally dropped off in front of my uncle's house, I stood there with my few items under my arm and gathered my resolve, not sure that anything I could say would sway him. At 102 pounds, much skinnier than when my Mendota relatives had last seen me, I could tell that Uncle Fausto and my cousins were shocked when they came out to welcome me. Uncle Fausto's first words were, "Are you hungry?"

Before I could answer, an ice cream truck playing cheerful organ-grinder music came down the road with a throng of dancing children following behind. Uncle Fausto gestured toward the truck and asked, "Want an ice cream?" Thanking him profusely, I had the pleasure of trying my first-ever rainbow-colored, push-up sherbet. Savoring its creamy, sweet deliciousness, I was in heaven. And it was a mere morsel compared to the hearty dinner that Uncle Fausto set out that evening. I realized that I could easily forget about working and just enjoy the good life for the next two months. Yet no sooner did that thought occur to me than an image arose of my family back in Mexico, sitting around the table each night and subsisting on the most meager diet.

That evening I began my campaign with Uncle Fausto, telling him what an asset I would be in the fields. Again, he forcefully refused. But after a lengthy back and forth, my uncle said, "Okay, give me five good reasons why I should give you a job."

I don't remember the first four, but I clearly remember the last one: I looked Uncle Fausto in the eyes and said, "Because we need it at home."

He studied me thoughtfully, saying nothing. Finally he nodded his head. "Fine," he said, "if you're ready to go at five A.M., I'll put you to work."

That next morning, I waited outside by Uncle Fausto's truck fifteen minutes early, eager to prove myself. No special treatment followed. I was dropped off with a crew of mostly men and started at the bottom of the migrant-worker ladder—pulling weeds. By the end of my two months, I had moved up several rungs, from pulling weeds in the cotton and tomato fields to picking and hauling the crops, working with sorting and counting machines, and finally taking over one of the coveted tractor-driving positions.

During breaks, I kept to myself, pulling out a book I'd brought to keep up my studies and to feed my mind so that I could focus on the physical challenges of work and not be overwhelmed by menial or difficult tasks. I was proud that I could work harder than anyone else, not because of a difference in abilities but probably because of the urgency that drove me—the strong sense of purpose that came from the knowledge that every penny earned would put food on the table for my parents and siblings and would allow me to help improve my family's status quo.

When I did socialize at night with my cousins and my uncle, the main subject of interest was boxing. And it was in this context that I would be given the nickname "Doc," perhaps as a hint of things to come. But there was no medical connection, at least not for many years.

In Mexican culture, people are often given more than one nickname; we might have several that are loosely related to one another. On my first visit to Mendota with my family, most of my nicknames had been Americanized versions of Alfredo—from Freddy, to Alfred, Fred, and Fredo. At fourteen, as I was introduced to *Rocky*, the classic underdog, I was given a rash of new nicknames. First was the affectionate "Ferdie" that my uncle dubbed me in honor of Dr. Ferdie Pacheco, the famous boxing physician who had been Muhammad Ali's beloved cornerman and personal doctor. Then he and my cousins started calling me Dr. Pacheco, which then morphed into "Doctor" and ultimately just "Doc."

When everyone in the fields heard my family calling me Doc or Dr. Pacheco, they assumed that the nicknames explained why I read so much and was so intense and meticulous in everything I did—as if each task were a matter of life and death. Some of them believed that I was a doctor!

Looking back, I know that part of my intensity stemmed from my percolating anger that my family's situation hadn't improved. Some of my anger was directed at my father, no doubt, because so much had fallen on my mother's shoulders. He blamed himself for the loss of the gas station, but after five years, I thought it was time for him to move on. Yet he was stuck. But even more intense than the anger was the war I was fighting against a rising feeling of hopelessness. The only way I knew to combat it was to work myself to the bone and squeeze every cent out of every second. After two months of this extreme regimen, while refusing to spend any of my earnings, I had dropped to ninety-two pounds. My normally round face was drawn, with sunken cheeks, and I had to punch three holes in my belt to hold up my pants.

Uncle Fausto frequently pointed out that I needed new clothes. Finally, he announced that whether I liked it or not, we were going to go shopping on my last Sunday in Mendota. "Okay, Dr. Pacheco," he said, as my cousins and I entered the men and boys' store that sold an array of popular brands, "buy yourself a new wardrobe."

I stood there frozen, not wanting to even look at the clothes, or worse, to spend a dime of what I'd earned. But how could I disobey my uncle, whose generosity had allowed me to prosper?

Seeing my paralysis, Uncle Fausto shrugged and proceeded to pick out two pairs of jeans and two shirts in my size that he knew I would like, and then headed for the cash register. When I argued that such items could be bought more cheaply in Mexico, he appeared not to be listening. "Doc," he said, "give me your wallet."

"No," I refused.

"Freddy, give me your wallet."

Tears streamed down my face. My cousins lowered their eyes. Finally, I gave in, removed the money, just over fifty dollars, and paid for the clothing that I desperately needed, and secretly wanted.

Uncle Fausto taught me an important lesson on that shopping trip. He wanted me to know that taking care of myself wasn't selfish and that while sharing the fruits of my labor with others was admirable, hard work should bring a few personal rewards too. To put a fine point on that message, the next day, when he and my cousins took me to the Greyhound station, just before I boarded the bus, Uncle Fausto surprised me with the gift of his Walkman, complete with tapes of American rock and roll. He had seen me pricing tape players at the store and knew how badly I wanted one. It was one of the most generous presents I'd ever received.

One of the few gifts to rival it came within a day, upon my return home. When I stepped off the bus in Mexicali, Mamá burst into tears the moment she saw me—ninety-two pounds of skin and bones. But I told her that I had something for her that would make her feel better. When we were home, just the two of us in the kitchen, I reached into my right sock, under the ball of my foot, and removed the roll of bills that I had protected with every molecule of my energy on the bus ride back to Mexico. About fifty bucks less than one thousand dollars. The amazement and relief that shone on my mother's face when I turned the money over to her—enough to feed us for a year and put money away for the future—was the greatest personal reward that I could have received.

·   ·   ·

I had been back from Mendota for nearly a year when my mother finally persuaded me to buy a pair of used boxing gloves so that I could realize my dream of working out at a gym in Mexicali. By then, I'd gained back the weight I'd lost, and before long, I was working my way up to lightweight status at 130 pounds. Part of my motivation, I confess, was that I was tired of having my butt kicked, being a target, and having to surround myself with bigger guys for protection. A part of me also entertained the idea of getting revenge against a particular punk who had embarrassed me many years earlier. Later, to my shame, I used my boxing skills outside the ring to call him out on the street and beat him badly—a wrong that would be on my conscience for years. I would then learn the truth of the Kaliman philosophy "Revenge is a poor counselor."

But when I was pummeling the punching bag, all I knew was that life had been beating us down and I had to find a new way to respond. My stint as a boxer taught me that I could do more than bob and weave defensively in the face of a challenge; my training helped me fight back, even to be the aggressor when necessary. The first two of my three fights in the ring—which I won—easily confirmed this conclusion. But in the third and last fight, in which I faced a physically overpowering opponent who left me to taste my own blood, I wasn't so sure—especially when he knocked me to my knees just before the bell in the last round. Still, I had a choice—to quit or to stand up and finish the fight, even in defeat. By choosing the latter option, I learned an essential lesson: it's not defeat I should fear; more important than whether I won or lost was how I responded to being knocked down and thrown off balance.

Though this was my last official fight, boxing had given me what I needed at the time—an opportunity to hit back. I also discovered that, like those corner breaks that allowed me to recharge during fights, there were ways to recharge my batteries in other pursuits. Eye-opening! But I still had plenty of anger, as there was a need for a surrogate to blame for the misfortunes that had gone on for too long. Rather than taking my fight to the ring, however, I started reserving my anger and rebellion for the forces, institutions, and authorities that most controlled my life. At this time, the major injustice that ate at me was the ongoing bifurcation of the social classes in my country that devalued human beings in the bottom economic strata, as if only those at the top with political connections, wealth, and means were worthy of respect and opportunity. Part of my fight was not to allow those values to get to me.

Always, my grandparents provided a guiding light for how to respond productively to hardship. Now they were getting up in years and both battling serious illnesses. Though I understood in theory that they wouldn't be around forever, Tata Juan and Nana Maria had always been so much larger than life that I couldn't imagine their being taken from this world.

Yet on a day like any other day, one of my cousins arrived at the director's office of my school to request that I be released from class, explaining that my grandfather—afflicted by metastatic lung cancer—was dying and had asked for me. We sped to my grandparents' home, and as I rushed into Tata's room, I thought I was too late. He seemed to be staring off into space, already gone in spirit. When I approached him, however, I saw that his eyes were shut.

"Tata," I said softly in his ear, leaning in close, one hand on his shoulder and the other on the weathered skin of his cheek. "It's me, Alfredo."

"Oh, yes," he replied with effort. "Alfredo."

My tears began to fall helplessly. In recent months, with cancer slowly and painfully killing him, I had visited often but rarely gotten him to talk much. Though I had seen him declining, I wasn't ready to say good-bye.

In the otherwise silent room, the sound of his breathing and the ticking of a small clock near his bedside were unforgettable. Then my grandfather slowly opened his eyes and asked softly, "Do you remember when we would go to the Rumorosa Mountains?"

"Yes, I do. Always."

"Me too. You used to call 'Tataaaahhhh! Tataaaahhhh!'"

"I remember."

"You know," he said, just before he closed his eyes and offered a final smile, "I really enjoyed those times."

Tata's dying message assured me that I should not be afraid to climb mountains, no matter how treacherous, and that I could even take joy in doing so. He wasn't telling me how to do that but wanted me to know that I could continue to call on him whenever I felt lost.

After Nana Maria passed away two years later, I felt her presence with me too—though her message was to be careful and to look out for pitfalls. I hope she forgave me for not being at her side more when she was dying. After a lifetime as a healer, helping to bring hundreds of lives into the world, Nana went to the grave knowing that no one had ever died in her care. But I was surprised to learn from my father that until the end, she was afraid of death and especially the loneliness of not knowing what was on the other side. My father also told me that in spite of her fear, when her time came she was ready. Nana discovered what many of us will never know until we are there—that no matter how many times we defy the odds, we all reach the moment where the only way out is surrender. Until then? Give it everything!

.   .   .

Christmas 1985 was eventful for a few reasons. At the age of seventeen, almost eighteen, I was on my way to becoming one of the youngest students ever to graduate from the training program at the teaching college that was my stepping-stone to the future. With excellent grades and teachers' recommendations, once I graduated I would wait to see where I would be assigned in Mexico to begin my journey as an elementary school teacher. I also had a wonderful girlfriend at the time, a beautiful, bright young lady from a well-to-do, respected family. Our courtship was new, but we were both serious enough about our futures to enter into a meaningful relationship.

After many difficulties, I was confident that brighter days were around the corner, as I told my cousin Fausto and his friend Ronnie when they drove down in Fausto's truck from Mendota for the Christmas holiday. My hope, I explained to them, was that I'd land a plum assignment for my first teaching post, ideally in one of the bigger cities close to home. The government sometimes sent newer teachers without the right family connections to out-of-the-way locations where there was little money to be made and few options for pursuing further education. But given my excellent academic record, I was sure to be rewarded with the right job—or so I expected.

In the best of moods, we decided to drive into Mexicali to join some of my friends for holiday parties. With Fausto's truck, we had wheels and could make the scene in style—a big plus for me, given that I usually had to ride the bus to such destinations and then walk an additional three miles or more in extreme heat or cold. We were so mobile, in fact, that not long after arriving at the party in Mexicali, Fausto and Ronnie suggested we continue on to other parties across the border in Calexico, California.

Small problem. I wasn't carrying my passport. Since I hadn't planned to cross the border, I'd left it at home. Fausto offered to drive us back to my house for it, but I didn't see a reason to drive two hours just for a little piece of paper. By the time we did that, the parties would be over. "Never mind," I told Fausto, "I won't need it. They hardly ever stop us."

We approached the checkpoint at the border crossing. The agent, seemingly in a cheery holiday mood, started to wave us through when something appeared to catch his attention and he gestured for us to stop.

Standing at the driver's side, the American agent asked Fausto, in English, where he was headed. Fausto, without an accent, explained that he was from Fresno but was visiting family for the holidays and was just going across the border for a party.

The agent nodded. Then he asked Ronnie, "Where are you from?"
Ronnie answered, "Fresno." The agent took him at his word.

Hoping to avoid more questions, I pretended to be looking very closely at something outside the window, up in the sky. The agent said, "You! Where are you from?"

"Fresno," I answered, mimicking Fausto and Ronnie's tone and pronunciation. My knowledge of the English language in this era was close to *nada*.

"And how long you lived in Fresno, son?" the border agent asked.

"Fresno," I nodded and smiled, clueless.

The agent then asked for documentation and, of course, I didn't have any.

Within seconds, a group of agents surrounded the truck. After much discussion, they allowed Fausto and Ronnie to go but detained me. A full two hours of interrogation followed, during which I repeatedly insisted that I had simply forgotten my passport and meant no harm or crime. I knew that I couldn't give them my name, however, because they would then suspend my passport for good. I also couldn't tell them what I did or where I was from. But I couldn't lie.

A Spanish speaker, the border agent who stopped us wanted blood. He could see I had nothing on me, as I was wearing only lightweight shorts, a tank top, and flip-flops. He began to threaten harm to my loved ones, even though he obviously didn't know who they were. Not getting anywhere, he locked me in a freezing cold room, as close to a cell as I would ever inhabit. Curling up in a fetal position in a futile attempt to get warm, I cried myself to sleep, certain that my life was ruined.

Before dawn, another agent came to unlock the door and found me on the floor. A compassionate man, he was clearly upset with the other agents for holding me in such conditions so long without food and water. The agent apologized, handed me money for breakfast, and sent me on my way.

Lesson learned. My better judgment had clearly been clouded. The idea that I didn't have a plan in case I was stopped was bad enough. But in thinking that I could deceive the border patrol agent who first approached the car, I stepped over the fine line between confidence and arrogance. With due remorse, I resolved never again to travel without my passport.

After that ordeal, I wasn't sure that I wanted to travel again. But extenuating circumstances changed my attitude. Much to my shock, as soon as I graduated from college, I learned that, because of the political situation in Mexico, my academic credentials hadn't helped me get the assignment I'd wanted. Instead, I was to start work right away in a very remote, rural area. The better jobs in cities near universities had all gone to students from wealthier and politically connected families. How could the fight be so blatantly rigged? What about merit? What about talent and hard work? What about justice and equality?

Without realizing it, I was already applying what I'd learned of the American dream from my two visits to the San Joaquin Valley, first at age eleven and then at age fourteen. I wanted to believe that I could travel to Faraway in my own country and have adventures, meeting opportunity and success along the way. I wanted to believe that I could be like my hero, Benito Juárez, and come from nowhere to make important contributions to my country. I most wanted to believe that poor and politically ignored people like me were not powerless. For a decade, during which economic troubles exacerbated poverty and suffering, the once-thriving middle class had been left in the dust. Now I was finding out that the promise that had sustained me—that people like me who had sunk to the bottom could eventually alter our own circumstances—was nothing but a fairy tale.

My future was suddenly in question. Did I even want to be an elementary school teacher? Had I really excelled, or had learning just come easily to me? As I relived the recent years of my education, I realized that I'd felt little passion for my subject matter and now, more than ever, resented this system that had lured me in with promises it couldn't keep. Had I chosen my path because becoming a teacher was practical, because someone else had done it and had left me a trail? Had I given up on the dreams that had roused my fighting spirit from the time I was a little boy?

Everything at this point appeared more difficult than before, and at times my situation seemed hopeless. At moments, I even wondered whether my life was worth living, whether anyone would miss me if I died. Yes, I had a family that loved me and a girlfriend who thought I had something to offer. But perhaps they were mistaken. Maybe everyone would be better off without me.

No one was able to explain to me that I was probably suffering from an overdue bout of depression or that my disillusionment was probably age-appropriate. No one was there to mention that this dark period would help me in years ahead—allowing me to empathize with patients and to understand their struggles.

One image kept me from losing all hope: the memory of my mother's jubilant face when I returned from Mendota and handed her my earnings. That hard-earned cash proved that people like me were not helpless or powerless. That was worth something, I had to admit. And I also took some comfort from a dream that had come to me during this time of near despair. In it, a shadowy stranger assured me that better days lay ahead and that I could be the architect of my destiny, although I would have to leave all that was familiar to do so. I asked the stranger how I would know that I was on the right path. He told me that a woman would appear to accompany me at the right stage of the journey; she would be fair-haired and have green eyes.

The dream gave me few other specifics. However, clinging to the image of my mother's face when I'd returned home from working the fields the last time, I decided I could still become a teacher if I made a few adjustments in my plan. If I returned temporarily to Mendota, I could earn enough money to buy a car and also put aside some of my earnings to supplement my meager income when I returned to Mexico to begin my community service job. Uncle Fausto kindly agreed to put me back to work at the ranch, where I enjoyed my reclaimed status as Dr. Pacheco. Before long, I accumulated seven hundred dollars of earnings and this time needed no persuading to buy myself a wreck of an old Thunderbird at a local used-car dealership.

My dream of fixing up the car's interior like a Las Vegas attraction—with photos of movie stars, a pair of dice, some religious iconography, and a cassette player for blaring the heavy rock I now loved—would have to wait. But in the meantime, that wreck of a Thunderbird traveled much farther and back again than its makers probably ever imagined.

.   .   .

Toward the end of 1986, as I approached my nineteenth birthday, I felt my life's journey was nearing a crossroads. While I fought the idea of leaving Mexico for longer than a stint here and there and refused to give up wholly on finding a teaching position that would pay me a small salary, deep down I knew that it was only a matter of time before I migrated north.

I thought of my girlfriend, of course, and the possibilities of building a life together. But what could I offer? Then I recalled all my nights on the roof watching those fast-moving, action-seeking little stars—all going somewhere exciting, beyond the limits of my imagination. There was my answer, as certain as the fixed planets that I now knew hovered in the night sky.

Again, the opportunity to continue working at the ranch in Mendota was central to my thinking. The idea was to go there for a couple of years, returning periodically, like Uncle Jose, with money and help for the family. I hoped I could soon rise to Uncle Fausto's level, which would enable me to put aside enough money to come back to Mexico and study at the university. I wouldn't need political connections because I would be a man of means unto myself.

With that plan in mind, though I hadn't made a final decision or revealed my thoughts to anyone other than Gabriel, he and I decided to go up to Mendota for a few weeks before Christmas to earn some money for the holidays. We would then bring Fausto and Oscar back with us just before New Year's to enjoy the local festivities. After that, I would drive my cousins back home and either drop them off (as Oscar was finishing high school and Fausto was in his first year at Fresno State) and return home or stay at least until the following summer.

True to the plan, we worked in Mendota over the holiday, and then a few days before New Year's Eve, I rounded up my cousins and Gabriel, and the four of us hopped into my Thunderbird to make the now-familiar drive through central California toward San Diego and then east to Calexico to cross the border for home. After my earlier ordeal, I made sure to carry my passport wherever I went, so I wasn't worried about the border crossing, even if we were stopped. Besides, I thought, lightning rarely strikes twice in the same place.

Not so fast!

We weren't stopped that day. But on New Year's Eve, now back in Mexico, the three of us decided to drive back over the border to Calexico, at which point a couple of border agents stopped us and asked to see our passports. We showed them the documents, and everything was fine—until the agent asked when I had last entered or left the country and where I had been. "Fresno," I said. "Travel. Visit family."

Fausto and Oscar waited in the car as Gabriel and I were escorted into a room, where a two-hour interrogation ensued. The agents had nothing on us. Finally, they asked if we'd ever worked during our travel and family visits to the United States. "What?" I asked indignantly, as if that notion were the craziest thing I'd ever heard. All this time I had been working with only a tourist visa—clearly illegal. Now I was sweating bullets, but I managed to appear cool.

When they were about to let us go, one of the agents said, "Fine, let me take a look at your ID again."

But instead of letting me pull out the paperwork to show him, he grabbed my wallet, where he immediately found fairly recent pay stubs, issued in the United States, with my name on them. And there was a pay stub with Gabriel's name on it, too.

We were now officially in trouble not just for working without a permit but for lying about it.

And that was how lightning struck twice and I had my passport confiscated, as did Gabriel. When we came outside, Fausto and Oscar were waiting in the Thunderbird. I got behind the wheel and followed the agent's directions as he pointed us back south toward Mexico.

If I had been at all ambivalent about leaving home and spending a longer period of time in the United States, that incident sealed my fate. Granted, I had no passport, no legal means of crossing the border again. But that technicality wasn't going to stop me from executing a new plan. There was no time to make my good-byes, no time to explain myself or express my regrets to my friends or my girlfriend.

I had searched my heart and looked to the wisdom of my grandparents, who seemed to be sending me the same message: go! The time to leave home, family, and everything I knew in this world had arrived. There was no need to be afraid or to think that I couldn't do it. All I needed to take with me was Tata Juan and Nana Maria's lasting guidance and everything that I'd been blessed to learn in my eighteen years. That, and the sixty-five American dollars I had to my name.

As I devised the strategy I planned to execute, auspiciously, on New Year's Day, 1987, I spent the hours before dawn sitting outside in the darkness without a star in the sky. My thoughts wound back to my trips to the mountains with Tata Juan as we made our way to the little town of Rumorosa, along the steep edges of the Sierras. I remembered how dangerous the road was and the fact that many cars had fallen down the cliffs in terrible weather and in other mishaps. And yet my grandfather had chosen not the safest route but the one that provided the most interesting little stops along the way. While Tata was as eager to get to the cabin as I was, he didn't agree with me that the shortest and most direct route between two points was best. He wanted to show me what I would miss if I focused only on my destination.

Desperate situations—like the one in which I found myself on the eve of my nineteenth birthday—require desperate choices. Having made my decision, I couldn't allow any regrets or second thoughts to deter me. Don't look back, I told myself. I had to go forward to find my destiny, crossing the border fence to see where the path on the other side would take me. I had to act boldly, decisively, and immediately. And I had to climb to the top and jump.

THREE The Kaliman Maneuver

How did I do it?

Even today, I'm not sure how I managed to jump the fence to start a new life in California. Throughout the years since then, I have often said that I was propelled by a combination of audacity and naivety. Why else would I defy gravity and risk injury, incarceration, and even death to cross the border? Without a certain degree of ignorance about all the things that could go wrong, it would have been much harder to screen out disabling thoughts. If I had been more realistic and had considered the pitfalls in greater depth, I might not have made the journey at all.

But I was not entirely blind to the risk I was taking on that New Year's Day in 1987. When I watched the sun rise over the fields of home for possibly the last time, I was fully aware that the strategy I'd crafted during the night might fail. If anything, life had taught me not to be afraid of failure. What made me more afraid was *not* trying to embrace the world just beyond my reach. My fear was that I would *not* go for it, *not* give it my very best shot. And that wasn't audacity or lack of worldly experi-

ence. It came from the belief that I had valuable assets to offer—my passion (Quiñones stubbornness) and boundless energy, even if I didn't yet
know how to harness it in a meaningful way.

These resources likewise came into play in my approach to crossing the border without documentation. Certainly, desperation added
fuel to the fire. But the scientist inside me was also already at work.
Remembering Tata Juan's advice, I realized that I had to veer off the well-
traveled path to build a promising future. And anticipating the advice of
the great scientist Santiago Ramón y Cajal, whose writing would influence me greatly in my career, I knew instinctually that I needed to think
clearly, plan my strategy carefully, and never give up. Of course, having
just put away my school books to prepare for full-time work at the lowest rungs of agriculture, I would have laughed at the notion that I could
become a scientist one day—let alone a *neuro*scientist.

Not that my plan was perfect. As any science-minded person could
have told me, most real breakthroughs come about through a process of
trial and error, repetition and adaptation, imaginative leaps, and—even
though we are not supposed to admit it in the scientific world—the all-
important commodity of good luck.

Indeed, there was nothing very scientific about my decision to defy
the conventional wisdom that the safest way to get across without capture by the border patrol was to make a hole at the bottom of the fence
or tunnel under it. According to lore, if not fact, people who attempted to
scale the fence, as I planned to do, and then tangled with the barbed wire
were the ones who sustained the worst injuries, and some even died.
Although armed vigilantes were not prevalent at the time, most of the
stories about shooting fatalities at the border involved people who had
been trying to go over the fence rather than under it.

Perhaps it was the underdog in me—the boy who was used to being
challenged and who wanted to do things differently—that opted to go
the dangerous route. And being of a rebellious mind-set anyway, I found
no allure in going the easier way—or so I tried to explain to Gabriel,
Fausto, and Oscar on the evening of January 1, as the sun began to set
during our drive to the drop-off point in Mexicali.

"Doc, you're crazy!" cousin Oscar scoffed from the back seat of my
Thunderbird, where he sat next to Gabriel. "Nobody *jumps* the fence."

What he meant but didn't need to say was that nobody jumped the fence in the middle of Calexico. Actually, lots of people found remote stretches of the fence to climb. But attempting to do so in the middle of town was so bold as to be nuts.

From the front passenger seat, I glanced over at Fausto, who was behind the wheel. In his kind, intelligent fashion, Fausto suggested, "Well, I think we're using the word 'jump' as a euphemism, right Freddy?"

"Exactly." Then I explained that my move would, in fact, be more of a Spiderman climb up the eighteen-foot fence, followed by a hop over the barbed wire and a leap toward foreign soil—culminating in a flying descent and a pantherlike, spring-loaded landing, reminiscent of the Kaliman maneuver that I'd never mastered.

Although Oscar and Gabriel expressed misgivings about this outlandish plan, we were all pumped by the excitement of the undertaking.

For all the risk that the gravity-defying portion of the crossing would entail, the rest of the plan was much tamer and had fewer potential pitfalls. Or so I insisted while explaining that Fausto should stop the car a few blocks from the stretch of border fence where I would attempt "the maneuver."

Fausto would then drive west the three miles or so to the main crossing gate where cars went from Mexico into the United States and, from there, slowly make his way through the streets of Calexico to our designated meeting place behind the house of one of our relatives. My intention, the moment I landed on the other side of the fence, was to race off in an entirely opposite direction from the Thunderbird, kill some time in order to lose the trail of any suspicious border agents, and eventually wind back to our spot. From there, after we made it out of town and onto the highway, the plot would thicken as we implemented a few measures to avoid the immigration checkpoints—which actually posed the biggest obstacle for most border crossings.

Today, with the many changes in technology, many more checkpoints along numerous transportation channels, and much tougher measures along the U.S.-Mexico border, this plan of mine would not work—for good reasons. Immigration issues have grown much more complicated, and we have much work to do in figuring out how to reach fair-minded reform with all of those considerations.

In some respects, however, things haven't so much changed as they have intensified, including economic extremes in both developing and developed countries. For the poor and the powerless, literal hunger and a quest for opportunity are enough to compel them to risk everything, even their lives, to cross the border. Meanwhile, anti-immigrant resentment has grown too, mainly against the poor, undocumented workers who provide cheap labor.

As I would learn later on, developed countries will always welcome the Einsteins of this world—those individuals whose talents are already recognized and deemed to have value. This welcome doesn't usually extend to poor and uneducated people seeking to enter the country. But the truth, supported by the facts of history and the richness of the immigrant contribution to America's distinction in the world, is that the most entrepreneurial, innovative, motivated citizen is the one who has been given an opportunity and wants to repay the debt.

Of course, I was unaware of these complexities as I prepared to cross the border. For me, the fence was the dividing line between oppression and a fighting chance, between stagnation and hope. It was that simple. What's more, at the time the United States had unprecedented demand for cheap labor that was dependable—decent, hardworking, able. What this said to me was that I was needed. Upon this stage, my drama was set.

At precisely 8:30 P.M., it was do-or-die time. I approached the fairly remote stretch of the border fence a couple of blocks beyond Mexicali's city limits. As I slid into place, crouched next to a bush between two light towers, I was relieved to see that I cast very little shadow. I knew, however, that when I moved closer to the fence, I would be plainly visible to anyone in the vicinity. No motion detectors were present in this era, but even so, one wrong move, one flinch of a muscle, could cause the endeavor to fail.

Behind me a few hundred yards, hiding behind a tree in the darkness, were Gabriel and Oscar, watching my attempt to make history—to do something none of us had dared consider or witnessed before. From their vantage point, I assumed, the lighting would allow them not only to see me scale the fence but also to look across to the spot in Calexico where Fausto would pick me up. Pumping myself up, I imagined that their challenge would be to stifle their cheers when they saw the Thunderbird speed away—and to avoid any other noise or movement that would attract the attention of the Mexican police who patrolled the border on our side.

At 8:31 P.M., I seized my moment, filled my lungs with air, and knowing that I was being watched by my brother and younger cousin, mustered every bit of courage and showmanship I had to propel myself up the fence and pull out all the Kaliman stops. Even though Gabriel and Oscar were rooting for me to get over the fence safely and smoothly, I knew that they would be equally excited to see me bite the dust. Oh, ye of little faith, I thought, just as it hit me that I was really doing this thing. In an instant, I understood what all my years of agility training had prepared me for. I sprang into the air and vaulted over the top rolls of barbed wire with a jump, hop, and a leap, positioning my body the perfect distance from the fence, moving down through the starless winter night with the grace of a bird. As I landed majestically on my feet, I was utterly exhilarated. Yes, yes, yes, I had done it! The eagle had landed. I had pulled off the maneuver! Just a small glitch. Based on my scientific calculations, I had decided that I needed three minutes to get from one side of the border to the other before speeding away on foot into the streets of Calexico. But my calculations were wrong—by thirty seconds. Out of nowhere headlights blasted into the darkness, momentarily blinding me—amid the screeching of brakes of the border patrol car arriving on the scene and the churning of dust as the two agents threw open the car doors and suddenly stood on either side of me.

So much for pulling off the maneuver. Humiliated, I felt like a total loser. I could only imagine my brother and cousin rolling on the ground, laughing uncontrollably. Despite my audacious, scientific, visionary thinking, the fireworks had just fizzled. Now what? Morosely, I prepared to be lambasted not only as a menace but as an incompetent one at that. To my surprise, though, the border agents were a rather affable duo. In fact, in the annals of law enforcement, my capture was as routine and benign as they come.

I was then chauffeured in the military-style Ford Bronco back to the main crossing station, where I was led into a room for booking. When prompted, I gave the agents a made-up name, knowing they wouldn't push the issue. I was a scrawny, defeated-looking kid who appeared to be all of sixteen, without even any facial hair. They had nothing to gain from rubbing my face in my defeat. Without saying anything explicit, the agents appeared to be sympathetic—as if they knew the kinds of challenges that had driven me to risk life and limb to cross the border without papers. But everyone has a job to do. And they did what they always do—kicked me back to Mexico, out the rear door to head home on foot.

Memorably, it was right there, as I plodded along the three miles in the direction of my failed border crossing—where I'd last seen Gabriel and cousin Oscar—that I did some serious soul searching. I was crushed. How could the path of last resort lead only to a dead end? But then I asked myself if perhaps only my ego was hurt. In my mind, I put myself back in the ring and decided to be my own cornerman, to summon the Dr. Ferdie Pacheco as well as the Ali in me. Sure, I was knocked down. Yes, my timing was off. But was I going to collapse and cry? No way. I was going to hit back and give it my all once more—this time with a revised plan and new calculations.

Reinvigorated, I sprinted toward the crossing point, eager to share my new approach with my brother and cousin. I assumed that they had watched the whole debacle unfold and couldn't wait to see me eat crow.

But the two of them had no idea what had happened after they saw me fly into the darkness. As I would learn months later, while I was being booked, Gabriel and Oscar were about to be booked by two Mexican policemen who had picked them up simply because they looked suspicious, hiding behind a tree for no apparent reason and looking young and naive—one of them (cousin Oscar) well dressed in U.S.-bought clothes. Never having been in trouble, they figured that matters could not become much worse when the officers put them in the police car. But after driving for several minutes, the policeman in the passenger seat turned around and noticed a near-empty bottle of beer at Oscar's feet.

The policeman behind the wheel was outraged as he turned to his partner. "We just got these kids in the car, and they're drinking?"

With that, Gabriel and Oscar were dragged into the station and soon escorted to a jail cell, at which point they dug into their pockets. Gabriel had only a few dollars to fork over. But Oscar ended up paying something exorbitant—like a hundred hard-earned bucks.

That drama was still playing out for them when I arrived back where I had attempted my over-the-fence maneuver an hour earlier. I wasn't sure what to do next. All I knew was that I was lucky because I had a choice: either to throw in the towel and give up, or, as I had learned in boxing, to get back on my feet and try again. This decision was a crucial test of my mettle, and it taught me a lesson I have carried with me ever since—that the best successes often come after multiple failures; the key is to try again and again without losing enthusiasm and focus.

Given the choice, I decided to go for it again—the same strategy, only better. To that end, I spent the next hour hugging the ground right next to the fence, below a few bushes, and studying the movements of the border patrol. Instead of giving myself a three-minute window, I would need to condense my movements into two minutes and thirty seconds. In my first effort, I'd moved too soon, and the agents had spotted me in their patrol car's rear-view mirror.

Some would have thought it folly to repeat the same move, from the same spot, that had led to my capture the first time. For me, it made perfect sense. The border agents wouldn't be looking for me to come back within a couple hours and try the same thing that had failed before. Who would be that crazy, right? They had to be thinking that lightning wouldn't strike twice in the same place. I knew better!

So again I climbed to the top of the fence in a matter of seconds and flew over it to the other side. My flight was much less elegant this time, as I came within a hair of getting tangled in the barbed wire at the top of the fence and then bit the dust and fell to a less-than-cushioned landing. But before I'd even planted myself on the ground, I was running so fast that my feet cut air, with the motion of my legs carrying me as fast as the wind. With my heart bursting out of my chest, I moved so fast that I nearly tripped again, coming close to crashing to the dirt. Instead I moved even faster, careening down alleys, over more fences, under clotheslines draped with laundry, and across fields, stirring up a badass pack of dogs that barked in chorus as they chased me through the city.

At last, I reached the neighborhood where Fausto was supposed to meet me. Magically, when I turned the last corner, I saw him there, waiting in the darkness in my Thunderbird.

He approached slowly, reaching across to throw open the door, and I leapt into the car with it still in motion. As I caught my breath, we high-fived, neither of us saying a word, and he drove us away from the border, moving along the well-lit main drag of Calexico until we blended in with all the cars driven by local revelers continuing their New Year's festivities from the night before. We then turned west and wound around until we reached the highway leading toward San Diego, which thankfully had no checkpoints.

Now came phase two of the strategy, which called for Fausto to drop me off at the airport in San Diego. Here was where the plot became much more complex and where the outcome was going to depend less on science than on luck. I had heard that some people paid smugglers six hundred dollars to orchestrate and implement such a plan, but with only sixty-five dollars to my name, I had no choice but to devise my own makeshift version.

Not knowing what to anticipate, I was on pins and needles. From the moment my passport had been confiscated, I'd been on an adrenaline rush, catching only a few hours of sleep here and there. Exhaustion should have set in by now. Not a chance! My heart beat faster as Fausto and I reviewed the logistics of the next step. To avoid the Indio checkpoint, we needed to separate in San Diego and then reconnect in Los Angeles—probably in the early dawn. In these pre-9/11 days, airport security and requirements for showing one's ID were not as stringent for short domestic flights as they were for transcontinental and international travel.

My gamble—which was huge—was that I would be able to buy a ticket and board a plane for the very short flight to L.A. (thus avoiding the checkpoints along Fausto's driving route) without having to show my ID. But, of course, this wasn't an original idea, and ticket agents were sure to be on the lookout for people like me. So on the way to the airport, Fausto had helped me memorize and rehearse answers to some of the questions I might be asked. Being a good mimic, I listened to his pronunciation of key phrases—"A ticket to Los Angeles, please"—and then repeated them, practicing my best American accent.

Only after Fausto dropped me off in the middle of the night at the San Diego airport and sped off into the darkness did fear really set in. As I stood in line at the airport ticket counter, I began to panic, afraid that immigration agents would suddenly appear and surround me. Although I was dressed in stylish American Bugle Boy slacks and a preppy Le Tigre polo shirt, I doubted that my attire was fooling anyone.

When my turn arrived, I walked up to the woman at the airline counter, concerned that my heart would beat right out of my chest. I summoned every memory I could find of past successes at mastering my fears: driving a car for the first time at five years old, overcoming stage fright at my first public speaking event, turning menacing bullies into bodyguards. These thoughts quieted my nerves and I said with as much charm as possible, still keeping it cool, "A ticket to L.A., please."

"Next flight out, sir?"

"Yes, thank you." I almost added "my lady" like Tata Juan and threw in a small doff of my imaginary hat.

The cost of the ticket was sixty-three dollars and change.

I paid for it and nodded graciously, carefully tucking away the dollar and coins that I had left and looking around to determine where to go next. Without a better option, I decided to follow the early-morning crowd and fortunately ended up at the plane's departure point. The flight was surreal, astounding, and stomach-churning. Not once was I asked for identification or questioned by anyone in authority. Even so, I didn't exhale until we landed in Los Angeles and pulled up to the gate.

But now the plan lost all scientific control. Since Fausto hadn't known what plane or what airline I was going to take, he had simply said that he would do his best to be there to meet me when I disembarked. If I didn't see him when I got off the plane, the plan was for me to wait for him near the lower level of the terminal entrance by the baggage carousel—though we had no idea that the airport had numerous terminals. So I wasn't alarmed when he wasn't in the gate area to meet the plane or even when a few hours passed and he hadn't arrived at the terminal entrance where I'd arrived. Though somewhat concerned, I thought perhaps he had driven back to Mexicali to get Oscar and would eventually show up.

While the past two days had flown by, the hours now slowed to a sluggish crawl. Of course, I wanted to run victory laps around LAX, but until we were on the road to the San Joaquin Valley, I wouldn't be able to relax. Besides, I was famished, even after spending my remaining dollar and a half or so on a cheeseburger at the first spot I found—Burger King. To distract myself from worrying about where Fausto was, I decided to explore the airport and spent the rest of the day listening to the fantastic array of conversations, languages, and dialects. At one point, weak from hunger, I went to sit in the food court, hoping to spot leftovers at other tables. A few tables over, I saw a couple with two children dash off to catch their flight, leaving their trays behind. With the agility of a gazelle, I went over to bus the table, discreetly feasting on the food that would have gone to waste otherwise.

The food revived my energy and spirits, but by late afternoon, I was frantic, ready to give up on the long odds that Fausto and I would ever find each other. The prospect that I'd have to make it on my own suddenly became real. True, I knew no one in Los Angeles, had no money, and spoke practically no English. But if my road had brought me here, I would follow it out into the city: someone would recognize a hard worker and give me a job sweeping floors or pumping gas. And just as I resigned myself to this fate, right as I stepped onto the down escalator—in a terminal far from where I arrived—to make my way into the cool of the evening, there was Fausto coming up the escalator on the other side! Unbelievable! What were the odds? We could have circled the airport for days, never finding one another. But here he was! I will never forget the moment when I saw his face and his warm smile grinning up at me.

We jumped into my Thunderbird and peeled out of the parking lot, into the chilly night air of Los Angeles, California. Before I could get a sense of the city, we veered off and away, onto the freeway, following the signs north. Once we were out of the city limits, I finally allowed myself to hoot and holler and to thank the saints above for the miracle of this opportunity.

If memory serves, the date when all of this came together was January 2, 1987—my nineteenth birthday.

FOUR Lessons from the Fields

Winter is often the most grueling season for the year-round migrant worker.

I learned this hard truth a short time after my return to the San Joaquin Valley, along with a series of other eye-opening discoveries about the new path that I had chosen. Besides the cold, wet weather that greeted me upon my arrival, I was confronted by the fact that the year-round work cycle was very different from the short stints I'd worked at the ranch before. Seasonal workers move from farm to farm and crop to crop, depending on the growing season, so any preconceived ideas I had about what I could expect for the coming months at once became irrelevant. Because the seasons had just changed, there was no work picking the crops where I'd been working last. This was the cue to move on to the next job and the next employer.

When I went to speak to the foremen at nearby farms, most had already filled the bulk of the jobs. They were impressed that I could fix machinery and drive anything on wheels, but these skilled, supervisory positions were usually earned only after long periods of moving up the ladder. I realized that no matter where I landed—and no matter which season or crop, I'd need to get used to starting over every time I moved. And with each move, I would have to get to know a different boss, who had to answer to a different owner, as well as find my place in a different group of co-workers. The only familiar element—whether the crop was cotton, tomatoes, corn, cauliflower, broccoli, grapes, or melons, all of which I helped cultivate over the next eighteen months—was that one or two of the workers would remember me as Doc.

Fortunately for me that winter, after a couple of days staying with Uncle Fausto, I was hired on at one of the huge neighboring ranches. For the next few weeks, I lived in my car, basically homeless, until I could add enough to my savings to proudly pay three hundred dollars for the first home of my own—a small camping trailer I could park at whichever farm employed me, not too far from where other migrant workers were housed in busier seasons.

On the first or second night after taking up residence in the trailer, I discovered it had several almost unfixable leaks. This coincided with my discovery that the cold of winter in Mendota was much more oppressive than that of the Baja. Clearly, I was not prepared for the bone-chilling wetness of those frigid nights and early mornings, especially as I attempted to acclimate to a much more intense work regimen than I had known before. But I was not about to admit that I couldn't handle it, so I decided that I would embrace, even celebrate, the hardships and see them as educational. Who, me, worry about the weather and admit to feeling more alone than ever before in my life? Not a chance. And to prove it to myself, I decided to love my leaky trailer all the more for its flaws—not to mention for its ugly, awkward blue-green trim. I was still my father's son. If the weather was cold and the work was grueling, so be it. My belief was that I was being tested—physically and mentally—and that if I could get through this pass successfully, nothing could stop me. If something happened to shake my confidence, I could live with that. If I could fight back by making light of the problem as not such a big deal, I would prevail. That's how I chose to view my leaky trailer—not as the trappings of poor me but as a palace!

Then I learned that one of the most menial and most challenging jobs for any farm worker was the seasonal requirement of moving irrigation lines. Wouldn't you know it? That was my winter job—the first test handed to me, just in time to bring me seriously down to earth. To some, this trial by fire might have been nothing but a choice to put up with the job nobody else wanted. But for me, that would have been defeatist. Instead, I had to figure out how to take it in stride and excel at it. My inspiration? Bruce Springsteen, champion of the working class, whose "Born in the USA" was already an anthem for me, even though I wasn't born here. To demonstrate my rugged individualism, I bought an all-terrain vehicle, a Honda 175 motorcycle (red, my new favorite color), a rarely seen three-wheeler—which I could drive in the fields as well as on the road.

Moving irrigation lines was worse than I'd heard. The task was to move twenty-yard-long sections of the lines from one row of cotton seedlings to the next, picking them up at one end and then at the other, shifting them bit by bit. The ground was a nasty consistency between mud and quicksand. Anyone wearing boots or shoes would sink precipitously into knee-deep mud and become stuck. I could move twice as fast if I went barefoot, though I still sank down in the mud to my knees and my feet were quickly torn to shreds, becoming frozen and bloody. And that was my life—pretty much all day, every day, in the cold. Brutal!

The physical toll included exhaustion, discomfort, and lots of pain, but the real challenge was the mental test—the need to confront my fear of the discomfort, my dread that the hours would elapse too slowly, my resistance to the sheer monotony of the repetition and the menial labor, my insecurity that others might look down on me because I worked in the dirt, and my own maddening impatience for the work to be over.

At first, I survived by daydreaming about my unfolding master plan to make a lot of money as quickly as possible and return to my country triumphant—no longer the child of a poor family or a teacher who couldn't afford to do the job for which he was trained, but a man of stature, wealth, and options. However, this fantasy started to wear thin once I had collected a few paychecks. With my wage of $3.75 an hour—actually 50¢ more than the minimum wage at the time—I began to realize that I would need much longer than a year or so to accumulate the kind of savings I'd imagined I would put away in that time.

So I reminded myself that I would not labor here for the rest of my life; my work on these California farms was only that first step toward saving enough to return home and acquire a university education. Other steps would come. But just as important as seeing the big picture was learning how to be in the present moment and to inhabit the little picture—to intensify my concentration on whatever task was at hand. Little did I know that learning to wield this sword of intense, pure focus would serve me well in the future—from moving irrigation lines to picking tomatoes to battling brain cancer.

I learned that with focus came patience—a commodity that I'd never had in great supply. And, ironically, my patience was what enabled me to move up rapidly at each new job that I was given. Patience—which is as necessary for tending crops as it is for conducting Nobel prize–winning research—also nurtured joy and a passion for life. Without joy, of course, we're left with drudgery and even hopelessness. Passion further encouraged me to do my best, no matter how menial or small the job. Some might think me crazy to find passion for field work. But I learned to love the labor as a treasure I had unearthed in the San Joaquin Valley, one that made me rich forever and that made me feel like the alpha male I wanted to be. This period in the fields was my time in the sun, my opportunity to rise, and I wasn't going to let the bitter, cold winter or irrigation lines or leaky trailers stop me.

And rise I did. Before the season was over, I had worked my way up from moving irrigation lines to driving one of the biggest, baddest, most intricate pieces of farm equipment of the era. Manufactured by Caterpillar, it looked like a space-age dragon and could practically fly, able to plow soil in wide swaths—provided, that is, that the driver could maneuver it with the utmost precision.

I loved driving that dragon, sitting up in the cab with my coffee and breakfast, seeing the steam rise from the hot thermos and my breath escape into the cold air, as I raced a pack of wily coyotes that were determined to jump into the cab and get to my food.

When the winter season finally came to an end in late March, I rejoined the crew working for Uncle Fausto. There at the ten-thousand–acre family-owned ranch that had been founded during the Great Depression, I was inspired to learn some of the history of this Greek family and discovered that the owner's grandfather had come to Ellis Island and migrated west, starting as a seasonal farm laborer and working his way up until he had enough money to start a small farm of his own here in the heart of central California. It was wonderful to imagine the stages of growth of that first harvest and picture the crops flourishing over the years so that future generations of his family would be the beneficiaries of his dream. Where else but in America could such a success story be told? What was to stop me from eventually cultivating a ranch of my own? Nothing!

Nothing, except that every time I rose to the top of the class at one job, the slate was wiped clean as soon as I moved to the next job, and I had to start fresh. Fortunately, I moved up rapidly, sometimes on a daily basis, other times within a week, until finally I was the head of a crew. This progress was a reminder that while patience was a virtue, I preferred the motion forward—like those speedy stars I loved in the night sky.

But whether moving slow or fast, I had many moments of doubt. One such incident took me by surprise during a lunch break when I decided to converse in Spanish with the kid who worked behind the counter at the little market out in the middle of nowhere. By now, I had invested in my first Spanish-English dictionary (kept in my hip pocket, always at the ready) and had even started a journal in which I was attempting to write my thoughts in my very broken English. Most of the time, I placed my lunch order in English and got little reaction from the teenager who worked there, who was clearly Mexican-American—probably first generation.

On this day, being my natural, gregarious self, I said something in Spanish about the beautiful spring day and then parted with, "Have a pleasant afternoon, brother."

Saying nothing, the kid stared back at me in revulsion. No, his look was one of disdain. Even derision.

In that instant, I felt as devastated as I had at six years old when the big kids played me at marbles and stole money from the gas station cash register. When I analyzed the exchange at the market, I realized that the teenager's embarrassment at our shared ethnicity had less to do with me than with his shame, perhaps, about his parents, who may have been migrant workers. I got it. But his reaction planted a seed of insecurity in me, really for the first time, about my accent and about being Mexican. Before long, the tiny thing had taken root, unwanted though it was.

Shortly thereafter, out in the field one day, I was helping one of the guys on my crew, when the son of one of the owners walked by and looked my way yet didn't show any sign that he had registered the presence of another human being. That was how he looked at all the laborers. Were we invisible? Did he not realize that we were there working to the best of our abilities to bring in his family's harvest, increase its profits, and enrich him too? In his eyes, we were not individuals with names or identities; we were nonentities, even faceless.

I wanted to give him the benefit of the doubt, but another encounter made that tougher to do. Our paths crossed this second time when I was given an opportunity for extra work in the evenings and on the weekends—cleaning the ranch house belonging to the young man's family. Later I would visit more opulent mansions, but at that time, when I arrived at the house and stood outside of it, the sprawling home looked like it could be on *Lifestyles of the Rich and Famous*.

Nervous and excited, I rang the doorbell. When no one arrived to open the door, I tried knocking. Nothing. Finally, I rang one more time, and the same teenager threw open the door, apparently annoyed. Saying nothing, he pointed me toward the cleaning supplies, gestured to the main part of the house, and left me to fend for myself. I concluded that migrant workers were perceived as not only faceless but voiceless.

Later, I could look back at these encounters and recognize the early lessons they had taught me about the need for compassion and caring for the many patients who all too often are treated as faceless and voiceless in institutional and even family settings. The treatment of migrant workers also stayed with me as a reminder to acknowledge the contributions of everyone at the hospital, clinic, or lab—from orderlies and janitors to nurses and technicians, on up to doctors and administrators. Everyone has a name, a face, a voice. And these experiences of being marginalized would keep me from seeing others only through the lens of their job, or their diagnosis—as anything other than a fully alive person and valued human being.

Lack of access to care for migrant workers hit very close to home one abnormally hot summer afternoon when I was summoned to the corn-field with urgent calls of, "Get Doc, tell him to hurry, his uncle Mario has collapsed!" Everyone knew now that I wasn't a doctor. But because Uncle Mario was my father's brother who had come up from Ensenada to work for the busy season, I was the obvious person to summon.

It wasn't a stretch for me to determine that dehydration had contrib-uted to my uncle's collapse. With water and salt tablets, he was going to be fine. But even so, I thought he should be checked out by a real doctor. Yet when I talked to the third in command on the job site, Asunción—"Chon," as we called him—he looked at me like I was *loco*. Medical ser-vices for migrant workers?

This incident wasn't just about my uncle. Sure, he hadn't had a heart attack or a stroke. But, then again, what if he had? We had no access or advocates. My God, I remember thinking, we're naked out here—completely vulnerable, less than nothing. Uncle Mario felt that way too, apparently. Not long after his collapse, he packed up and returned to Ensenada.

In isolation, these incidents didn't alter my desire to do well for myself. I still believed that I'd come to the ultimate land of opportunity. But I was beginning to understand that without the benefit of an education, hard work would not be enough to get ahead.

This lesson became even clearer whenever I saw Cousin Fausto, who was thriving at Fresno State. He credited his success to the pretty young woman he had met and would soon marry. Through her influence, he had connected to God and faith in a way that would guide him from then on. Fausto, I should add, always seemed connected spiritually. A tenacious, infinitely generous soul, he always looked out for others.

"You know," Fausto urged me about six months into my journey as a migrant worker, "you should take some classes at Fresno State. It would be good for your social life!"

"I'd love that," I told him. "But I don't know where I'd find the time."

Also, my application for a worker's authorization, which was required to attend college, hadn't been approved yet.

The encouraging news was that in the wake of the 1986 amnesty legislation passed by President Ronald Reagan, the state of California was reforming its policy toward migrant farm workers. If you were able to show that you had worked in the United States for a certain number of days in the previous year, you qualified for a worker's authorization. You could then apply for a temporary green card and eventually an actual green card. So once I had a worker's authorization, my plan was to enroll in night classes—anything to improve my English. In the meantime, I'd have to stick to my pocket dictionary.

Thanks to these changing laws governing migrant work, by summertime, more of my family members were able to join me in the San Joaquin Valley. Among the first to arrive were my sister Rosa and her husband, Ramón Ramirez. Expecting their first child, they were hopeful that Ramón could obtain work at the ranch where I was working. Fortunately, he was hired right away, and they became my neighbors, parking their spacious (or so I thought at the time), well-insulated trailer not far from mine.

Even though Ramón had been a friend of mine, I had not been happy when I'd first heard that he and my sister were getting married. She was sixteen years old, even younger than our parents had been when they married. But as I got to know Ramón better, I concluded that she could not have chosen a better spouse—truly her soul mate. Even before the fateful day in the not-too-distant future when Ramón would help save my life, I had other reasons to appreciate the greatness of his heart and his determination.

Soon after the two of them settled in at the ranch, the next wave of family members arrived—including my parents and my younger siblings, thirteen-year-old Jorge and nine-year-old Jaqueline. Gabriel had decided to remain in Mexico until he completed the technical college program he had begun. I admired his decision and knew how tough it was to stay behind on his own, especially since, to save on rent, he had moved into our grandparents' house, now turned into a funeral home. Talk about ghost stories!

From the moment I raced across the muddy field on my three-wheeler to greet my parents, I could tell that Mamá wasn't prepared for the changes that had occurred in me during our time apart. But she didn't say anything other than how happy she was to see me.

Years later, Mamá admitted the distress she felt that day. "To see your face dirty from the mud and working the fields," she said, "it made me sad. You had studied to be a teacher. You had graduated three years ahead of everyone. You had changed, and it wasn't how I expected to see you." Later that night, she told Uncle Fausto as much.

"What do you mean?" my uncle asked her.

"Dirt on his face, all sunburnt, wearing jeans caked with mud. But I know it's only temporary."

My uncle said, "Flavia, your son has a future here. That's how he will always look."

His words were so chilling to my mother that she decided not to tell me. But his pronouncement that I wouldn't resume my path toward a profession outside of field work had saddened her so much, she later confessed, "All my hopes began to go down."

Papá too must have felt mixed emotions when he saw me back at the ranch. He could take some pride in the fact that I was moving up the ranks; but he had to accept that I was far from the world of books and learning that he wanted for me. Then again, I wasn't putting stock in what he wanted. Probably I was still angry that he hadn't managed to do more to alter our family's circumstances after the economic hardships knocked us down so far. I suspect that this anger, at times, drove me to prove that it was possible to pull oneself up again after being knocked down, that sometimes a man has to do what a man has to do. But no matter what, I adored my father and was sad he seemed to have lost his fire for pursuing his destiny.

Mamá and Papá soon left the ranch, having decided to go farther north to find employment in the more industrial area near Stockton, at the northern edge of the San Joaquin Valley. They anticipated that the schools there would be better for Jorge and Jaqueline. A short time later, Rosa and her family decided to head to Stockton as well. When they tried to talk me into joining them, I declined, explaining that I had some exciting irons in the fire in Mendota—including my own trucking business!

Thinking expansively, I began to dream of my new enterprise: I'd start small and grow my fleet, then eventually hire all of my family members, present and future. I would call the company something like Q Trucking and emblazon the name on all my trucks with a logo of a bright yellow comet on a black high-gloss background!

Partnering with my cousin Hector—who claimed to be a mechanic—I made a down payment to Uncle Fausto on an old truck and went to work. After investing the little money I had saved, I was sure that my produce-hauling skills would beat out those of the competition. As I worked with Hector to rebuild the truck and its engine, I realized not only how much I loved the feeling of grease on my hands but how much I enjoyed using my brain and my hands at the same time. Even though I was not on the road toward education, I was far from lost. As Tata Juan had encouraged me to do, I was exploring other avenues in search of fulfillment, happiness, challenges, and adventure.

Everything about my business venture worked like a charm, other than the strange noises the truck was making.

Hector assured me, "It's nothing, don't worry!"

So I didn't worry, until the day I was driving down Highway 99 with a truckful of broccoli and saw a tire roll in front of me. Who in his right mind would lose a tire in the middle of this busy highway? The answer came pretty quickly. With a clunk and a bang, I went skidding into a ditch, watching broccoli fly all over the road.

"What kind of mechanic are you anyway?" I asked Hector when I saw him.

He shrugged sheepishly, "Not a very good one?"

So much for the trucking business. With my savings diminished, I returned to the Greek family's ranch for the fall and winter season, once again starting at square one, weeding and picking cotton. But before the winter was over, I'd risen to the top again, driving the big dragon Caterpillar, the massive John Deere tractors, the imposing cotton picker, and the space-age tomato picker fit for an astronaut, once more plowing the fields and racing the coyotes.

By the time the spring season rolled around, my brown corduroy wallet was full again with uncashed checks, my work authorization papers were in order, and I was promoted yet again—on a par with the third in command. Not bad. And that was more or less the context in which a life-altering conversation took place one afternoon with my cousin Oscar.

A handsome young man with a strong, square jaw, Oscar would later pursue an education and become a teacher. But at the time, he was focused on climbing the ladder of success at the ranch and on supplementing his income by hauling melons with his own truck.

Oscar didn't seem to have the same sense of adventure or humor that his older brother and I shared. Oscar was just as bright, tenacious, and hardworking as the rest of the Hinojosa family, but he tended to be cynical about anything that sounded overly ambitious to him. In any case, he was instantly pessimistic when I mentioned my latest decision to enroll in night school and improve my English. He might not have realized the extent of my insecurity about my thick accent and limited language, but he must have known that without more education, I would never have any options other than to keep struggling at barely a subsistence level. Yet he appeared to be personally offended by my plans.

Nothing could diminish the education I had acquired in the fields. The experience had been a blessing, and I had learned from the best— the everyday heroes who till the soil and bring forth the harvest. As a year-round worker, I had known the thrill of picking a tomato from a vine that I had planted. But at twenty years old, I couldn't accept that I'd reached the pinnacle of where a field worker could go. With an education, I imagined myself landing a management job at one of the big food companies—why not? Then, after making some real money, I would return to Mexico with options to have, be, and do whatever I chose. And the first step toward realizing this beautiful dream was to learn more English.

Initially, Oscar didn't say a word. But then, he started to laugh, as though laughter was the only reasonable response to my apparent absurdity. "Don't kid yourself!" he finally said. "School to learn English? C'mon."

At first, I didn't react and managed to let his comment roll off my back.

Oscar had been through his own rough times, dealing with the divorce of his parents at a young age, but it occurred to me in this instance that he didn't really know what it was like to live in poverty or to go without access to the opportunities and education that living in the United States afforded—including the freedom to believe in and go after the American dream. So I shrugged off his laughter and said nothing.

Oscar then became serious. "Look," he said, "you don't need the dictionary or night classes. Why waste your time? In a year and a half, you've accomplished what it took Chon eleven years to do. You're at the top of the food chain already!"

Still not saying a word, I felt a prickle of anxiety start in my stomach and journey through me.

Oscar continued, "This is where you're supposed to be, Freddy. You're gonna be the foreman before too long!"

My heart banging like a bass drum in my ears, I couldn't catch my breath. I got it. Of course, I got it. He wanted me to pull my head out of the clouds, to protect me from filling myself with big ideas and setting myself up for disappointment. But in so doing he was killing the dreams of that little boy who had stood on his roof with a slingshot trying to hit a star.

"Look at where you are," he said again, not without admiration, "you belong here. You'll always be in the fields. You're never gonna leave. You will spend the rest of your life in the fields."

Upon hearing that awful statement, I felt as if Oscar had cut me open and taken my heart in his hands to squeeze it with all his might. Even in memory, I can conjure the physical reaction I had at that moment—my heart crushed by the weight, power, and certainty of his grim prediction.

Maybe he was right. For as long as I stood there, frozen, shocked, and hurt, I was never going to leave the fields—and to think otherwise was simply fooling myself.

There was only one thing to do, other than to remain there like a statue. I signaled to Chon that I was going on break and then, feeling the weight of the world on my shoulders, jumped on my three-wheeler and flew across the muddy tomato field for the last time, roaring down the dirt road to the nearest pay phone. Deep inside, it had been wired into my DNA that there were only two options when facing difficulties:

either alter them or adjust yourself to meet them. In the long run, I had made the right choice. But after the drama of the moment subsided and by the time I picked up the phone, I realized that the people who had believed in me might be disappointed.

My tail between my legs, I called my parents, who were then staying with relatives in Stockton. Without hesitation, they agreed to come pick me up. Within two days, I'd arranged to leave my trailer behind and to store my three-wheeler until I could come back for it. During those forty-eight hours, I had time to second-guess my decision, especially now that I had no idea what the future held. I was leaving the security of a decent job as a migrant farm worker for the unknown. The picture of this new future was murky—as if I'd opened a door into a darkened room and couldn't find the light switch. Waiting for my parents and younger siblings to round the bend to pick me up, I could feel my former bravado seeping away.

From the instant that I saw my father behind the wheel of his latest automotive disaster—a phlegmatic Gremlin he had recently bought, mainly because he liked the color, an ugly mustard yellow—I began to smile. At that moment, the ugly mustard yellow Gremlin was the most beautiful sight in the world.

We put a few of my belongings in the hatchback and then set off on an unforgettable journey. As we left Mendota and I glanced back at the rusty train tracks that had brought me here all the way from the outskirts of Palaco, Mexico, and that were now leading us north, I marveled to think of the audacious, naive nineteen-year-old who had come here a seeming lifetime ago. Now I was starting over. Not once did I hear a word of criticism or even a question about what had happened or about dashed hopes and dreams. In fact, the mood in the car was—dare I say—celebratory! Soon someone told a joke, and a series of hilarious stories and anecdotes followed. In short order, we were laughing so hard that we were wiping our eyes and holding our sides.

Then the singing began. And we had to contend with the Gremlin's idiosyncrasies. To prevent overheating, Papá had to pull over and pour water into the radiator every thirty minutes or so, also adding oil each time for good measure.

Traveling no more than fifty miles per hour, we had so much fun that we didn't care if it took us five hours to make what should have been a two-hour trip. As we pulled into the gritty streets of Stockton, scanning the signs for our new address, I remembered those earlier trips to the Sea of Cortez and how they would stay with me long after I'd returned home. In the same way, this delightful journey would linger in my heart for a long time to come, allowing me to safely cross the border from all that had been before to whatever was coming next.

.   .   .

My enrollment in night classes at San Joaquin Delta College inaugurated a period of great growth and learning for me. The next order of business was to secure employment. Although my new job could have been viewed as a plunge to the bottom of the food chain, when I was hired on to shovel sulfur at the port, I figured this move was just another test—not a permanent sentence.

Compared to my port duties, moving irrigation lines had been a cakewalk! The smell of sulfur—which came to live inside my nostrils and coat my clothes, skin, and hair—is not a sense memory easily forgotten. The odor is commonly compared to the smell of rotten eggs or untreated sewage or the worst case of flatulence. It's no accident that descriptions of hell include the punishment of fire and brimstone, otherwise known as sulfur.

But getting to and from this job in hell was pure joy, thanks to a few significant purchases. After saving up some seven thousand dollars, I finally was able to buy two items I'd once only dreamt of: first, a pair of Ray-Ban sunglasses, and second, a brand-new red Nissan minitruck, my first vehicle that had never been owned by anyone else.

Over the next several weeks, I became a top customer at the Pep Boys auto supply store, investing my sulfur-shoveling earnings into souping up my low-frills truck until it became my vision of the ultimate American ride. With multiple speakers for my car stereo and a kit system that let me lower the car in sync to the music, I was the man! To show my international side, I hung furry dice in the front window and put a stuffed animal in the back window of the cab—a striped, orange, smirking Garfield.

Whenever I parked the truck at work or at the community college, I straddled two spaces to avoid getting scratched or dinged. With my hair long and a couple of Native American earrings dangling from one ear, blasting tunes that ranged from Guns N' Roses to James Brown, I got a lot of stares—just as I did dashing across campus in heavy work boots and splotchy overalls, cradling a stack of books in my arms like a baby.

Most of the time, I was oblivious to the effect I was having, but one day when a friend caught me getting out of the truck, he commented, "*Vato,* none of this computes. But, Garfield? I mean, what's your story?"

My story for over two years had been that I was going to go home to Mexico after I made it big. But in truth, I could feel a new pull tempting me to consider the possibility of putting down roots here. The mere thought scared me into facing up to the hard fact of the matter—that I hadn't succeeded at any of my earlier plans. All this time, I had delayed my return home because of demands put on myself and the belief that others would see me as a failure if I didn't have any money or substantial achievement to show for my time in the United States. The only way to get past defeat and past the fear, I realized, was to return to Mexico for a visit and see how I felt. Why not? Suddenly, in the middle of a Friday afternoon at the port, with another four hours to go until the shift was over, I decided that I was going to do it! After work, I'd shower, change, and then hop in my ride and drive through the night and into the morning—my legal documents in order—and storm into Mexicali with my music and my minitruck rocking out to the beat! Then I'd cruise out to Palaco and drive to the outskirts, on past the old gas station, and down to my grandparents' house to surprise Gabriel. Why hadn't I thought of this before? Road trip!

Fatigue set in early in the drive, but as the hours and miles passed, I adjusted. The night was memorably dark, with rain threatening and clouds obscuring the stars. The farther I got from my family in California, the more concerned I felt about the fact that we still had only a tenuous hold on any form of security. The way forward seemed as unclear as it had been when I had first crossed the border. Why did life continue to be so hard?

But just before the first signs of daylight, I felt a strange lightening of this load. The shift was subtle, but I welcomed it as much as the sight of rolling fields of farmland, curving down through the valley as I turned east—with the sunrise throwing out bands of golden light, illuminating spots here and there.

As the sun came up, I suddenly felt renewed and relaxed, strong in the belief that all things were possible. And just at that lofty moment, as my imagination ran wild with grand ambitions for the future, I spotted a VW van in my rear view mirror. Being familiar with American culture by now—or so I supposed—I nodded knowingly to myself, expecting to see hippies within, holdovers from the culture that had reigned in earlier years. Instead, as the VW van passed me, I saw the faces of two people, a man and a woman, looking out at me from the back window. But then I looked more closely and suddenly realized that those pale circles in the window weren't faces. They were naked butts! What? Why on God's earth would anyone do such a thing?

Not until much later, while watching an Eddie Murphy movie, did I learn about this popular American prank called "mooning." Clearly, I had a lot more to learn about American culture. In the end, I was still a country boy from the Baja.

But after thirty-six hours back on home turf, I felt less connected than ever to where I'd grown up. The first sign that I was not being welcomed home as a returning hero was when I stopped off in Mexicali for something to eat and returned to my pickup to discover that the side window had been broken and my Garfield was stolen!

It was wonderful to reunite with Gabriel and to learn that he would soon join the rest of the family in Stockton. I was also entertained by how easy it was to fall into the old ways of relating to family and friends. Everyone was as they had always been, it seemed—everyone except for me. When I ran into my ex-girlfriend, some of my guilt lifted about leaving without warning; she had moved on and was in a new, happy relationship. Years later, she would tell me that she had understood my leaving, that she believed I was going somewhere special, "somewhere that none of us had dreamed."

On the way back to Northern California, I felt that my visit home had been a way to gain a sense of closure. I had needed to reconnect to my roots, in the land where I was raised. But my home turf now seemed small and provincial, a place where I could no longer grow. Nothing was firmly resolved. One thing, however, became clearer than ever: I had to push past the limits of my education, to expand my scope of knowledge.

So, as my first order of business upon my return to Stockton, I took out the community college catalog and circled three courses that appeared intriguing. None of them were offered during the evening, so I had to figure out how to rearrange my schedule with a different job to accommodate them.

Meanwhile, I resumed the daily grind of shoveling sulfur and scraping fish lard—the greasy deposit of entrails that collects at the bottom of ship tankers, creating a sludge with a clinging smell that is possibly worse than the rotten-egg smell of the sulfur, something unimaginable. I joked that I must have been crazy to leave the fields—only I wasn't joking!

The toughest test was enduring the slights of two co-workers who seemed to go out of their way to make me feel beneath them. One in particular made no effort to hide his contempt. Even though he was Chicano, probably second- or third-generation Mexican-American, he apparently resented my background and my ability to move up in the sulfur-shoveling business. In any case, he didn't hold back from making derogatory references to the fact that I was from south of the border, labeling me a "wetback" and embellishing the term with other stereotypical adjectives like "stupid," "lazy," or "dirty."

While his attacks added to my insecurity, I wanted to understand why he disliked me so intensely, especially because he was also of Mexican descent. Maybe he had issues with my long hair and earrings. Maybe he disliked my sense of humor and my way of joking that my skinny build had rippling muscles like Rambo's—my attempts to get a laugh from him and his sneering sidekick. Given the history of racial strife in the Stockton area, I wondered if they had picked up some kind of loathing for the old country at home or in their neighborhoods.

One of my family's rude awakenings upon our arrival in Stockton was the discovery that it had recently been designated the most violent city in America—according to a television news report. Young, disenfranchised gang members of second- or third-generation Hispanic descent, along with African-American gangs and other cliques made up of newer arrivals from Southeast Asia, were engaged in full-fledged warfare. Drugs, guns, and poverty had contributed to a skyrocketing crime rate that we had unwittingly stumbled into in the search for steady work in and around the Port of Stockton.

Why none of us kids were drawn into gangs or drugs, I'm not sure. One reason was probably the strong foundation that my parents instilled in each of us that prevented us from being lured into those destructive behaviors. At the same time, only Gabriel and I pursued education at the higher levels. Our younger siblings—who came of age while attending school in Stockton—didn't value higher education in the same way, perhaps because of the chaotic atmosphere that pervaded school and the streets.

None of us were immune to threats of street violence. This became clear one Thursday morning when I had a close call while speeding off to work. In my haste to fit in a stop at a little market for a bag of cashews and a soft drink (the lunch of champions in those days), I thoughtlessly zipped in front of a large white truck with dark-tinted windows, inadvertently cutting it off. Not thinking much of this encounter, I parked and was about to head into the market when I saw the white truck pulling up next to me and the driver's window rolling down to reveal the huge barrel of a gun pointed squarely between my eyes.

"You're gonna die!" thundered the person holding the gun. Then I heard the ominous click of the trigger being cocked.

My heart dropped. My breath stopped. And so too, apparently, did the part of the brain that controls bowel functions! Helpless, I didn't have time to be embarrassed. But as I braced myself to say good-bye to life, my assailant issued a harsh warning: "Don't EVER cut me off again!"

With that, the gun vanished, the tinted window rolled up, and the white truck roared out of the parking lot. Once I had caught my breath, I thanked God for sparing me again and vowed to become much more street savvy than my experiences so far had prepared me to be.

After all, I'd grown up in a rural setting, not even in a village, in virtually a third-world country, and had spent most of my time in America in the fields. City living required many adjustments. At first, my parents and younger siblings and I squeezed into one room with twin beds in an apartment building where we shared a bathroom with ten other families. After Gabriel successfully completed college and traveled north to join us, we rented a small house that accommodated the whole family, as well as Rosa, Ramón, and their beautiful baby daughter, Daisy, my first niece.

Adjusting to urban life wasn't easy for my father. He had no trouble getting short-term work doing manual labor, but those jobs weren't stepping stones to something better. Papá found his outlet, however, in fixing up and painting our rented house, soon turning it into a charming, colorful home in the middle of an otherwise rough neighborhood. My mother remained the pillar of the family, a genuinely optimistic realist. Throughout the years, if my life was ever hard, my struggles were nothing compared to Mamá's. Rarely discouraged by our challenges, she was able to secure steady employment, usually working in some form of quality control at local factories. With an education behind her, Mamá could have become an executive at any of those companies. Even without the means for such promotions, her counsel was regularly sought by co-workers and family alike.

My mother was certainly my sounding board, especially when I had to endure the racism of my two co-workers. Her advice about how to confront intolerance was so insightful that I later interviewed her for a college anthropology paper. In addressing the subject of cultural bias, she spoke about the need that some people have to see others as beneath them.

"I do not think there is such a thing as an inferior or superior race," she said. "However, I am perfectly aware that there is racial discrimination and injustice, not just in the United States but also throughout the world." Mamá admitted that discrimination would always be a part of life because of embedded attitudes that caused some cultures to see other cultures as inferior. But she saw a path forward for people who have been treated as lower-class citizens. "I think the only way to gain respect is by becoming educated. The only way to gain equilibrium in the system is to become leaders of the system instead of followers of the injustice."

Just as I was about to reach my breaking point in fish-lard scraping and sulfur shoveling, I learned from my buddy Gustavo—Gus for short—who was married to my mother's cousin, that an opportunity loomed. As luck would have it, less than a hundred feet away from where we shoveled sulfur was a team of welders who worked for California Railcar Repair, a company that refurbished the tankers that transported materials unloaded from shipyards to various industrial destinations. Gus worked as a foreman for the company at a different site. This information opened the door for my brother-in-law, Ramón, who had been trained in Mexico as a welder.

Exceedingly kindhearted, industrious, and intelligent, Ramón quickly proved to be a valuable asset with his welding skills and unusual strength, despite his slight, wiry frame of 112 pounds. Within a short time, Gus then put in a good word for me as well. Charming, tall, and brawny, Gustavo could have been an action-movie star if he had chosen to pursue that path. Instead, he had become a master welder like the man who raised him—his stepfather, Don Mateo, as we fondly called him. After Gus persuaded his bosses to start me out as a janitor in the shed, he and Ramón received the go-ahead to train me as a welder. I was then able to recommend my father to replace me as the janitor.

Before I had mastered my training, I had a harsh awakening about the dangers of the job and the importance of even the smallest of details. On this occasion, I failed to put on the eye shield correctly and burnt my corneas, suffering excruciating pain for which the only treatment was to lie in the dark with wet towels over my eyes. Once was enough. When I returned to working with the welding iron, I had to learn to keep my distance from the burning, melting lava that I was forging—melding pieces together and pulling others apart, building out the molten substance, playing with it, watching the intense red of the flame's core turn metal into liquid, but doing all this at a respectful distance from danger. Such lessons in the careful use of tools and protective devices would later translate to surgical settings—not that I was yet aware of this destiny. And yet I had begun to believe that a promising future was just around the corner, waiting to be uncovered.

.   .   .

Then, on April 14, 1989, my promising future came crashing down after my plunge to the bottom of the railway tank and my unsuccessful attempt to climb out—as I lay, unconscious, without oxygen, face down, dying.

Of course, I recall that moment not from my direct experience of it but from reports given to me years later by those who were there—accounts that were as difficult for them to give me as they were for me to hear.

For my father, all of his worst nightmares were realized the instant he saw Pablo's face and understood that my co-worker had let go of my hand. After he heard the thud reverberating in the tank, Papá's screams were momentarily silenced as he was joined by Ramón on one side of him and Gus, carrying ropes and a collapsible ladder, on the other side. They had arrived in time to hold Papá back as they looked down to see that I had fallen with my knees bent slightly under me, my body in a fetal position. I can only imagine my father's desperate frustration, knowing that he had been so close to being able to save me. By all accounts, including his own, he went mad, and with the sound of Don Mateo praying loudly as he still knelt by the side of the tracks, my father lurched forward, attempting to enter the tank, thrashing and fighting the others as they sought to calm him. The more they tried to reason with him, explaining that he would die if he went in, the more Papá fought off their efforts to restrain him. Gus reminded my father that he was too broad shouldered to fit through the opening, not to mention too old to risk the rescue. Thinking back to what Papá must have felt at hearing this, at the same age that I am today, I can't imagine how I would react if someone told me that I couldn't attempt to save my children's lives

Gus wanted to come in too but was also much too big to squeeze into the hole.

It was Ramón who pushed himself to the front, insisting, "I'm going in." Seeing the others' hesitation, he yelled, "I'm going in! Freddy's dying down there!"

Gus, knowing that he could lose both of us, agreed that Ramón, strong, wiry, and quick, was the only one who stood a chance of success. With meteoric speed, Gus secured a rope for Ramón and directed the team at the top to be ready to throw down the thin metal ladder. Ramón lowered himself down the rope as fast as he could. Halfway down, the fumes began to overtake him—like being horse-kicked in the stomach, as he would later describe the experience. He blacked out for a moment when he landed next to me but managed to rouse himself long enough to lift me onto my back, with my face up. My mouth had begun to foam, my tongue was sticking out, and my skin was turning purple. Ramón again started to lose consciousness and knew that he had to get out immediately if he hoped to survive. As he climbed up the thin metal ladder that had been dropped in for him, Gus reached down with one hand, grabbed Ramón, and pulled him out like a small animal by the scruff of his neck. By this time, Ramón was out cold. As soon as Gus laid him on the upper walkway, however, Ramón began to pound the tanker with his fist, slapping himself into an awakened, alert state—exerting enough force to push the others aside and insisting that he had to go back in.

This time, Ramón came down faster than before, with a rope tied around his chest and another rope to help pull me up. He knew that almost ten minutes had elapsed since I had first gone into the tank, and with the lack of oxygen at the bottom, I should have already been dead. Ramón also knew that he had only a few seconds to act before he too passed out. In those few seconds, he carefully tied the rope around the middle of my body so as to balance my lower limbs with the weight of my torso and head when I was pulled up. How he calculated the physics of this maneuver, I can't fully explain—other than that he must have tapped into his superhuman abilities, demonstrating not just exceptional strength, agility, and courage but a level of genius. Ramón miraculously completed the last loop of the rope without blacking out. But once he began ascending this second time, all his faculties faded, and he was pulled out unconscious again.

Now Gus took over and began the painstaking work of reeling me up, inch by inch, without any sudden or hurried movements that would cause an imbalance and send me plummeting again. One slip, one miscalculation, would have been disastrous. With this orchestration of complex maneuvers to save my life, Gus could have been a brain surgeon, the conductor of a world-class orchestra, a general mobilizing his troops. He was all of that, performing at the highest of his abilities—on my behalf.

During this do-or-die effort, Papá, Ramón, Pablo, and several others were right there helping, with Don Mateo still praying and another team readying the forklift that would set me down on the ground so I could be loaded into the back of Gus's Ford Bronco and taken to a nearby industrial clinic—where a waiting ambulance would rush me to the closest hospital. Because our site was in such a remote location, the roads weren't even marked on area maps, so trying to explain where we were to an ambulance driver would have been futile. Thus, this plan too was a feat of fast, inspired thinking.

As the story goes, Ramón and Papá never left my side and began to see signs of life in me during the ambulance ride—a couple of moments when I tried to speak but was too disoriented to make any sense. Though I remember trying to wake up—as when you try to wake from a nightmare but can't—I recall only a few blurry images of being transferred into the ambulance and strapped down. My first conscious recollection—when I was absolutely awake—is of opening my eyes, looking around, and finding myself in the hospital on a yellow transport table, with my father and Ramón flanking a young olive-skinned, large-nosed man dressed in white. I thought perhaps I had died and gone to heaven, and this man was an angel. But I soon learned that he was a doctor and I was in a hospital—for the first time in my life. Safe, alive, I had made my way back to true terra firma—the land of the living.

Not out of the woods yet, I was more nauseous than I had ever been in my life, with a terrible taste in my mouth and an awful smell that I couldn't shake. My stomach was in lousy shape too, churning with an empty, sick sensation. In addition, I was starting to become belligerent, fighting the restraints of the yellow stretcher and trying to stand up.

"Relax," the doctor told me, "what's your name?"

"Relax? I can't breathe!" While I fought the urge to vomit, I also began to calm myself and allowed the young emergency room physician to check my heart rate and set up an oxygen tent.

A series of medical tests followed. To the shock of everyone involved, the results showed no trace of oxygen deprivation or physical trauma. A few hours passed before I could form coherent sentences, but my father knew I was going to be fine when I noticed some very attractive female nurses and whispered to him, "Does my hair look okay?" Papá laughed in relief.

Nothing had been lost. On the contrary, in the days and weeks that followed, I came to the conclusion that I was more myself than I had ever been, if such a thing was possible. My brush with death seemed to have rewired and supercharged my brain, allowing my instincts and senses to operate at a higher level. I felt as if, in the moments when I had battled for my life, the adrenaline needed for survival had risen to a permanently higher level, intensifying my focus and helping me turn negative energy into more positive results. Mysterious, I know, but it's a phenomenon I would observe time and again in patients and others who must fight against their own mortality.

In the meantime, no one could understand why I didn't break any bones when I fell so suddenly after letting go of Pablo's hand. Was I just lucky? Well, that can be debated. But as for the heroism of Ramón, Gus, my father, and everyone else who played their part in saving my life, that was more than luck. And yet, because of the trauma and my fear that talking or even thinking about the event would conjure negativity, more years than I care to recall would pass before I could bring myself to raise the subject and thank them personally.

Papá was the only one to comment on the miracle as such. "You have been given a gift," he told me at the hospital. "Put it to use, Freddy. Life is short. Be good to others."

Perhaps seeing the doctor's example, as he stood by and provided the safety I needed, helped open my eyes to my father's meaning, even if I didn't make the connection. When I arrived home the next day, everyone could see at once that I was all right but needed to be alone. No one asked any questions when I went into our little living room to sit by myself in quiet solitude.

We had just moved into the house and had no furniture yet, so I sat on the hardwood floor—barefoot and without a shirt, just in my jeans— in a state of such intense introspection that I can still see, smell, hear, and feel every tiny detail of that night: the chilly evening air, the smell of the wood varnish on the floor, the noise of dinnertime and random conversations in the neighborhood, the sound of tires rumbling by on the asphalt, the mix of music from car stereos with the bass turned up high—all booming and drowning out the sound of my weeping.

Twenty-one years old, still with no facial hair (though I was determined to have a goatee once I got a chin whisker or two), I let myself cry it out. This was the first time that I had cried throughout the ordeal, and my tears were part relief, part gratitude, and part delayed trauma from having seen death and come back.

As I sat there, thinking of my father's words about the gift I'd been given, I felt overwhelmed. And in that moment, I decided never to think of those minutes close to death ever again. Whoever I once had been—seeking to prove myself by material means in order to go home a conquering hero—was no more. Instead, I had to go where the path didn't lead and see where it took me, using unprecedented levels of energy to reinvent myself, to move farther and with more passion in order to be who I was and to become who I was meant to be. As if transformed, I no longer cared about the trappings of wealth or dreams of riches that had motivated me before. Something better and more meaningful was out there for me, and I needed to search for it. And with that revelation, I stood up from the floor with a new level of confidence and drive.

Other than the long-postponed conversations that would occur much later on, my journal entry of April 19, 1989, remains the only record of the incident. In this brief mention, I noted that the doctor had told me how lucky I was, that staying at the bottom of the tank as long as I did would have killed most people. If I had been down there two minutes longer, I would have died.

Those two minutes were the gift that every person on the rescue team gave me. My father, I believe, played the pivotal role, amplifying everyone's sense of urgency. He gave me a fighting chance—thanks to his love and devotion and the speed with which he responded to his own premonition. *Two minutes.* My life!

PART TWO Harvesting

Another light at the end of the tunnel comes into focus—this time as I hurry toward a staff examination room. A yellow fluorescent light, it spills out of the open doorway into one of the long dark corridors of San Francisco General Hospital. Suddenly, hospital personnel, dressed in green scrubs, appear in the pool of dim yellow light at the end of the hall, waiting for me with somber expressions.

Out of habit, I wonder who the patient is and what dire diagnosis is cause for concern. Then I remember: I'm the patient.

Quickly reviewing the events of the afternoon, I pray silently, "Please, make this be a dream and let me wake up!" Bargaining, I'm even willing to let this be a nightmare. Anything to make it not true. This isn't the first time that I've wondered if I've just imagined the events of the past ten years. Maybe I did die in the railway tank and have been dreaming my life. Maybe the fantasy just caught up with the reality, and I'm about to find out that I'm not alive. But if this is real, I'm going to die for sure.

Even though it's only been two months since my first night on call as a neurosurgical intern—newly arrived to the front lines of battle here at one of the busiest Level I trauma centers in the country—it feels like a lifetime ago. That chaotic night when I was summoned to examine a patient with a gunshot wound to the head was quiet compared to most others. Continuing down the hallway to the waiting hospital administrators, I remind myself that the challenges of adjusting to the pressure are normal for anyone coming from the controlled environment of medical school and now thrust into a blizzard of uncontrollable situations. And for me, the sole neurosurgical intern in the department—compared to the squadron of interns in other departments—the unpredictability is multiplied a few times over. But even with the rigors of training—the brutal hours and the war zone atmosphere—not for anything in the world would I be anywhere else.

Earlier this day, in fact, when I arrived at work after a few hours' sleep, primed to stay awake for the next couple days, I was in high spirits, grateful to be training with many of the giants in my field and serving in the trenches with individuals who were now like members of my family. The opportunity to train at the University of California, San Francisco, was a source of immense pride. The institution had long been in the forefront in developing proactive responses to trauma—starting in the 1960s, when drug use and street violence surged alongside the cultural revolution of the era. In the 1980s, San Francisco General Hospital had opened the first AIDS ward in the country, and it remained the acknowledged leader in the care of patients afflicted with HIV and related complications.

Yet even with my usual good mood that morning, I had an uneasy sense of impending trouble trying to push its way into my awareness. Everyone seemed slightly on edge, geared up for a higher-than-usual number of incoming and other emergencies. The shadowy feeling, I later concluded, was a premonition much like the one that had troubled my father ten years earlier when I almost died in the tank. For me, the flash of worry was so foreign that I put it out of my mind and focused on the work at hand.

There was, after all, a logical reason to be on guard. As any data analyst might point out, and as experts in health care and law enforcement understand, certain times of the week, month, and year tend to bring a higher incidence of life-threatening accidents and violent crimes. For instance, the number of 911 calls increases dramatically in the periods before, during, and after holidays. One theory is that people experience higher levels of anxiety and depression during these periods, which can be complicated by money worries or increased drug and alcohol use.

We were experiencing such a period, as the demands put on everyone not only intensified from Labor Day on but were further aggravated by the area's economic woes, which were then starting to hit the rest of the nation. Around the Bay Area, the word was that the dot-com boom—like the gold rush that had put San Francisco on the map—was about to go bust. All of these developments translated into a greater need to manage the outside chaos with order, care, and precision inside the hospital.

These undercurrents weren't in my conscious thoughts as I joined interns and residents from orthopedic surgery in a rotation in the AIDS ward. This wasn't my first time working among HIV-positive patients, and I understood the risk of infection for health care workers as well as the precautions we needed to take when doing basic procedures. By the late 1990s, the medical community knew that some HIV-positive patients were also positive for hepatitis C. But as I was to learn this day, when a senior resident and I went to run a battery of tests on a patient with full-blown AIDS, sometimes the precautions aren't enough.

Everything happened so quickly and yet so slowly, as though I could see an accident about to occur but couldn't stop it. The scenario began to play out when the senior resident gestured toward a patient's room and asked me to follow. The moment we entered the room and approached the patient, a terrible smell assaulted my senses—the kind of smell that accompanies death, not fully present but seeping unmercifully into the room. As I entered, I saw only the patient's fearful eyes, open and staring at me, hooded in bony sockets, appearing to be his last defense against death and reflecting the agony of being devoured by his disease. At first, I could hear only the shallow rasp of his breathing. The sound was interrupted by the voice of the senior resident asking for my assistance, while holding up a huge hollow-bore needle, no ordinary hypodermic, before using it to drain fluids that I knew would include contaminated blood—and asking me to put pressure on the entry point. As I got into position, the resident's hand lost control, and the needle, like a demon possessed, flew into the air and down again, driving deep into the exposed skin of the upper part of my hand near my wrist.

And now, seconds later, here I am, in a state of shock, instructed to go down the dark hallway toward the hospital personnel who are waiting silently for me. I know that when I step across the threshold into the light of the exam room, I will undergo a series of tests and be given grim odds.

Nothing in what follows alters those expectations. In describing the intensified triple-therapy cocktail that I'll be taking for one month, the hospital officials spare me the lurid details about the side effects of the drugs. Instead they tell me that these drugs can be effective in treating the early stages of HIV. Whether the therapy will be successful or not, only a full year of regular testing will tell. A year of not knowing.

In my numbness and shock, I ask a few questions, trying to hold on to hope, but the answers convey little other than that I'm in a very dangerous situation and should brace myself for the worst. I'm informed that I'm not simply facing the possibility of contamination; I have been contaminated. The triple-therapy cocktail has so far not proven effective for needle sticks from patients with full-blown AIDS and/or highly contagious hepatitis C. The patient whose blood and bone fragments were in the hollow-bore needle that shot into my veins has both. But the most chilling news is that in the history of the hospital, the one incident most similar to mine resulted in a sera conversion: the person stuck with a contaminated needle did become infected but didn't convert and test positive until a year later.

"You'll want to start the medications now," a nurse says, as I force my limbs to move. A doctor lets me know that I can return to the rotation as soon as I make any personal phone calls, if I need to do so.

Walking back out to the hallway, I reach for the wall to steady myself, trying not to sink to my knees in fear. I feel as if I have a time bomb inside of me—with no way to know whether it will explode or not. Even as I fight the tears, I feel my eyes burning, my breath ragged, and a painful knot in my throat.

I can't help but recall the adage that lightning isn't supposed to strike twice—which tells me that although I survived the first time, I'm not going to make it this second time.

I think back to the stories told on Día de los Muertos, in particular, the moral that if you cheat death once and send its armies packing, it returns even more lethally the next time. Though I'm not a superstitious man, I have come to believe that no matter how lucky you are, the odds eventually turn against you. The mocking voice of the enemy echoes the same taunts about my chance for survival that it delivered when I was in the tank: "You can't" and "Who do you think you are?"

Nothing in the form of hope can be summoned.

As I try to compose myself and continue back down the hall to make the necessary phone calls, I pass by fellow residents and hospital co-workers who know me well, and I realize they too are at a loss for words. But their expressions tell me everything I need to know—for now, I am a dead man walking.

FIVE Courting Destiny

During the uncertain days that followed the AIDS needle stick in 1999, I thought a lot about earlier times in my life when I had managed to overcome crises and challenges. Ten years before, in 1989, after I'd survived falling in the tank and had made up my mind to go out in search of a new path, I found myself having to hop another series of fences every bit as formidable as the one at the border. Again, a combination of audacity and naivety had propelled me forward. So had everything I'd learned during my two memorable years at San Joaquin Delta College.

By working the swing shift at California Railcar Repair, I could attend classes at the college during the day. I was now head of a specialized team at the company, earning an impressive ten dollars an hour. My mornings were exercises in split-second timing. I'd arrive at the library at 6:00 A.M. when the doors opened and then study until classes began, at which point I'd race from one lecture hall to the next, finishing up the last class without a moment to spare. I'd then fly outside, jump into the red pickup, and screech into the job site just in time for the afternoon shift.

On the weekends, I also started running races for track-and-field events at the college—not because I needed to be busier but because I needed to burn off the excess energy that seemed to have intensified since the accident. If I had an extra fifteen to twenty minutes to spare in this schedule, I enjoyed pausing to eat my lunch outside in the quad, sitting on a bench or on the grass.

During one lunch break at approximately 11:30 A.M. on a sunny California day, as I sat on a cement ledge next to a fountain and a fish pond filled with bright orange-red koi, I was so lost in thought that I didn't notice the two beautiful young women walking toward me. One of the two, a tall, slender eighteen-year-old with long blonde hair and what I would soon observe to be entrancing green eyes, had not been as oblivious to me. In fact, I learned much later that she had already spotted me zipping across campus many times and had wondered where exactly I was headed in such a hurry and had been intrigued by my style—the ponytail, the earrings, the paint-splattered jeans, and the Red Wing work boots. How had I not noticed her before—a knockout who exuded intelligence and warmth?

True, I was easily intimidated in social situations at this time, self-conscious about my accent and culturally unaware. But that hadn't stopped me from dating or developing romantic relationships. Nothing serious, of course. But I was nonetheless a red-blooded Latin male and wasn't entirely clueless. On this day, however, I was clueless, though everything else was crisp and vivid in my focus—the gurgling of the fountain and the splashing of the koi in the pond, the pleasant spring weather, and the dance of students across the quad, many of them gathering in small groups to converse, study, laugh, argue, and flirt. Mainly I was interested in my sandwich. Before I could take a bite, however, the two young women (who were sisters, I later learned) had invited themselves to sit down, one on either side of me.

Bidding *hasta la vista* to any shred of confidence, I sat frozen. When the tall blonde initiated a conversation, I was too self-conscious about my accent and limited English to get out more than a guttural sounding "Hi" before dashing away. I couldn't get out of there fast enough!

The two young women must have mistaken me for someone else, clearly. So I put the encounter out of my mind. But some weeks later, the bewitching young woman approached as I was standing in the quad, discussing a calculus assignment with my classmate Mike. With a slight tilt of her head, she asked, "So, Mike, are you going to introduce me to your friend?"

"No way," said Mike. "I'm not going to introduce you two!"

For a second, I thought I detected some jealousy but then I dismissed it; why would he be jealous of me? I later learned that he did in fact have a crush on her and didn't want the competition. None of this, however, made a dent in my thick skull, nor did it dawn on me that she was in any way pursuing me.

No matter how frequently her path crossed mine, I still didn't put two and two together, until one day at the school swimming pool, where I was doing rehab for a groin injury I'd suffered on the track. As I high-stepped through the water, wearing a weighted vest and vigorously pumping my arms, I saw a vision emerge from the pool like Venus rising from the half shell.

For a moment, I simply gawked at her, but then the vision spoke. "Hi!" I had seen that smile, those green eyes before! But wait. Was she talking to me? I looked to the left. No one there. I looked to the right. No one there either. She nodded, as if to say, yes, I'm talking to you. Again, "Hi!"

Mumbling something that was neither English nor Spanish and was unintelligible even to me, I nodded back, hopped out of the pool, made a sharp turn, and dashed into the men's locker room. When my heartbeat finally slowed, I realized that this was the same amazing young woman who had approached me in the quad and later asked Mike to introduce us. Though I eventually learned that she was a competitive swimmer and worked as a lifeguard, the only thing I could think about then was the incredible fact that she had just said hi to me. Not once but twice. What was she trying to tell me?

To think her interest was anything other than platonic would have been a stretch. For one thing, she was a classic beauty and all-American, maybe of Scandinavian descent, while I was Hispanic and foreign born. But more than that, her cool confidence, her strong sense of who she was, and her open, inquisitive nature convinced me that she was out of my league. She was probably much too brilliant for me to be able to hold my own with her.

After this encounter, I began to notice how often she happened to show up in the library soon after I arrived in the early morning. Wow, I would think, this young woman is quite the scholar! Eventually, when I still didn't get the hint, she more or less gave up on me and decided, hey, this man is clueless! She was sure that I wasn't interested.

But as an insurance measure, she approached me one more time in the quad, extending her hand and saying, "Hi, I don't think we've been officially introduced. My name is Anna Peterson."

"Alfredo," I replied, shaking her hand, "how do you do?" Too formal? Quickly, I added, "But most people call me Freddy."

"I like Alfredo," she insisted. And that was that.

Thank goodness for her perseverance. If the official introductions had been left up to me, it would have taken much longer for me to learn the name of the person who was to be the love of my life and the woman I was destined to marry. But another two years went by before that awareness finally set in.

In the meantime, we were able to develop a friendship without the pressure of dating. Anna, I quickly saw, was one of the most caring individuals I'd ever met—always looking after family members, friends, and even strangers, showing constant concern for the well-being of others. The youngest of three girls, she had been raised mainly by her mother, a schoolteacher, after her parents divorced when she was very young. Anna's father—who had his PhD in oceanography and worked for the California Geological Survey—had remarried when she was about eight years old and had two more children, giving her a half sister and a half brother.

Though I sensed there were painful experiences in her past, Anna wasn't one to hold on to negativity or to wear her troubles on her sleeve. Her attitude was that facing up to those challenges had made her a stronger person. This was conjecture on my part since Anna was a deeply private person, although I could see from the start that she was fiercely independent. Early on, I was impressed to hear how she had begun work at a young age. In addition to working as a lifeguard, Anna had started her own swimming classes at a local pool, offering scholarships to children who had no resources or who had disabilities. Family clearly meant everything to her: I could see how attached she was to home and how close she was to her mom and older sisters.

Raised in Manteca, a small rural town south of Sacramento, where she still lived, Anna dreamed of becoming a veterinarian, as she mentioned during a casual conversation one day.

Inspired by her ambition, I asked in my halting English, "For you love animals?"

"Oh, yes," Anna smiled. She described her pets and the array of injured creatures she snuck into her house or adopted—birds, cats, snakes, goats, geese, dogs, horses, pretty much every species. Being practical, she planned to pursue a teaching career that would allow her to obtain work and start earning a living faster. Her goal was to move out of the house sooner rather than later.

Although Anna and I had grown up in different cultures and countries, I recognized that we had many values in common: family, respect and admiration for others, resilience in the face of tough challenges. Still, I was too self-conscious to contribute much to the conversation about myself. So it was easier to keep things at a safe distance when we ran into each other—a nod, a wave, a smile, and then I was off and running!

Later, when I had started dating someone else and I spotted Anna with the tall basketball-player boyfriend she was seeing by then, I felt a twinge of regret—though I didn't know why. I did not know then that love not only can conquer anything but works its way into our most primitive brain activity and before we know it, becomes part of our DNA. Something on a deep level was already signaling to me that we were meant to be together, but more time had to pass before the message would finally get through.

What did get through were the vital influences of some outstanding educators who were less concerned about giving me answers than about challenging me to ask questions—encouraging me to veer off the beaten path and explore material for no other reason than to find out what was there. In some cases, the subject matter wasn't memorable. But there were meaningful exceptions—for example, when I was able to study with Professor Richard Moore, who taught English as well as a life-changing course, at least for me, called Film as Literature.

In his regular English classes, Professor Moore taught the fundamentals of literary criticism and composition writing, giving me the chance to begin to write coherently and meaningfully in English, a skill that would be so necessary over the course of my education and profession. Though he stressed the importance of the rules of grammar and careful organization, he also insisted that papers convey a strong point of view ably supported with clear, substantive arguments. The opportunity to express my own strong point of view on the page was a new, empowering experience.

As a mentor, Professor Moore may also have recognized that movies had already played a powerful role in shaping my worldview. He amplified that awareness by helping me appreciate the power of *all* movies: classic, nonclassic, great, good, and even bad movies. With his glasses, neatly trimmed beard, bow tie, plaid shirt, cardigan sweater, and sports jacket, Richard Moore looked more suited to the Ivy League than to the community college auditorium in which he taught Film as Literature and screened films like Federico Fellini's *La Strada* (starring my countryman Anthony Quinn). In awe of him, I always tried to avoid his scrutiny in this class of two hundred students. But no matter how hard I tried to hide, slumping down in a seat in the middle section, he would find me. Maybe his radar picked up on my ponytail or my work clothes and their metallic railroad smell.

"So, Mr. Quiñones," Professor Moore would begin, "what do you think of Stanley Kubrick's decision to shoot *Dr. Strangelove* in black and white?"

Listening intently, I would struggle to read his lips and then translate mentally. "I like it very much," I'd murmur nervously. "The black and white showed contrast."

He would stroke his beard and nod in such a way that I doubted he understood what I had said any more than I did!

But it was thanks to such exchanges that I was pushed to improve my skills in speech and debate class, eventually refining them enough to become a team captain. Looking back, I now know that my command of the English language still had a very long way to go. In fact, I wasn't a great debater. But I built my power of persuasion on a clear point of view and wasn't afraid to take a strong stand on an issue while also managing to use my shortcomings to my advantage. How? My secret weapon was to smile confidently as I spoke, secure in the knowledge that my opponents couldn't understand me very well. Though the judges had my written arguments in front of them and could follow along, my opponents didn't and couldn't counter any of my arguments. An unconventional way to win, I know, but it worked.

Perhaps because I had arrived at community college without knowing anyone, without a reputation following me from earlier schooling or from my socioeconomic background, I had nothing to prove to anyone but myself. The sky was the limit. The atmosphere was so conducive to growth and learning that I made the dean's list regularly and became a member of the honor society and its steering committee. Set to graduate in the spring of 1991—at the ripe old age of twenty-three—I figured my school days were over.

Not so fast, I was informed in my next-to-last semester. I'd missed a critical piece of information, as I was shocked to find out when one of my professors asked if I had applied to any universities yet. Until that moment, I didn't know the difference between an associate degree from a junior college and a degree from a full four-year program, nor did I understand the difference between private and public institutions or between a state college and a highly ranked university. All along, I'd assumed that community college was the beginning and end of secondary education.

"Not really," my professor said. "This is just a start."

How could I have not known this? Was I wrong to think that because I had completed a class in industrial psychology and found it to my liking, the academic portion was over and the course would launch me into a promising career?

My professor gently explained that such questions could be answered by an advisor at the counseling center. In fact, he was surprised that I hadn't taken advantage of the availability of advisors before.

Not sure myself, I wasted no time in setting up an appointment with an advisor and then turned to Peter Dye, a classmate and one of my closest friends, for his insights. Peter expressed his own surprise that I hadn't known there was more education to come. He had made previous references to the application process, but I hadn't understood what he was talking about. The lesson at hand was a cautionary tale, reminding me not to be afraid to ask questions in the future if I didn't understand what others were talking about.

Then again, Peter acknowledged that since I was the first member of my family to seek higher education in the United States, my naivety about the system made sense to him. But the reality, he went on, was that if I wanted to go into industrial psychology, I would need to put in at least another three years to complete an undergraduate degree and then probably a few years of graduate school and fieldwork.

Five years or more before I could earn a decent living? I was crushed.

Peter tried to cheer me up with a pat on the shoulder, telling me, "Freddy, if you applied, you could probably get accepted into the UC system. There are also private schools that might offer you minority scholarships."

"The University of California?" In thirty seconds, I went from depressed to curious.

"Sure. Berkeley, for instance." The university was ranked in the top five schools nationally, he continued, noting that it accepted only a small percentage of applicants. "But you never know." Peter—star of the debate team and a tall, competitive athlete—was versed in the art of persuasion, and he knew how to tap into my desire for a challenge.

"Berkeley, huh?" The very name resonated for me.

As I mulled over this bit of news, I thought of my cousin Armando, who, as a Harley Davidson–riding intellectual, had come of age in the 1960s in Mexicali. Though he never finished college, Armando was an avid reader and student of history and had followed the cultural revolution of the era, much of which had played out at UC Berkeley. It was a magical place, according to Armando, and because of him, it was already a part of me.

UC Berkeley existed only in a dream, far beyond my reach. Nonetheless, I decided to shoot high, just as Tata Juan had told me to. So I not only applied to Berkeley but applied to several other California undergraduate programs as well. William & Mary was the only out-of-state college to which I applied—mainly because Peter and his family said that it had a strong debate program and offered scholarship funding for some financially needy students.

When an acceptance letter and a generous offer of financial assistance from William & Mary soon followed, I was stunned. Had the admissions people made a mistake? No, Peter assured me, not at all. When I looked at the photographs of this picturesque, centuries-old university campus, I was enchanted. How could I say no? Then I decided to do some research to find out exactly where Virginia was. Somehow, I'd missed a minor detail: the school was all the way on the other side of the country, where I would be cut off from everyone I knew. The thought of being separated from my family for months at a time was too daunting. Instead, I pinned my hopes on getting into one of the UC schools.

While waiting to hear back from them, I set out to secure new employment to help pay for the next stage of my education. My days working on the railroad as a welder and painter were numbered. Considering that the company was billing its customers as much as five hundred dollars an hour for my services, I should have been making a much higher salary and receiving medical benefits and more, but instead my wage was capped at ten dollars an hour. At the time, the need for benefits wasn't a priority, and I honestly thought my bosses were paying me a fortune! On that salary, after all, I'd been able to put myself through community college and to help buy my parents a house. The main issue wasn't dissatisfaction with refurbishing railway tankers either. It was simply time for a change. No viable options presented themselves until Gabriel mentioned offhandedly one day that I'd always been a poor man with expensive taste. True! Whenever I went to the nicer mall in downtown Stockton, I was particularly drawn to an elegant boutique that sold imported designer clothing for men. Why not apply there? I was hired on the spot—ponytail and all!

With my hours at the store, my track-and-field activities, and the studies for my last semester of community college, I was too busy to worry about the status of my remaining college applications. Or so I pretended. Really, I was on pins and needles! All the members of my family sweated through the process with me, and we were all thrilled when the next-to-last response came in from Berkeley—an acceptance letter! *Ecstatic* is too plain a word to describe my reaction. Though part of me could not believe that the letter was real, I was overjoyed. The very next day, an envelope with the embossed return address and seal of Stanford University appeared in our mailbox.

When the family gathered around to watch me open the envelope from Stanford, I prepared myself for a rejection, joking that my parents and siblings were making too much of this moment and trying to let us all down easy. Then I scanned the first few lines and jumped down to the verdict, took in a small intake of air, and immediately folded up the letter and returned it to the envelope. Everyone drew in close and began offering comfort, assuring me that this rejection wouldn't matter.

"Who cares what they think, anyway?" said Gabriel, as he grabbed the envelope from my hands and opened it himself. When he saw that the answer was yes, he shook his head. "You really had me fooled!" I was proud to receive acceptance letters from two top choices, and I was even happier that everyone in the family could share in the honors.

Now came the tough part. Stanford or Berkeley? The tuition was higher at Stanford, a definite minus. But in the end, the reason I went with Berkeley had to do with my cousin Armando, who had never even been there! Maybe it wasn't the wisest way to choose. But as usual, once I decided, it was a done deal. No looking back.

.   .   .

Though Berkeley is only an hour and a half from Stockton, I could not have been less prepared for the culture shock if I'd gone to Mars. The first sign that the university was in a different universe from community college was when I received my first test back in an anthropology class.

As the teacher's assistant walked down the aisles matching names with tests, handing them out slowly, I was horrified to see the grade

at the top of my exam—a C! This couldn't be right. I'd read the material backward and forward. My notes from the professor's lecture were
impeccable. Were these trick questions or something? Whatever had
gone wrong, my heart plummeted.

Seeing my shock, the TA asked, "Did you study the Black Lightning
lecture notes?"

"Sorry?"

I found out that these notes, developed by teaching assistants for the
classes they taught, were sold at the campus bookstores. Since the TAs
were often responsible for developing the exams, students knew that
these notes would offer clues to what was going to be on the test. I was
grateful to have this insider's knowledge early on—with enough time to
do well on subsequent tests to bring my grade up in that class.

Eye-opening! In the past, I'd assumed that conquering the material
and burying myself in the books would take me a long way and back. I
now understood that IQ was not just book-based; rather, you had to be
broad-based and keep your ear to the ground for knowledge that might
come from unlikely sources. Brilliant book smarts could still be an asset,
but so too was the ability to organize your time, know who to ask for
guidance, and be savvy about who was a reliable resource. This was a
whole new world!

The UC Berkeley experience rarely offered a dull moment. Though
I started living on campus in a dormitory—and was fascinated by the
array of exotic men and women who congregated in the living room
of my suite and talked with a dazzling sophistication way above my
head—I quickly moved into an apartment in Oakland, where I could
study more easily and share expenses with a couple of guys who were
experiencing the same culture shock I was. We could compare notes on
some of the crazy happenings and figures on campus—like the Hate
Man and the Naked Man. An equal opportunity hater, the Hate Man
walked around flipping everyone the bird. He actually preached, "Hate
is love." The Naked Man wore only his trademark sandals and backpack.
Soon others started following his example. Many of these followers were
people who frankly should not have been naked in public!

No matter how many times I saw those two, or other unusual sights, on campus, I never came to see them as commonplace. They reminded me that I was still a kid from the outskirts of Palaco. Indeed, when Christmas break came at the end of the first semester, I was eager to go home and spend the holidays with my family. And I arrived just in time to squeeze in some hours at the men's clothing store and shore up my dwindling bank account.

One day when I was zipping through the mall on the way to work, I had a funny feeling that something important was about to happen. Not quite a premonition but something along those lines. Later, an hour or so into the shift, I glanced up and saw a familiar face. There was Anna Peterson, seemingly lost in thought as she browsed the display rack.

When she noticed that I was watching her, a lovely smile spread across her face. Seeing her green eyes got to me all over again. But since we'd lost touch and had become only passing acquaintances, I had no reason to entertain romantic thoughts.

As we chatted, I learned that she was finishing up community college and had been accepted to the University of the Pacific in Stockton, where she planned to pursue a teaching degree. When she asked how I liked Berkeley, I told her it was great but somewhat challenging. We left our conversation there, and she walked out of the store, ostensibly out of my life for good.

Not quite. Later during the holiday and then a few times during spring break, Anna happened to be in the mall and would stop by to say hello. After one of these visits, the manager of the clothing store, Yamil, piped up, "That girl really likes you, Freddy!"

"You're crazy, you know that?"

"No," Yamil insisted, and he reminded me that many people sought his advice because he was an expert in matters of the heart.

Since he didn't seem to be pulling my leg, I valued his opinion. The next time Anna was in the mall, I greeted her with a bit more flair than usual, inquiring, "How are you today, my lady?" After we talked about plans for the rest of the school year, I popped the question. "Would you mind if I dropped you a letter from time to time while I'm away at Berkeley?"

"Not at all."

I was so happy that we could now have a courtship—albeit long-distance and via the mail—that I almost forgot to ask for her address. Fortunately, Yamil quickly stepped forward with a pen and a pad of paper so that she could write it down.

And with that, a beautiful correspondence began. In the store that afternoon, I finally started to put all the pieces together. It had been two years almost to the day since she and her sister had approached me by the koi pond. Thanks to the stars above, I was beginning to see the light.

I was also thankful to the anthropology TA for giving me the heads-up on the Black Lightning lecture notes. Studying them helped me prepare for exams, enabling me not only to ace my other courses but to finish the year out with an A- for that class. Feeling on top of the world with nothing but great possibilities ahead, I joined my TA and a group of five students from the anthropology class at Caffe Strada, a popular meeting place at the center of campus. We were there to celebrate the end of the course—and my improved grade! Though I usually avoided drinking coffee because I didn't need the extra energy, I decided to indulge this time. To be at Caffe Strada—with the same name as the Fellini film that I loved—and to bask in the company of this bright, interesting group—was like a fairy tale to me. Thinking of the sacrifices of my parents and the encouragement of others, I felt exceptionally lucky.

As we were discussing the well-roasted coffee beans, foreign films, and our respective backgrounds, I wasn't too surprised to hear the TA describe an affluent upbringing with a private education, while the rest of my fellow students reported coming from a mix of privileged and middle-class families. Then the TA turned to me: "And where are you from?"

"From Mexico."

Looking me square in the eyes, the TA said, "You can't be from Mexico. You're too smart to be from Mexico."

An awkward silence followed. The conversation changed. I said nothing but was thankful that the swelling noise at Caffe Strada gave me an excuse not to voice the visceral reaction inside of me. Everything was amplified by the jolt of caffeine in my veins. But I couldn't believe what I had just heard. Like the day when my cousin predicted I'd never leave the fields, I felt as if someone had cracked open my chest and was press-ing my heart into nothing. This felt worse. This wasn't about me. It was about my people, my family, my ancestors, my entire history.

Years later, I can still recall the feeling of suffocation—my heart pounding, my body numb, and my hands clammy with sweat.

"You're too smart to be from Mexico," was not the worst thing ever to be said to or about me. But it brought up a backlog of more overt painful remarks in my past. How was this any different?

Just as I was later grateful to my cousin for the kick that got me out of the fields, one day I'd look back and feel the same about the TA's remark, which was more thoughtless and ignorant than mean-spirited. The ugly truth that those words revealed at the time, however, was that I had no defense mechanism to fend off their impact. Because of who uttered them, they planted seeds of shame in me that took root in my being, soon to become weeds and even twisted, thorny vines, constricting me like a vise and making me want to hide my background. I should have said or done something, and I'm not proud that the blow was landed because of my weakness—my embarrassment about who I was and where I came from.

I had much to learn before I could fight off the foe of insecurity. But I also used those words to spur me on—to prove them wrong. That thoughtless comment helped me to grow up, shed some naivety, and become more serious in my focus. It was a reminder that few would have the opportunities I now was getting. I owed it to myself and to everyone who believed in me to make the most of those chances, to make some decisions about my destination and then to accelerate.

Such was the task I took upon myself that day at Caffe Strada, sitting there, seething inside but saying nothing.

six Green Eyes

Unlike many who heed the call to go into the field of medicine—usually with aspirations they've nurtured from childhood though premed college classes—I came to the dream later, as one rediscovering a long-lost love. The fantasy of being a doctor had hovered in the distance during my youth, like other "Faraway" dreams. But at some point, the dream had seemed beyond my grasp and I let it go. Or so I thought.

When I arrived at Berkeley, I had the freedom to explore many avenues before committing to one pursuit. Increasingly curious about the field of law, I was excited when I was invited to a gathering of mainly Hispanic law students and young practicing lawyers. Once I got to the party, it turned out that my expectations of meeting young versions of my hero Cesar Chavez—fighting for justice, righting wrongs, uplifting the underdog, changing the system—were somewhat overblown.

There was some of that, but the journey looked to have many more steps and appeared to be less exciting than I'd imagined. After twenty minutes at the event, I found I had nothing to add to the conversation. I was much more comfortable discussing math and science than politics and current events. Maybe my goatee, long hair, and earrings made me feel like a Berkeley radical, but my passion for revolution was more about challenging the status quo in the laboratory or advocating for more research into how the brain is wired or why we use such a small portion of our innate mental capacities. Human behavior fascinated me. But lawsuits and precedent-setting legal cases? Not my thing. This discovery was a big awakening.

At this point, something began to seriously stir in my emotional system about what I really wanted to do. But months would pass before the neural transmitters could get the message back to Command and Control in my head. What was I resisting? By my junior year, though I had no barometer for comparing my grades or rankings to others', I was thriving—multitasking as always. Two gears still drove me forward. One was for the dreamer and optimist in me who imagined, as I had from childhood, that I was destined to live forever. But the other was for the part of me that realized that life could be snatched away at any moment and felt I had to work hard at everything, as if each day were my last to live. So when I wasn't studying or hitting the gym, I was racing off to a variety of jobs—as a research assistant in the laboratory, as a private tutor, and as a TA in physics, chemistry, and calculus. Moving at that pace, I had become disconnected from the feeling I'd had when I saw the doctor upon awakening in the hospital after my tank accident, and from the promise I'd made to give to others what he had given me. What was the problem? It was, of course, my own insecurity. The mocking voices of *"you can't"* and *"who do you think you are?"* still ran the show.

Fortunately, there was someone very close to me who reminded me to ignore those voices: Anna. After months of courtship via the U.S. postal system, we were officially dating at last, although we had a long-distance relationship. After we had gotten to know one another intimately in heartfelt letters, I had finally invited her on a first date—a movie and then a moonlight tour of the Berkeley campus. On our evening stroll, I took her hand in mine for the first time and felt it was the most natural thing in the world to do. I couldn't yet tell her that back in Mexico as a youth I had once received a message in a dream that a woman with green eyes was destined to be my soul mate. Not that I was embarrassed by that story. But speaking those words would have disturbed the magic. Without saying so, I suspect we both knew we would be together from then on.

Our families weren't so sure we were meant to be together at first, but no one had major objections. The only comment about the differences between us came from Mamá. When I brought Anna home to meet everyone, my tiny mother stood looking up at my new girlfriend and burst out with "Dios mío!" Turning to me, she said in Spanish, "Who have you brought home, a giant?" Anna laughed and took it in stride.

We did have our detractors. Whenever we were out together, holding hands while standing in line for the movies in Stockton or driving through higher-income neighborhoods, we saw people's condescending looks. My red pickup with the booming sound system and hotshot hydraulics didn't help. At the pool where Anna worked as a lifeguard, a co-worker went on a rant, mocking her for dating someone who was "a greasy Mexican." The words "dirty" and "lazy" came up too.

Anna did not hesitate to confront the bigotry for what it was. Usually, my role was to reassure her that the latest slight was no big deal and that I was used to worse. Yet her emotions showed me how deeply she cared, which only brought us closer. And when I talked about my career goals, Anna was the ultimate cornerwoman—on my side, believing in me no matter what I chose to do.

What was I to do, then? The moment of truth hit me one evening as I was jogging across campus. Memories suddenly sprang to life, reminding me of everything I had learned—without knowing it back then— from Nana Maria. Not the techniques for delivering babies or preparing remedies and herbal cures. The only family member who learned those was my father's sister, my aunt Nela, who just like her mother was a born healer and a beautiful human being. Unfortunately, I was too young to learn those older folk-medicine traditions. But what I did observe in Nana was her 100-percent investment in the care of her patients; she knew her gift as a healer and greeted each day with optimism, fulfilled by doing good for others in their time of need.

Whether I had the same gift for healing, I didn't know. But I knew that the joy that came from helping others was part of my makeup, passed on to me in my DNA. More importantly, I had the desire. My decision was clear: I had to become a doctor! But where should I begin?

The moment I posed the question, answers followed, as did a wealth of guidance. In particular, three mentors stepped forward to steer me in the right direction. The first was Joe L. Martinez, then a professor in Berkeley's Psychology Department and the head of the laboratory in which I worked—exploring research projects in neuroscience. Through his recommendation, I applied for a Ford Baccalaureate Scholarship that allowed me to support my undergraduate studies at UC Berkeley while doing lab work, mainly in neurobiology.

Dr. Martinez said very little in passing conversations. When he did, he spoke in a soft, unassuming voice that would rise only when he wanted to make an important point, striking me with the lightning speed of his brilliance. Other times, he would listen closely, looking at me with his inquisitive eyes as if trying to read my mind.

Professor Martinez treated all his students and colleagues as equals. Even amid the dog-eat-dog battles for distinction in the world of science, he believed that all clashes of ego should end at the door to the labora-tory, where everyone was gifted, regardless of background or pedigree. Under his wing, I was introduced to the writings and legacies of the masters like Santiago Ramón y Cajal.

Considered the father of the field of neuroscience (among numerous other distinctions), Cajal ranked up there with Newton and Galileo, with discoveries that included his Nobel-winning studies establishing the modern neuron doctrine. By magnificently detailing the existence of individual neurons, his work provided the foundation for everything yet to come in our understanding of the nervous system and the brain.

When I read Cajal's slim volume *Advice for a Young Investigator,* I fell in love with its simple but multilayered guidance—especially the message, echoing Tata Juan, that only by veering off the well-traveled path could scientists make new discoveries. Cajal also believed that anyone could do science. Anyone could do *good* science, he wrote, as long as he or she worked hard and had the "intense motivation needed to succeed." While warning against carelessness, bias, and an overreliance on precedent or theoretical logic, Cajal laid out a roadmap for doing good science that

As a baby with my mother, Flavia, 1969.

Above: At age four, ready to "conquer the world," according to my grandfather, Tata Juan.

Below: In first grade *(front row, behind the letter F), 1973*. This was not too long after my baby sister Maricela died.

Above: Holding my bike without brakes, along with (*left to right*) one of my cousins, my brother Gabriel, and my maternal grandfather, Jesus, who loved animals and at one point raised calves, around 1973.

Below: The PEMEX (Petroleos Mexicanos) gas station where I worked every day after school. We lived in two rooms behind the station—on top of the gas tanks! Financial problems forced my father to sell the station in 1977.

Above: I vividly remember this man and his burro in the Rumorosa Mountains, where Tata Juan and I had our adventures. *(Front to back, left to right)* Me, my brothers Jorge and Gabriel, sisters Rosa and Jaqueline, paternal grandparents Maria and Juan, and my mother, 1978.

Above opposite: The cinder-block and mud house we lived in from 1974 to 1982. I used to go to the roof of this house and look at the stars.

Below opposite: The house we moved to in 1982, which had belonged to Tata Juan and Nana Maria. This is where I watched Nana Maria interacting with young mothers after delivering their babies.

At age sixteen, 1984.
I loved my boots, which
I wore for Mexican folk
dancing and special
occasions.

Celebrating graduation
from teaching college,
with *(from left)* my father,
my mother, and my
brother Gabriel, July
1986.

Above: The border, seen from the American side, January 1987.
This is where I jumped the fence.

Below: My leaky trailer in the fields of the San Joaquin Valley in
Mendota, California, where I lived from 1987 to 1988.

Above: At San Joaquin Delta College's Learning Center, where I tutored students in statistics, 1990. This is around the time I met Anna. Due to necessity and lack of time, I was beginning to go for the long-haired look.

Above opposite: Repairing a motor with my cousin Hector, 1987. When this engine blew up, I learned the hard way that Hector was not a very good mechanic, though I was even worse.

Below opposite: Working as a welder *(far right)*, April 1989. Only a few days after this picture was taken, I fell into the tank car that had carried liquefied petroleum.

Above: With Anna Peterson, a few weeks after we started dating, 1993. Even in those early days, we suspected we would be together for a lifetime.

Above opposite: Reunited and happy, with all our family members now in Stockton. *(From left)* Rosa, Gabriel, Papá, Mamá, me, Jaqueline, and Jorge, 1989. My mom was so pleased that we were all together that she let me get away with baring my chest on this important occasion!

Below opposite: Saying a few words at my sister Jaqueline's quinceañera celebrating her fifteenth birthday, 1993. *(From left)* My father, Cecilio Ramirez, Jaqueline, my mother.

Above: At the Día de los Muertos anatomy lab at Stanford Medical School, the first time I saw a human cadaver, 1993. My friend and mentor Hugo Mora, who took this picture, likes to remind me that my shaky reaction wasn't exactly that of a future brain surgeon.

Above opposite: Graduation from UC Berkeley, with my mentor Joe L. Martinez, June 1994. Joe believed in me, nurtured my appetite for scientific discovery by taking me into his laboratory, and taught me not to fear failure and instead to fear not trying.

Below opposite: With Esteban González Burchard, another key mentor, who helped persuade me to pursue medical school in 1994 and whose path later crossed mine both at Harvard and at UCSF (photo taken at Hopkins in 2008). Esteban has been a trailblazer in respiratory medicine, science, and advocacy for minority students.

Above: Anna's and my wedding at the home of Ed Kravitz, February 1996. Ed brought Anna into the room on his arm because her father could not be there. It was a small but beautiful ceremony.

Above opposite: Studying in Vanderbilt Hall with Reuben Gobezie during my first year at Harvard Medical School, 1994. I continued to take notes in Spanish during lectures and later translate them into English—an exercise that helped me both to retain information and to better my English skills.

Below opposite: With Anna and Wells Messersmith during a trip to Washington, D.C., in 1996. When Wells took us to see the White House, I wondered if I would ever be able to call myself a U.S. citizen.

Above: Graduation from Harvard, carrying six-month-old Gabbie and shaking the hand of Surgeon General David Satcher, 1999. While I gave the commencement address, Gabbie stood up, smiled, and acknowledged every round of applause as though she were the speaker!

Opposite: In Faneuil Hall, Boston, after my citizenship ceremony, 1997. Only ten years earlier, I had been an illegal homeless migrant farm worker, and now I was living the American dream as a Harvard medical student and proud U.S. citizen.

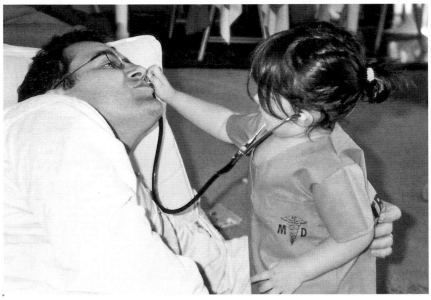

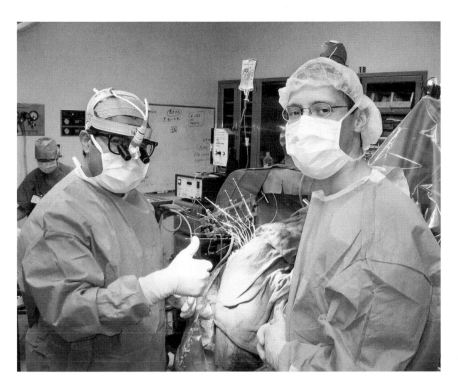

Above: In the OR at UCSF with Paul House, a young attending physician, doing brain surgery and mapping the brain in a patient who was awake, 2004. I am grateful to all the patients who have trusted me to work inside their brains—a gift I do not take for granted and that I receive with the utmost respect and gratitude.

Above opposite: Going-away party with *(back row)* Ed Kravitz, Ken Maynard, David Potter, me; *(second row)* Kathryn Kravitz holding Gabbie, and Anna, 1999. I was on top of the world—having graduated from Harvard with honors, enjoying time with my beautiful family and friends, and even receiving some media attention—but little did I know what a hard road lay ahead.

Below opposite: Being "doctored" by Gabbie, 2000. During this time, when I was taking triple drug therapy after having been stuck by a contaminated needle, I would come home after days of not seeing Gabbie, and she would want to play with me. However, I would often fall asleep within minutes of lying down on the couch.

Above: The Dr. Q Team in front of the dome symbolizing Johns Hopkins's high purpose, 2008. This highly committed group is a multicultural and multidisciplinary array of postdoctoral fellows; graduate, medical, and undergraduate students; physicians' assistants; and administrators.

Above opposite: Neurosurgeons Geoffrey Manley, Michael Lawton, and Mitch Berger, UCSF graduation dinner, June 2005. I wish I could include pictures of all my mentors, but I would need several volumes to do so.

Below opposite: With *(from left)* Anna, Don Rottman, Paul Watson, and Don's companion Dana Kemp, 2008. I was touched to receive the Olender Foundation's America's Role Model award from Don that evening, since only a year earlier we had been in the operating room fighting his brain tumor together.

Holding a photograph of Aaron Watson, with Paul Watson and Ava Watson Dorsey at my side, at the first annual Creating Hope Motorcycle Ride, sponsored by the Brain Cancer Research for a Cure Foundation, 2009. Twenty-six members of my research team joined us to welcome the participating motorcyclists.

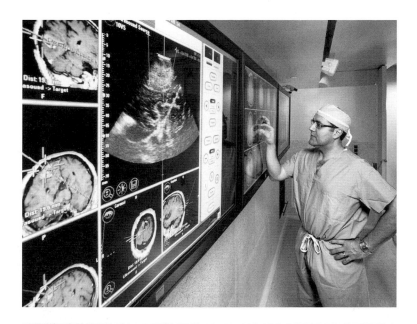

Above: Studying MRIs and planning the surgical resection of a patient with a brain tumor in the intraoperative suite, OR12, at the Johns Hopkins Bayview Hospital, 2009. In this suite we can image the brain at the same time we are doing surgery. Photo by Keith Weller.

Below: Straddling two worlds, 2009. I've always depended on the labor of my hands, both as a farmworker, toiling in the fields, and as a surgeon, laboring to mend and heal. Photo by Chris Hartlove.

With David, Olivia, Anna, and Gabbie, 2007.

emphasized three main steps: first, think clearly; second, design your experiments appropriately; and third, work extremely hard and never give up. Cajal was insistent that scientists not only conduct research but also write about their findings so that others could continue the work. Santiago Ramón y Cajal thus sharpened my desire both to improve my writing skills and to conduct research that mattered enough to be published.

A short time after I studied under Dr. Martinez, he left Berkeley to become the director of the Cajal Neuroscience Institute at the University of Texas at San Antonio, one of three research institutes in the world that bear Cajal's name. As the director of an internationally renowned summer program in neuroscience and ethics in Woods Hole, Massachusetts, Joe would later include me as a faculty member and lecturer in this annual event—opening yet another door.

Because of Professor Martinez, I decided early on to make research an important component of my focus—even while I continued to expand my interests. Through his influence, I learned to seek answers to scientific and medical mysteries in the least likely places; he also helped me see that when unraveling the knottiest, most complicated questions, the key is to think as simply as possible, sometimes by going back to basics. If we want to cure cancer, for example, we have to understand how it originates and spreads.

In science, many would say that intellect is what separates the good from the great. Another group might say that the difference rests in the power of imagination and the ability to see what others can't. Albert Einstein once ventured a definition of a great scientist that added another quality. He agreed that intellect, imagination, curiosity, and even lucky accidents are all important to the work of good scientists, but he believed that those come second to a more important trait that distinguishes the great scientist: character.

Joe Martinez exemplified character, never forgetting who he was and where he came from. A member of a prominent New Mexico family, Joe could trace his lineage back to the Spanish Inquisition, when his ancestors—believed to be Sephardic Jews—were expelled from Spain and then fled to the New World in 1507, settling in what became Mexico. These ancestors, the Martinez family, were among the first settlers in New Mexico in 1598. Joe embraces his family's centuries-old history as part of his identity and extends this respect to all branches of the human family. That he is an American is an accident of history: the result of Mexico's cession of Nuevo Mexico after its defeat in the Mexican-American War in 1848.

When I sought his advice about pursuing medical school, Dr. Martinez admitted that he would prefer to see me pursue a doctorate in research. But he urged me to apply to all the top Ivy League institutions.

The thought was intimidating. Surely, he was just trying to pump me up. But Joe said, "Alfredo, this isn't only about you. Wherever you land, you'll be creating opportunities for others. If you remember that, you'll be surprised how far you can go."

I had a similar conversation with a Stanford medical school student named Esteban González Burchard, who turned out to be a trailblazer for me in a multitude of ways. My introduction to Esteban came about by happenstance when I started making phone calls to medical schools about summer research programs. Naively, I had simply worked my way through the phone book to make these calls, not realizing there was a much more formal protocol. And when the admissions people at Stanford saw how lost I appeared to be, they suggested I talk to Esteban, who graciously took my call and many, many more. Although he was only a year older than I, he had shot up to the top of his class and was soon to graduate before going on to a stellar career that would take him from the Stanford University School of Medicine, where he was earning his MD, on to Harvard for his residency in internal medicine, and then to UC San Francisco, where he joined the faculty in 2001—ultimately pioneering a specialized area of pulmonary medicine and research. Little did I know when he first took my call how closely our paths would be intertwined.

Early in our talks, I learned that we shared similar backgrounds. Esteban's mother was born in Pomona, California, to Mexican immigrant parents. With great determination—including periods when she herself went to work in the fields as a migrant farm worker—she taught herself English at the age of twenty and put herself through college. Upon graduating, she became a teacher, later raising Esteban on her own in a rough San Francisco neighborhood. Esteban thrived as a scholar and athlete and further stood out because of his warm, outgoing personality—factors that gave him an edge in applying to college and med school. Esteban told me, "Ambition is terrific. But everyone applying to med school is ambitious. You're interested in research and that's important. But you're not alone. Find out what it is about you that makes you different from everyone else. That's what med schools are looking for."

Esteban recommended that I contact a man by the name of Hugo Mora—also known as Obi-Wan Kenobi to the people he mentored. Aha! The name was familiar. When I had started making phone calls to area universities in pursuit of summer research assignments, no one had much information to give me, but invariably I'd hear that the guy I needed to call was this fellow Hugo Mora.

As part of the Hispanic Center for Excellence, Hugo oversaw a federally funded grant from the National Institutes of Health. His charter at the time was to identify and recruit minority candidates for careers in health and medicine. Everyone spoke of him with such respect that I couldn't wait to talk to him, although I couldn't imagine how he could live up to his reputation.

Not a problem. The instant I heard his voice and the music of his deep, passionate Chicano inflections, I recognized a catalytic converter of energy and other people's potential. Hugo suggested that we meet at a place on Bancroft Avenue near campus—Caffe Strada.

When Hugo asked, "Do you know the place?" I answered emphatically, "Very well!"

Before hanging up, he added, "And bring your grades, transcripts, test scores, anything you've got."

For the next twenty-four hours, I scrambled to pull together every bit of information I could, though I didn't think there was much on paper that showed how far I'd come. Arriving early for our meeting, I fought a wave of uncertainty. Maybe I was getting ahead of myself to think I could be accepted into med school. Who was I trying to fool? Only five years had passed since I'd left the fields. I still couldn't get very far without my Spanish-English dictionary. Clearly, I was out of my league and should prepare myself to be let down easily.

As Hugo Mora entered the café, all those thoughts vanished. If he had told me that I was capable of leaping over tall buildings, I would have believed him. Short, solid, with dark straight hair, full eyebrows, and thick native features, Hugo had a cordial, dynamic manner. He greeted me, sat down, and reached for my papers. Then with great enthusiasm he began to read, continuing until he finished every word.

Finally he raised his head and said, "*Vato*, with your grades, these awards, what you've accomplished in three semesters, you could definitely go to Harvard Medical School."

What? My first reaction was to acknowledge that Hugo was a very nice man, giving me wonderfully positive reinforcement. But I thought to myself, "This amigo is clearly living *la vida loca!*" I told him a little bit more about myself, thinking he would then see that there wasn't enough beyond my good grades to distinguish me from other applicants. Plus, I wanted to stay in California—at which point he suggested applying to Stanford and UC Davis or UC San Francisco. But he insisted that I seriously consider going to the East Coast.

Though Hugo understood my not wanting to be far from my family, he urged me to go where I could have the most impact, echoing Dr. Martinez's opinion that I could be a pathfinder for others. Indeed, breaking such new trails was the cause of Hugo's lifetime, one he had embraced since childhood when his family left Mexico. A brilliant thinker and writer, Hugo had intended to get a PhD, but before completing his degree, he found his work as a champion for students like me taking precedence.

We spoke that day about Hugo's sister, the beloved Magdalena Mora— famous for the activism she had begun in high school, working for immigrant rights and other issues related to women and labor, and for her significant writings about subjects of interest to the Chicano community, written at a time when we had too few voices telling our stories. Amazingly, she accomplished all of that in twenty-nine short years of life, one of the reasons that Casa Magdalena Mora, a residential program for Hispanic students at Berkeley, had been established in her lasting honor.

When Hugo spoke of her, I could tell that the family still grieved over the sudden loss of such a vibrant, inspirational young woman who had everything going for her.

"How did she die?" I asked.

"A brain tumor," he answered. "Cancer."

This was the first time I'd known anyone who had dealt with brain cancer. Though I wasn't aware then that battling this disease would become the cause of my life, I often think back to this introduction to its devastating effects—remembering Hugo's work and everything he did for me. I thought even then that his sister should still be here and that more should be done to improve our understanding and treatment of this insidious, deadly disease.

But before I could join in this effort, I had more hoops to jump through. A week after our meeting, Hugo called to remind me to fax over an application for a summer research program at Cornell University in New York. The deadline was the next day, and the application called for a research essay, which I hadn't written, mainly because a summer at Cornell seemed like pie in the sky. When I hemmed and hawed, Hugo laid down the law: "Listen, *vato*, our people haven't had opportunities like this. You are going to do great things! You have an opportunity to go to the Ivy League, Cornell University, for a summer research program with the coroner's office. If you want the chance, it's yours. Get me the essay bright and early tomorrow."

Minor complication. I had a final the next day that wasn't going to be easy. What to do? Study and blow the application? Or write the essay and risk flunking the final and ruining my grade point average? Hugo Mora showed up at my apartment unannounced, another cornerman, and sat with me until I did both.

The exam went well, but I had to wait several weeks to receive the verdict from Cornell—during which I had a heart-to-heart with Anna about the demands of medical school and a career in medicine. We weren't officially engaged, but we were heading in that direction, and I had to know whether she was prepared for a steeper climb than she might have originally expected. Still unaware of the full extent of the challenges, I knew enough to realize that the road ahead would require years of study and training, much more debt than earnings initially, and long hours away from home.

While I don't recall Anna's exact words, I do remember the light in her green eyes when she put her hands in mine and told me how she used to watch me run across campus at the community college and ask herself, "What's up with this guy? Where is he going in such a hurry?" The way that I went zipping by, she said, convinced her that I was a man on a mission and my sense of purpose had appealed to her.

"Oh," I joked, "and not my rippling muscles like Rambo's?"

Anna laughed. "I always knew you were going somewhere. Now I know where. And I want to go there with you." I still had a year and a half to go at Berkeley, and she needed another two and a half years to complete her biology teaching degree and student teaching. In the past, Anna had talked of teaching school for a while and then later resuming her education to pursue her dream of becoming a veterinarian. Though the plan was still a possibility, I also knew that there would be practical considerations to balance when the time came. Then again, if we had been able to handle the separations and challenges so far, we figured the future couldn't be too different. Little did we suspect how many more tests we would have to weather.

One of these tests arose a short while later on a windsurfing excursion with Anna's sister and her date. We had never been out swimming together, partly because I avoided any competitive activities in the water—not the least because I had never really learned to swim and Anna was highly accomplished in this area! But windsurfing—with the speed of the boat and the use of upper body strength—was right up my alley. In fact, it was so much fun that I didn't want to stop. But Anna was ready for a break after a few hours and decided to swim back to shore.

After she took off at a brisk clip—in her element as a distance swimmer—I thought it would be less than gallant not to swim back with her and, probably with the help of some ego, I called it a day and headed back too. In no time, I almost caught up with her, my competitive nature causing me to push myself mentally to try to compensate for my lack of actual swimming skills and the fact that I was already fatigued. If not for what began as a tiny leg cramp, I probably could have reached the shore first. Or so I would like to think! But the small twinge suddenly exploded into a whole-body cramp. Suddenly I was sinking and flailing in the water.

"Cramp! I have a cramp!" I gurgled loudly enough for Anna to hear me, and—lifeguard that she was—she immediately turned back to come to my rescue. While considering how my ordeal might make for a very embarrassing story one day, the pain of the body cramp and the inability of my feet to touch the bottom of the lake sent me into a panic. Unable to catch my breath, I was convinced that I was going to die and initially fought off Anna's effort to get me to surrender to her help. But her soothing voice and calm confidence eventually allowed me to relax and avoid pulling us both down, at which point we were able to wave down a group of boaters, who gave us a ride to shore. When we reached dry land, I tried to inject some humor into the situation by saying that I was just testing Anna's skills. But we both knew that she had saved my life.

The shoe was on the other foot a short time later when we took a memorable trip to Mexico. We started at the Sea of Cortez, where I wisely avoided doing much swimming. To my lasting joy, the place had not lost any of its magical beauty. We then drove into Mexicali, where I was proud to introduce Anna to some of my relatives still living in the area and to show her the places where so many of my memories had formed. To wrap up our getaway, we stayed overnight at a little place in Rosarito Beach and dined on tacos from a small stand. Big mistake. Though I had an iron stomach and was immune to the notorious Montezuma's revenge that afflicts many American tourists, Anna had no such immunities.

By midnight, the violent vomiting and diarrhea had begun. When Anna showed no improvement by 3:00 A.M., I knew we had to get to the hospital in San Diego—a couple hours away. As the sun rose on an otherwise peaceful and picturesque Southern California morning, the contrast between the beautiful day and the scene of desperation when I pulled into the hospital parking lot and lifted Anna into my arms could not have been more stark. All of 110 pounds, Anna lay like a rag doll, dehydrated, barely breathing, while my own breathing became more labored as I carried her into the emergency room. I'd never seen anyone in such a perilous state. The threat of losing her was real and terrifying, evoking the memory of losing my baby sister to diarrhea.

The medical staff went to work with great efficiency but had a difficult time establishing an IV for hydration, even when anesthesia personnel were called in. With every minute that passed, my frustration grew; I knew that time was of the essence. Finally, a more senior nurse appeared and established the IV without a second to spare. Anna pulled through, thank God, and we both recognized that this test had brought us even closer.

When I later told my family about the ordeal, I was surprised by how upset my father was that I didn't get Anna to the hospital sooner. His distress made me realize that he was still haunted by my baby sister's death and by the memory of almost losing me as well. His reaction also showed me how much he cared for his future daughter-in-law.

.   .   .

Cornell turned out to be nothing like what I had expected from the Ivy League. Far from being inside lofty towers, all of us in the summer program spent much of our time riding along with police officers and members of the coroner's office—walking into scenes of death, madness, and mayhem, most of which were the violent aftermath of suicides. The purpose of our research was to compare how males and females chose to commit suicide. What we found, consistently, was that while women accounted for a much larger percentage of suicides than men did, men used much more violent methods.

Not only did I find this work fascinating, but I had the great fortune to be mentored by Dr. Bruce Ballard, who ran this program geared to promoting minority premed students. An associate professor of clinical psychiatry and the medical school's associate dean for student affairs, Dr. Ballard was deeply committed to opening doors of opportunity for minority students, much as doors had been opened to him as an African-American. I saw his commitment firsthand when he sat me down toward the end of my two months at Cornell and said, "Alfredo, before you go back to California, I think it would be worth your while to take the train to Boston and visit Harvard Medical School." He added that while I was there, he hoped that I could meet his mentor, Dr. Alvin F. Poussaint.

Though Dr. Poussaint's fame grew in later years when he coauthored *Come On, People* with Bill Cosby, at the time he was already an icon— a leader in the civil rights movement and a distinguished researcher exploring links between violent racism and various forms of mental illness. In addition to being a professor of psychiatry and associate dean for student affairs at Harvard Medical School, Dr. Poussaint was also the director of recruitment and multicultural affairs.

Deeply grateful to Dr. Ballard for taking an interest in my future, I explained that I couldn't make the trip to Boston. The ticket wasn't "in the budget."

"Don't worry. We'll arrange for your expenses." Without spelling it out, he made the arrangements and, I suspect, paid for the ticket from his own pocket and sent me on my way. Years later, I told this story when presenting an award to him for his contributions to student advancement in the field of medicine. And when the organization honored me with a $15,000 grant for any uses that I chose, I couldn't think of a better way to express my gratitude for what Dr. Ballard had done for me than to set up a fund to pay for visits to Johns Hopkins Medical School for students who couldn't otherwise afford the trips.

That summer, when I arrived in Boston and stepped outside the train station, I remembered being eleven years old and dreaming of going to Faraway. I was sure I had arrived at that elusive place. Meeting Dr. Poussaint was amazing. Handsome and vibrant, he had the ability to make everyday conversation sound like oratory, and he also made me feel instantly at home. Since I hadn't applied to medical school yet, I had no reason to read anything into his parting words to me: "I believe we may be seeing more of you, young man. I certainly hope so."

That meeting fired me up, boosting my desire to aim as high as possible. Back in California, I said as much when I ran into Mike from community college—the guy who wouldn't introduce Anna to me way back when. Maybe his reaction was sour grapes, but he couldn't have been more discouraging about my prospects for getting into a medical school like Harvard or Stanford. It was next to impossible, he said, for someone like me to get accepted. When I shrugged, saying that I'd wait to see how I did on the MCATs (the grueling tests required for medical school applications), he laughed, warning me, "You're wasting your time." I later learned that he had been trying to get into med school and had failed to pass the test the first time around.

Much as I tried to ignore his skepticism, my doubts returned when I sat down in the fall of 1993 to fill out the med school applications. Who was I kidding? Just as I started to reconsider my prospects, the phone rang. It was Hugo Mora, who didn't even bother to announce himself as he asked, "You need a ride to Stanford for Día de los Muertos?"

Hugo didn't explain that the event at Stanford was a conference for minority premed students, designed to provide information about applying to medical school and obtaining financial assistance, nor that the main event would be an anatomy seminar in which we would dissect cadavers. Once I heard "Día de los Muertos," all I needed was the date and time and I was on my way. Day of the Dead celebrations connected me to my roots—to the days when our Aztec ancestors celebrated the last corn harvest before winter arrived. The ritual merged this ancient celebration with the Catholic religious holidays of All Saints' Day and All Souls' Day at the beginning of November. My associations with the traditional celebration had remained happy through the years—the music, the parades, the costumes and masks, and the altars adorned with marigolds and special items belonging to the deceased to ensure that their souls would enjoy coming back for a visit—and lots of candy!

The Stanford student group that sponsored the conference skillfully connected the holiday's cultural traditions with the work of those who study medicine, especially during the anatomy and dissection demonstration. Even though I felt queasy and may have looked pale in the photo that Hugo took of me that day—this being my first encounter with a cadaver—I was inspired by the lesson that we need to respect what the dead can teach us and to honor those people who depart from this world and leave us their bodies so that we can learn more. The event also helped me realize that when dealing intimately with the dead, as physicians do, it is healthy now and then to put on the mask and dance in the face of death, defying and mocking it with celebration, passion, and joy.

After the conference, I was pumped enough to apply to several top medical schools, and I was elated to receive acceptances from almost all of them in the months that followed. The one exception was the place I thought would be the most likely—the University of California, San Francisco, the medical school associated with Berkeley. Though I was disappointed (and mystified about why I was accepted at Stanford but not UCSF), the rejection lit a fire inside me to try to attend UCSF in some capacity in the future. That chance would come when I applied for a residency several years later—a much harder, higher hurdle.

While I continued to be wary of the East Coast—arguing that the stuffy Ivy League atmosphere was not for me—I couldn't say no when Harvard offered to fly me there for a visit in April 1994. Since my official interview had been in San Francisco, this trip was my chance to get a better sense of the program (and to realize I was as guilty of stereotyping as anyone else).

Just before I left, Dr. Joe Martinez called me into his office and silently handed me a yellow Post-It with two names written on it: David Potter and Ed Kravitz. Puzzled, I looked at the names on the Post-It. Who were these guys?

"Just meet them," he declared. Then, tongue in cheek, he added, "Or I'll break your legs."

As instructed, I made appointments on a Saturday morning to meet these two legends. By the time I arrived for my appointment with Dr. David Potter, I'd learned enough about him to be thoroughly intimidated. The former chairman of the neurobiology department at Harvard Medical and a full professor overseeing landmark laboratory research, he came out to meet me in the grand old foyer and took me back to his surprisingly small and simple office, which helped put me at ease. He was a stately and distinguished gentleman with white hair and a white beard and eyes that blazed with intelligence and warmth.

Dr. Potter came from the sort of background that I mistakenly thought was a Harvard requirement. He was from a very wealthy family that had come to the United States from England centuries before, enabling him to receive the most privileged education, including a stint at Johns Hopkins as a young faculty member. Yet, despite this background, here he was, a man of incredible vision who knew how important diversity was to the future of science and medicine and to the future of the United States and the world.

"Tell me, Alfredo," he asked in his warm, inviting manner, "would you like a cup of coffee?"

A trick question or a personality test? Not one to refuse a kindness, I answered, "I would love to have a cup of coffee."

He then proceeded to make two cups of coffee in the most purposeful, ceremonial way I'd ever seen—taking out his beans, coffee grinder, and European coffee press that looked a bit like a laboratory beaker. After pressing the grounds just so, he took out two mugs and carefully split the coffee between them.

With everything else he would teach me, I never forgot that gesture. Nor did I forget his courtesy when we wrapped up our conversation. "It was so nice to meet you!" he said. "Thank you for coming. Now, I understand you are to meet with Ed Kravitz next, so why don't I show you the way? You can keep your coffee with you."

David Potter, moving quickly for a man in his sixties, then walked me all the way to Dr. Kravitz's office and said good-bye. Just as welcoming, Ed Kravitz ushered me into his similarly modest office. His desk was piled with papers, and a large, comfortable blue sofa took up much of the space in the room. With a beaming smile and lots of energy, Dr. Kravitz gestured for me to have a seat. Rather than asking about my academic interests or background, he wanted to know about me. So, with my cup of coffee in my hand, sitting on his blue sofa, I told him an abbreviated version of my journey so far, as he nodded, laughed, and allowed his eyes to mist over once or twice.

Then he told me his story, which was very different from Dr. Potter's. As a poor Jewish kid who had grown up in the Bronx, he had not done exceptionally well in his early school years. More street smart than anything, he said, he didn't get much attention for his intellectual capacity until his last year of college, when he landed a research position at the Memorial Sloan-Kettering Cancer Center in New York City. Through science, he had found his passion and undergone a transformation, proceeding to become the youngest-ever full tenured professor of neurobiology at Harvard—at age thirty-one. He had accelerated meteorically, coming out of nowhere.

We spoke briefly that day about the history of neurobiology at Harvard Med. The department, revolutionary in its day, was founded in 1966 with Stephen W. Kuffler as the chair. Previously, the study of the brain

had been treated like a poor stepchild, often lumped into other departments as an afterthought. By bringing together experts from different
disciplines—anatomists, physiologists, biochemists—to start to give the
study of the brain its due, the department dramatically advanced the
field. Kuffler brought in a team he believed would be pioneers with him,
including Potter and Kravitz. Until that time, Harvard had been like a
country club that tended to bar admittance to Jews, African-Americans,
Latinos, Asians, and other immigrants, as well as women, with a few
exceptions. All that would change with Ed Kravitz and David Potter. But
not without a fight.

Dr. Kravitz told me about the day in 1968 when Dr. Martin Luther
King Jr. was assassinated and he decided that the cause of his lifetime
would be to recruit and train those who had been disenfranchised. He
and his colleagues went up against a faculty board ready to fight to the
end to protect the status quo. As a full tenured professor, he would not be
easy to fire. But he had adversaries who were dead set against opening
up the admissions process. Full of fire to do what he believed was right,
Dr. Kravitz went before the board and announced that he was going to
launch a movement for the recruitment of more minorities to Harvard
Medical School. This was the time, this was the moment, he told them,
and they could try to stop him, but history could not be stopped. And
that was the beginning.

The following year, sixteen African-American students were admitted
to Harvard Medical School as part of the class of 1973. At this writing,
over one thousand physicians from minority backgrounds—Hispanic,
African-American, and Native American—have received their medical
degrees from Harvard. In 2010, 21 percent of the students entering med
school were from underrepresented groups. Meanwhile, there had only
been twelve women in the 1969 graduating class of Harvard Medical
School and by 1998 the numbers had changed so dramatically that fifty-
two percent of medical students were female. Dr. Kravitz and Dr. Potter,
along with Dr. Poussaint when he arrived in 1969, helped contribute to
these changes.

My visit to Harvard left me with nothing but wonderful first impres-
sions of the medical school and especially of the two mentors poised

to have an incredible impact on me. Dr. Potter and Dr. Kravitz treated me like family from the start. They believed in me, never doubted that I would succeed, and supported me at every turn. By example, each would teach me how to persevere and put my energies toward issues that matter.

Years later, after I had gone on to my residency and become a young faculty member at Johns Hopkins, I found myself at a dinner seated next to one of the titans of medicine, a gentleman raised in the South who was considered almost without peer among fellow neuroscientists. At Hopkins, no policy to recruit Jewish or other minority faculty members had been instituted until some time after minority barriers were broken at Harvard. And at the scientific society meeting where the dinner took place, I looked around and realized that as a person of color, I was still very much in the minority. But I knew that I wouldn't have been there at all if not for Kravitz and Potter.

When my dinner companion asked about Harvard, he mentioned that he knew David Potter and commented, "I never understood him. He was so brilliant. He could have done anything. He could have won a Nobel Prize if he wanted to. But he wasted his career with this issue of bringing people of color to science . . . " Not bothering to finish his sentence, he waved his hand dismissively.

Hurt by his remark, I felt better a short while later when David Potter was honored at a standing-room-only gala attended by three dozen world-renowned scientists, including some Nobel Prize winners whom he had mentored. How thankful I was at that joyful occasion that my mentors in 1994 had made sure that I wouldn't turn down the opportunity of a lifetime.

·   ·   ·

Though I was tempted to go to Stanford and stay closer to my family and to Anna, meeting Kravitz and Potter just about sealed the deal for Harvard. And if I had any remaining fears of the unknown and concerns about whether I could handle the challenges, a trip back to Mexico to attend the funeral of my maternal grandfather Jesus put everything in perspective. After decades of being a widower, my grandfather had finally remarried, to a woman half his age, and become a new man. For two years, he and his wife traveled and lived life to the fullest. The spirit of adventure that had always been inside of him had finally been set free.

On the drive back to Berkeley after the funeral, I realized I would be crazy to pass up a chance to see the world beyond California and walk through the door of opportunity that had been opened for me. If I didn't take the risk, I'd never know what I had missed. My grandfather had lived only to work and waited until old age to enjoy himself and pursue his earlier dreams. I also thought of my brilliant and attractive cousin— the only person in our extended family who graduated from college in Mexico, a young woman with every possibility at her doorstep. A freak accident had cut short her life soon after I left for the United States, dealing a blow to her head that caused her to die instantaneously from bleeding in her brain.

End of the debate: I would go to Harvard, if not for myself, then in memory of my cousin and my grandparents Jesus, Tata Juan, and Nana Maria. And I would go for the children I hoped Anna and I would have.

Hugo, Joe, and Esteban were delighted by my decision. But then Joe and Hugo raised an issue they knew was going to be a tough sell.

Joe Martinez broke the news gently. "You need to consider cutting your hair."

"My hair?" My beautiful long hair that my girlfriend loved and that was part of my distinctive style?

"Yes," Joe went on. "And the goatee and the earrings. You should get rid of them."

Feeling like Samson, I was heartsick and convinced that my strength would be zapped the minute I lost my hair, which the ladies loved and the gentleman envied. Hugo took me out for a beer and set me straight. "Alfredo, your hair doesn't define you. It's what you do that defines you. You have to let it go."

I argued that my exotic look was disarming to others. People didn't expect a guy with a ponytail and earrings to get top grades. It was my element of surprise.

"No, that's history, *vato*." He wanted me to see that East Coast attitudes weren't necessarily the same as those at Berkeley. People might misjudge or stereotype me for superficial reasons, so I would be wise not to give them ammunition. He finally won me over by reminding me, "Harvard will not only open doors to you but also to others, and you have to represent all of us."

Once I agreed, I set out to find an affordable hair stylist who would not butcher me. I interviewed candidates for weeks and finally located someone who promised not to make me look too boring. Instead, as Anna noted, he attempted a type of Latino jerry curl on me.

Not until the packing was done, the good-byes were over, and I was on the airplane did I decide I liked the haircut. I had to admit I would have been out of place with my more bohemian look. Even without my distinctive hair, I stuck out among my fellow med students that fall of 1994 when I started Harvard Medical School.

Much of my self-consciousness about being different wore off when I participated in an informal version of a ritual that has become known as the "white coat ceremony"—during which each student is presented with a short white physician's jacket to wear until graduation. Putting on my white coat that day, glancing down to see "Harvard Medical Student" on one side, embroidered on the pocket, and my name on the other side, I felt as if I were donning Superman's cape! No, even better—I was going to be a doctor!

Another ritual followed, as all the incoming first-year med students (about 140 of us) waited for our assignment to one of five academic societies, all equally desirable: Cannon, Castle, Holmes, Peabody, and Health Science & Technology (HST). Like fraternal orders from the heraldic ages—or the different houses at Hogwarts in the Harry Potter series— these societies existed to help every Harvard med student flourish in the work ahead, instilling a "one for all and all for one" team mentality. The school issued no grades: all courses were pass or fail. There were no rankings in the class. We were all assessed to be the cream of the crop, all equals.

My joy in knowing that I would be part of this atmosphere—where I would be mentored by some of the leading minds in medicine and some-day mentor others—could not be subdued. While waiting to hear my assignment, I wanted to jump up and down and turn back flips! Instead, I bit my thumb and adopted a serious expression, a habit that would become more pronounced over the years whenever I felt excitement that I couldn't contain. And then, to make everything perfect, I was assigned to the Castle academic society. A fairy tale come true!

That afternoon in the cafeteria at Vanderbilt Hall, after my first Castle Society study group meeting, one of my classmates escorted me to a table of fellow first-year students so that we could start getting to know each other. Everyone else at the table had been born in the United States, and most were from the East Coast and from old wealth. Emphasis on *old* and on *wealth*. Many had surnames that dated back to the Mayflower, and a few were descended from inventors and famous figures in academia. They told stories of going to private boarding schools, then to Ivy League undergraduate colleges, spending vacations skiing the Alps or watching tennis at Wimbledon. Their wide exposure to art, music, culture, and travel was astonishing to me. While my studies at Berkeley had introduced me to names such as Picasso and Van Gogh, some of my new colleagues had original paintings by these artists in their homes!

And yet, I didn't feel intimidated. I knew that some of them probably thought that I had made it to Harvard through an affirmative action program and that I wasn't up to snuff. But because that wasn't the case, I tried simply to be myself, hoping that people would get past the accent and get to know me and value what I could add to the conversation.

Finally, one of my classmates turned to me and asked, "How about you? How did you get here, Alfredo?"

I was comfortable enough to answer rather matter-of-factly, "I hopped the fence."

Everyone burst into laughter. They thought I was kidding. How little they knew!

When the laughter subsided and I didn't continue, probably looking startled at their reaction, my classmates realized I wasn't joking but instead hadn't understood the question—which was not about how I had come to the United States but about my educational path. They then asked more leading questions about my three years at Berkeley and about what had led me to Harvard Med—the last destination on the planet I could have imagined on that night seven years earlier when I had hopped the fence, not once but twice.

I started to talk about my days as a migrant worker but, feeling self-conscious, stopped.

"No, please continue," said one of my companions, a handsome yet somewhat melancholy-looking young man who, I had learned, was descended from aristocrats in the worlds of academia—with a famous father and a family tree that went back generations and included many "who's whos."

"Yes, go, on," everyone concurred.

Not sure if they were simply being kind, I wrapped up after a few more anecdotes, feeling nonetheless right at home.

When everyone stood up and took off to go to bed or hit the books in preparation for the first official day of classes, the melancholy-looking student hung back and walked with me outside.

"You don't know how I envy you," he began. "I know that sounds strange, but you have no expectations to live up to. No one has come before you to set the bar to a level you'll never reach no matter what you do."

I could see he was in a lot of pain, so I said, "Yes, I never thought of that."

"The pressure is unbearable. Crushing. It's like an elephant standing on my chest. Sometimes I can't cope."

His comments left a profound impression, and I thought long and hard about them afterward. I had assumed that someone with his background was to be envied. Now I felt new appreciation for my parents, who had only encouraged me through the years. When the time came to raise my own children, I would reflect back on our conversation this night and decide never to put pressure on them to live up to expectations other than their own. But at this moment, I didn't know what to say, so I put my hand on his shoulder, acknowledging that hardships come in different forms. This gesture seemed to cheer him a great deal.

Later, my friend went through a more drastic depression and attempted suicide. Depression, I later learned, was not uncommon for med school students, who not only had to cope with academic pressure but were also exposed to the pain and suffering of others. Such pressures were all the more intense for someone like my friend, who may not have wanted to be a doctor in the first place.

That night he thanked me for listening. Then, with a smile, he turned to me and said, "You're really lucky, you know that?"

"Yes," I told him. I couldn't have agreed more.

SEVEN

From Harvest to Harvard

My first few months of medical school taught me the importance of approaching the study of medicine as both a sprinter and a marathon runner. With a course load that included anatomy, physiology, immunology, and pharmacology, my time was divided between attending classes, keeping up with assignments and exams, as well as going to the laboratory daily to do research. Whether I was studying on weekends or during many all-nighters, or reading on my feet in the lab in between experiments, I was so caught up by these demands that the reality of where I was didn't fully hit me until that first winter.

Then, in November 1994, on an icy cold night as I was leaving the main administration building of the med school at around 2:00 A.M., the wonder of my circumstances finally dawned on me.

Instead of going outside into the freezing night air to get to Vanderbilt Hall, as I usually would, I decided to try an alternate route down a basement hallway that connected the two buildings. And as I was walking down this hallway, my feet moving over the ornate floor, laid with meticulous workmanship in little black-and-white square tiles, and my eyes taking in the rows of handsome cherrywood lockers that had been there for nearly a century, I suddenly had to stop and murmur something along the lines of "Ay, Dios mío!" Here I was at Harvard Medical School! How many of the most famous, revered names in medicine had walked these hundred-year-old hallways? Countless!

For my training as a physician and as a scientist, this moment in the wee hours of a winter morning was a critical turning point. It made me think about those who had come before me here—individuals who were among the elite of the medical world—and left me with a lasting sense of awe and humility to be following in their footsteps, walking the same halls they had walked.

I felt history scrutinizing me—reminding me of my responsibility not only to honor the institution, strive for excellence, and practice medicine to the best of my abilities but also to make the utmost commitment to my patients, who would place their lives and their trust in my hands.

From my earliest childhood, I had used my hands for everything from pumping gas and fixing car engines to making hot dogs, from boxing to picking tomatoes. That night, looking down at my hands, no longer bloody from the hard work of picking crops, I had a new purpose for them. I had chosen medicine after living through and observing true suffering, discrimination, and hopelessness. Now I could use my hands to take on the most devastating diseases and help patients to heal. In this electrifying moment was born the idea of becoming a surgeon—a way to use my hands to help others. History had opened the door to me, and I was standing on the threshold—ready!

This walk down the basement hallway became a rite of passage. Whenever I was beset by doubts or distractions, I could tap this memory to filter out the background noise and focus on what mattered. This focusing skill became one of the most important lessons to come from my Harvard education. During this first year, I also relived passages from childhood that had been long forgotten—as if these memories surfaced to give me guidance for the steep incline I was beginning to climb. In unsteady moments, I could feel Tata Juan's hand on my shoulder, as he used to place it there whenever we went to the mountains—

whether I was scared, overly excited, or overwhelmed by how high we had climbed.

.   .   .

Early on I discovered that Harvard provided a level of competition and collaboration that suited my temperament. It was a challenge to hold my own alongside fellow students who, besides being brilliant and educated in the finest institutions, had life learning that was foreign to me. They knew American history from their own family lineages. Many were descended from generations of physicians and were steeped in knowledge about the practice of medicine going back to premedieval times. Some had even been raised among artifacts from the earliest years of science—medical illustrations or early versions of scalpels and stethoscopes.

Of course I was intimidated. Not until my second year would I finally let go of the security blanket of my old Spanish-English dictionary. And only in the following year would I have my first dream in English. But time and again, throughout the five years of my training, including one year of research funded by the Howard Hughes Medical Institute and conducted during my fourth year at Harvard's Massachusetts General Hospital (known to locals as Mass General), I could draw on one advantage that helped balance out my doubts: my ability to focus on what mattered and to work as hard as just about anyone else. That focus came from the conscious choice, again and again, never to take for granted this golden opportunity that I was being given to learn.

All my professors, especially Dr. Potter and Dr. Kravitz, recognized my eagerness to absorb everything, and they sought to fuel my enthusiasm and motivation. Dr. Potter's door was always open to me, whether it was to discuss material he covered in class or to provide advice over a cup of his incomparable coffee. For the first two years of medical school, I worked in Dr. Kravitz's lab, where he was as immersed in the work as any of his students. Like surrogate parents, these two mentors also recognized my initial lack of an overall direction, seeing that I was like a kid in a candy store, sometimes all over the place. Each helped to ground me and offer direction that left a lasting influence. As one example, I was especially interested in their work identifying specific neurotransmitters in the brain and locating the parts of the brain that perform special functions—causing different kinds of behavior, helping to regulate temperature or memory, or influencing aggressive behavior. Their contributions and the body of work they had inspired had already made for life-saving advances and would continue to do so—in ways that would help determine my specialization.

Each in his own way, Dr. Potter and Dr. Kravitz taught me the value of pursuing the scientific method with relentless vigor. They also taught me the importance of pursuing a clearly envisioned line of research to its culmination, even when others dismissed it as impossible. Today, whenever I'm told that I'm overly ambitious for seeking a cure for brain cancer, I think of David Potter and Ed Kravitz, who raised me to filter out the noise of lowered expectations. As teachers, Potter and Kravitz were the epitome of commitment and passion, inside and outside the classroom.

David Potter showed me that I had been wrong to think that anyone who came from wealth or had an impressive pedigree couldn't relate to the struggles of everyday human beings. He taught the power of connection across borders, across differences. In the realm of patient care, this lesson was essential.

Ed Kravitz was passion and energy personified. A survivor of gastrointestinal cancer that had thankfully been resolved with surgery and a colostomy, he started every day with a game of tennis at Harvard Square. He celebrated life with the same rigor he brought to his work. As a mentor, he did so much for me personally and was a hero for showing that everything worth doing was achieved with effort and tremendous perseverance.

Dr. Kravitz also gave me a crash course in the truth of the saying that there is a thin line between a mentor and a tormentor. One day, excited about lab research I was doing on a steroid that lobsters use to go through their molting cycle, which we believed could be relevant in their aggressive behavior as well, I brought him an abstract for a short scientific paper I wanted to write. I was proud to be ahead of my peers in seeking publication and had been thorough in my preparation. Or so I thought.

When Dr. Kravitz handed me back the abstract with red lines slashing it to bits, I was stunned.

"Don't worry, Alfredo," he tried to reassure me. "There is still some work to do. This isn't a bad start."

Nodding stoically, I tried not to show that my stomach had just turned upside down in shock.

Dr. Kravitz looked back at me with an equally stoic expression. "You may be disappointed today because you think you've failed." Before I could answer, he continued, "But if you don't keep trying, you will be doomed!" His tone then changed as he let me know that he would be a hands-on advisor and guide the paper step by step. But what I had turned in, he reiterated, wasn't close to what it should be. Not an easy pill to swallow. But I persevered through many drafts and was much happier with the short paper that emerged, my first publication. In the process, Ed Kravitz taught me not to take criticism personally but rather to appreciate the underlying value, even when feedback wasn't what I wanted to hear. He wasn't picking apart my paper to decrease my confidence, only to strengthen and prepare me for the competitive world of scientific research. From then on, once I understood that he really believed in me and my capacity to learn, our relationship flourished.

Dr. Kravitz was the person who dubbed me "Lucky Quiñones" in recognition of a breakthrough I achieved in his lab, when I succeeded in cloning a lobster's neurological receptor, an accomplishment that yielded a paper we presented at a scientific meeting. No longer a late bloomer, as I'd always seen myself, I felt lucky to be part of important research so early in medical school. Apparently, I was having a growth spurt!

Ed Kravitz also encouraged me to embrace the power of irreverence. Whenever a special occasion arose—howsoever he chose to deem it special—he would spontaneously throw a party for us in the lab, whipping up his secret recipe for the most deadly margaritas in the world—a subject on which I have some authority! One Kravitz margarita was enough to get the party well under way, at which point we knew the lobster dance would soon follow. Through his extensive studies of aggression in lobsters, Ed Kravitz had come to the conclusion that scientists who work with animals soon start to look and act like their research subjects. So we were treated to the sight of a towering figure in the annals of neuroscience rocking out on the laboratory floor, red faced and doing the lobster dance!

Such parties were the highlights of my otherwise nonexistent social life. On most Friday nights, when my peers were going out to a local bar or knocking off early to see a movie, I was in my regular seat in the library or standing over a microscope in the lab or volunteering to go on rounds with more senior med students. Everyone—even those who were part of my new extended family—thought this self-imposed schedule was insane. At least at first. But as time went on, they saw not only the method to my madness but the magic and the joy that went along with it. I was out to prove that it was possible to focus like crazy, work harder than anyone else, and make it more fun than doing anything else. And I was intent on recruiting others. Before I was even aware that I was developing my "rainbow" (as I called the diverse collection of fellow med school students and research collaborators who became my home team), the group seemed to naturally coalesce—an updated version of the array of siblings and cousins I used to organize as a child.

At the core of this group were my two closest friends, Wells Messersmith and Reuben Gobezie, who had been like family from the moment we met at Vanderbilt Hall. We soon became the Three Amigos. Besides being two of the finest individuals I've ever known, Wells and Reuben were always there to watch my back.

Wells Messersmith was from the Washington, D.C., suburbs and had attended Williams College before coming to medical school. Blond and blue-eyed, he was a virtuoso violinist who had experienced such a dramatic growth spurt in recent years that he had to stop playing the violin when he reached six feet five inches. Instead he channeled his passion into his academic studies, eventually focusing in the area of gastrointestinal cancer and developing new treatments for stomach and related cancers.

Whenever Wells heard anyone make even the slightest racist remark about me or imply that I had gotten to Harvard through special minority treatment, he took the comment personally. As it happened, Wells had a brother who was African-American. He never emphasized the word "adopted"—even though the Messersmiths had adopted the boy at a young age. The two were just brothers. And that's how Wells made me

feel whenever he decided to challenge someone for making a dispar-
aging remark. Sometimes he wouldn't tell me about an incident, but I
would hear from someone else how upset he was when, for instance,
during rounds a patient might mistake me for the janitor and ask to have
me take out the trash.

I usually managed to take such comments in stride. Besides, I had
only respect for everyone who worked in the hospital—janitors, orderlies, everyone. As far as I was concerned, every person on the floor was
part of the team that was vital to delivering the best possible patient care.
Wells and Reuben were constantly amazed by my recruitment process.
Whenever one of them asked how I happened to know everyone, my
standard response became, "They're on the payroll."

Though I am technically not tall, I joked that I only appeared to be
short standing next to Wells and Reuben, who both towered above me.
At about six feet three inches, Reuben, who was African-American, was
a paragon of good looks and intelligence. Reuben's parents had immigrated to the United States from Ethiopia, where his mother had grown
up in a well-to-do family and his father had come from a more humble
background. In the United States, Reuben's father had worked his way
through medical school and become a successful physician in the Los
Angeles area. Reuben knew from an early age that he would follow his
father's path into medicine. For his undergraduate degree, he attended
Johns Hopkins, and when he graduated from Harvard Medical School,
he would stay on to do his residency in orthopedic surgery.

The three of us studied together, cooked and ate meals together, and
joked relentlessly. We were fiercely competitive, but I took the prize in that
department, as evidenced by a challenge that I once put to our classmate
Renn Crichlow. Canadian by nationality, part German and part black,
Renn was six feet three and two hundred pounds, as well as a three-time
Olympian and world champion kayaker. Toward the end of 1994, he was
preparing to take a year's leave of absence to train for the 1996 Olympics
and was spending long hours in the gym, cranking up his workouts.

I gave Renn a hard time about his training regimen, telling him I
doubted his workout could be much harder than, say, mine. As the champion of the Stairmaster, I was convinced no one could match my ability
on it, and what better way to test this theory than to challenge Renn

Crichlow? But Renn wasn't interested in a Stairmaster duel. Of course not, I thought, because, as a kayaker, he was all upper-body strength and hadn't developed his legs as much. Hoping to exploit his weakness, over breakfast I proposed that we train together and do his workout, thinking that once in the gym, he wouldn't refuse a Stairmaster competition.

Renn said flat out, "No, Alfredo. You would slow me down."

"Me, slow you down? C'mon, Renn, you're probably too busy flexing your muscles to work out for three hours."

Renn finally acquiesced, graciously offering me lighter weights to compensate for the differences in our size. Nonetheless, I insisted on doing as many sets and reps as he did. An hour into the weight workout, I could see this was nuts. By the ninety-minute mark, I was sweating bullets. But no turning back now. I had to get him on the Stairmaster and push it to the max. Once there, he would be dust! When we finally got to the Stairmaster, I was running on adrenaline and on an endorphin high, so I pushed us up through the levels until we reached level 20—where only Kaliman-worthy, gravity-defying speed could sustain us for the thirty minutes we did at the top.

Renn was not undone by my virtuosity. But I felt victorious for matching his pace for three hours. Over a much-needed dinner, I began to entertain visions of Olympic grandeur. Renn acknowledged that he was impressed, adding, "If you want to join me for the evening workout, please feel free." He wasn't joking. After dinner, he would return for round two of the same!

I declined, explaining that I'd be in the library studying until late. Or so I thought, until every muscle in my body started to break down and I had to limp back to my dorm room. In a violent attack of lactic acid, I fell to my bed in excruciating pain—as intense as if someone were battering my chest muscles with bare fists. By evening, I had a spiking fever and was delirious. Putting body weight on my limbs was so painful that I had to put pillows under each arm and leg, balancing in a way that only my bones were holding me together. How I made my way to the bathroom, I don't remember. But I do recall peeing blood.

The next morning when I wasn't at breakfast, Wells and Reuben knew something was wrong and came up to my room. When they knocked, I could only call weakly from the bed, "Yes?" I was lucky that my two friends were medical students. In no time, they had security personnel open the door so they could rush in with Gatorade and an IV bag.

This experience was a significant lesson to check out the competition before going into battle. Renn never once said, "I told you so," and eventually I was able to laugh along with everyone else. And we're still laughing!

As the Three Amigos, Wells, Reuben, and I brought different skill sets and strengths to our studies. When tests were coming up or papers were due, we pulled all-nighters together or shared resources as much as possible. But there was one occasion when they could do little to help me. I vividly remember the expression of concern on their faces when I admitted that I had put off studying for a major chemistry exam until the last night. Again, arrogance had clouded my judgment, and I had overestimated my own abilities. The Renn Crichlow lesson had yet to be fully learned.

My predicament had begun when I found out that the roof on my parents' house was in urgent need of repair. I felt compelled to go home and help. The way I saw it was that, sure, holding my own at medical school was tough. But I had a roof over my head. Since my parents couldn't afford to hire anyone to do the repair work and my brother was overwhelmed trying to fix it on his own, I made the decision to take a week off from medical school so that I could rush back to California and lend a hand. With the two of us, I figured a week would be plenty of time to complete the repair and stave off any further damage from the brutal rains to come. My plan was to return to Boston a week before the final and study at my usual warp speed. I saw no other option. Besides, what was a week in the scheme of things?

Unfortunately, the roof required twice as much time to fix as I had estimated, and when I returned to med school, to my dismay, only one day remained to absorb all the material that would be covered in our test. In this era, there were no electronic notes or opportunities to review classes on tape or other technological means of revisiting the lectures. My resources were the syllabus and the ability to put my head down and go to work.

Thinking that I'd made some good progress, I checked in with Wells and Reuben, who offered to review with me. But after discussing the sections I did know, it became clear to both of them that I was going to be up all night cramming on my own.

Wells warned, "You better go get the jam."

"Why?"

"Because you are toast!"

Much to his surprise—and mine—by the next morning, I'd distilled all that data into basic linked equations, diagramming them with Sostenes Quiñones flashy colors on a huge chart.

Wells was mystified as he looked at my color-coded diagram connecting the chemical reactions, making them simple to understand and remember. "Do you realize that you just learned what the rest of us have been wading through for days in a tenth of the time?" he asked.

In this instance, unconventional thinking had saved me from my own arrogance. Lucky again! Even luckier was the fact that Wells and Reuben, my staunchest supporters, valued my unusual approach to problem solving and time saving. But not everyone was as charmed by my ingenuity as they were.

A barbed comment from a fellow med student toward the end of the first year of medical school showed me that I hadn't yet shaken the shame sparked by the Berkeley TA's remark years earlier. Perhaps seeing me as a threat, he disdainfully suggested that all that time in the library was only a show—to convince others I was somebody that I wasn't.

As everyone in our study group that evening glared at him, I asked what he was talking about.

"Come on, Alfredo," he said with a smile, "you know that the only reason you got into Harvard is because of quotas."

I wasn't as disturbed by the comment as by its ability to get to me. Acting disinterested, I shrugged it off. But deep down the worm still turned.

.   .   .

"Who are you?"

I looked around to see who was speaking to me as I walked down the hospital corridor on this late Friday night during my second year of medical school and was surprised to see Dr. Peter Black, the Harvard professor and chief of neurosurgery at Brigham and Women's Hospital. I knew who he was and how well respected he was as a brain surgeon—an area that even at this stage I couldn't imagine was a destination for me. Being a general surgeon was daunting, but brain surgery was a realm reserved for the toughest, most driven matadors. It also appeared to be for those who came from wealth or were born into the world of neurosurgery.

Though Dr. Black and I had crossed paths before, we had never spoken and he didn't typically stop to chat with people on his way into the operating room. After I had introduced myself and prepared to continue on my merry way, he asked, "Where are you going?"

"An exciting Friday night at the library!" I'd actually been trying to spend more time at home on the weekends now that Anna had joined me in Boston, where we were living in a tiny apartment in the Fenway Park neighborhood, but she and I planned to watch some old movies on the VCR the following night, so this evening I planned to put in extra hours at the hospital and hit the books harder.

Maybe I was simply at the right place at the right time. Or perhaps the insightful Dr. Black read me very well and saw a young man open to possibilities and eager to know what lay beyond the door to the neurosurgery operating room. He probably also saw a young man who, though self-assured in some areas, still tugged around a feeling of insecurity about his legitimacy, aware of his outsider status.

But Dr. Black didn't remark on any such observations. He merely nodded, smiled, and gestured toward the OR. "Would you like to come in and have a look at a case?" As if I needed any enticement, Dr. Black added quickly that it would be an awake craniotomy.

Having only heard and read about the extraordinary advances of this kind of brain surgery—meaning that the patient was going to be awake during the procedure—I was dying to see it with my own eyes. I knew that whenever tumors threatened critical speech areas in the brain, performing an awake craniotomy allowed the surgeon to avoid intruding on those places. With the patient awake, the exposed brain would be stimulated with a device applying an electrical current. The patient's speech responses to the surgeon's questions would then show up on a map of the patient's brain. When a patient failed to recognize a picture or a word during this process, the surgeon could see this was an important area that shouldn't be touched.

There was only one answer to Dr. Black's invitation—"Yes!" I supposed he meant at some point in the future.

But, no, he invited me to change into scrubs and observe the procedure right then! Not expecting this incredible offer, I stood frozen, feeling momentarily lost. Then, like a racehorse heading for the starting line, I leapt at the opportunity. Literally! Within minutes, I was crossing over the threshold—from a past where becoming a brain surgeon seemed nearly impossible to a new realm in which it would become my passion. While I had shadowed surgeons in other disciplines and had watched their process with similar admiration, nothing compared to the awe I felt as I entered the operating room, more brightly lit than any surgical setting I'd seen before.

Awash in light, almost ethereal—with the patient lying *awake, fully conscious,* secured to the table and surrounded by a highly organized team of experts dressed in pale blue sterile gowns—the OR resembled an artist's rendering of heaven. This was Shangri-la, Xanadu, another universe.

Standing in the back of the room, I watched Dr. Black take over from the chief resident, who was attired in a strange uniform that made him look like a cross between an astronaut and a welder—complete with special goggles that had the refracting powers of a microscope and a spotlight shining brightly from his forehead into the patient's skull, which he had just opened. Dr. Black then suited up with goggles and a headlamp, which a surgical nurse plugged into a power source. Every action, every motion in the room was choreographed like a grand ballet. The focus was supreme—to the point that members of the team could communicate with each other without words.

Stepping closer so that I could watch Dr. Black's moves, my attention was drawn away from him by a sight I will never forget seeing for the first time: the human brain. All three pounds of this astonishing organ shimmered in the light, its color varying from red to white, from gray to clear. Soft, tender, majestic, the brain pulsed miraculously—dancing to the beat of the patient's heart. In that instant, I was struck by the thought that every experience, every journey, every story, every person the patient had ever known, every memory of his life had been captured in his brain. Suddenly, I realized how much I'd been taking for granted about this most beautiful organ of our body.

I flashed on how tentative I'd been in going beneath the skin of the cadaver at the Día de los Muertos conference—how ominous it had seemed to cross that border. Now, in this celebration in the operating room, I wanted nothing more than to know what part of this brilliant dancing brain controlled the patient's memory. Where were the centers for speech? Where was movement controlled? Where were the command centers for the heart and the lungs? And then as Dr. Black began to ask his patient questions while touching his instrument to the brain, I held my breath in wonder.

Despite the otherworldly nature of this first experience of watching brain surgery, I realized with surprise that I felt comfortable in that setting, as if I belonged there, as if this was something that I could do and wanted to do—indeed, had to do. Had I just stumbled into this arena by accident, or was the hand of destiny at work?

Later on I would look back and wonder what direction my career would have taken if not for this fateful encounter or the bit of good luck that opened the door to the operating room for me that Friday night. For that matter, I am always fascinated by the interesting turns life offers each of us. Yet I also recognize that these peak moments that seem to arise from nowhere do not come to us unless we look for them. Certainly, I had been looking for something, and I found it that night. Deep down, not in my brain but in my soul, I knew that neurosurgery was the path that I'd been seeking all my life.

Then came the inevitable friction between dreams and conventional wisdom. The naysayers became very vocal. Some told me, "You really don't know what it takes to be a brain surgeon," implying that my third-world background had not equipped me to take on this task. Because of my ethnic background, many higher-ups insisted, "You should really become a primary care physician." They would remind me of the shortage of health care providers in the poor barrios in the United States—a need they felt I naturally would want to address. While I saw the need too and desired to be of service to all communities, I also detected some bias in these comments. So my challenge was to weed through the input, separating valid advice from stereotyped judgments that I didn't accept. Most of all, I wanted to make sure that I had the commitment to go the distance, because the path was not one to be chosen lightly. Just as important, I had to be sure that Anna was on board. If I followed this route, not only did I have to commit myself to it, but once Anna and I were married and had children, I would be committing the whole family. With the difficult balancing act that would follow, I had to know that Anna was as much a part of the passion for this work as she would be part of the sacrifices.

During our many conversations, Anna showed only interest and excitement and did not once question whether I was reaching too far or suggest that I had made this choice to deliberately keep us in the poorhouse forever. Indeed, from the minute we pulled out of Manteca at the end of the summer before my second year of medical school—settling into our cross-country drive in "Pepe the red pickup" (as we named our ride), without air-conditioning and with just enough money for gas and a few meals—it was clear that we were on this adventure together.

After living with her mother and sisters in Manteca while I was at Berkeley and at Harvard, Anna needed to summon considerable courage to come with me to the East Coast. Not only did she have the culture shock of living in the big city of Boston, she had to make her way independently much of the time, since I was gone many long hours. But as was her nature, Anna embraced the experience. In no time, she found a job teaching science at a private Catholic high school about an hour outside of Boston and learned to navigate the treacherous winter driving there and back every day. Meanwhile, by some decorating magic, on no money, she turned our humble apartment into a cozy little home.

Well, not to fool anyone, there was nothing glamorous about being broke or trying to move around with the bathtub and the bed vying for floor space in the kitchen. I joked that we were reenacting scenes from *Rocky*, when he and his girlfriend, Adrian, are stuck in his shoebox-size house. Still, we learned how compatible we were when we were able to deal with these challenges harmoniously. Our only slight disagreement was about pets. When I argued that we had no room for a cat or a dog, Anna agreed. But a hamster, she countered, wouldn't take up too much space. A fair compromise. Before long, the hamster was lonely and needed to have a couple of other rodent companions. That was the beginning of the end of my having a say on the rising pet population. But if Anna's menagerie made her happy, I was fine with it. Actually, I loved watching her care for our animal roommates and observing how her earlier desire to become a veterinarian was still a part of her identity.

We both grappled with the fact that my pursuit of a career as a neurosurgeon would require her to sacrifice her dream. If our financial situation had been different, she might have been able to study veterinary medicine at the same time that I was in med school and residency. Then again, Anna was a remarkable teacher and had found great rewards in working with young people. More important, when the gift of raising children became a reality for us, she would make the decision to stay at home with them rather than try to work or tackle the demands of veterinary college. As extraordinary as this sacrifice was, I don't think she would have had it any other way.

In the meantime, Anna enjoyed being the honorary den mother to our growing rainbow of friends and colleagues, who frequently came over for potluck meals or joined us for movie watching on our used but dependable TV. We were like a circus act as we tried to squeeze as many people as possible into a living room that could barely hold a sofa.

Anna was so strong, independent, and easygoing that I rarely saw her upset. One time I did see her express unhappiness was the day I visited one of her science classes at the high school. Anna was excited for me to see her in her element and to have me speak to her class about medical school and deliver the message that anyone can aspire to become a scientist or a physician. When I arrived at the school, she sent me to the cafeteria to have a cup of coffee before my talk. But I was not to get my coffee because the man in charge, apparently offended by my accent, eyed me suspiciously, asked me what I wanted, and then told me to get the hell out of the teachers' lounge. Anna confronted him later, calmly but firmly explaining who I was and telling him that his rudeness was not warranted. She received a weak apology and fumed to me about the episode later.

Because Anna was upset enough for both of us, I let the incident go. But confusion lingered. What was it about my ethnicity that made me a threat? Why was someone, anyone, who was a person of color less deserving of a cup of coffee than someone else? Besides, I could have really used some coffee that morning after a sleep-deprived night at the hospital.

Another time Anna called me at the laboratory crying so hard she couldn't get her words out. Shocked, I told her, "Whatever it is, I'll be right there!" The med school was less than a mile away from our apartment, so I sprinted home, where I found her out in front of the building pointing up to our apartment. When I ran upstairs, I found the door knocked down and nothing left inside but some dazed and confused rodents. Whoever had broken in had taken everything we had.

When word of the burglary spread, friends pitched in to help us get by. Ed Kravitz and David Potter each wrote checks for five hundred dollars so that we would have enough for the required deposits and a full month's rent at a new place.

"Dr. Potter," I protested. "I can't accept this money. I don't know when I'll ever be able to pay you back."

"Nonsense," he insisted. "It's not a loan. You'll do for others what others have done for you. I have no doubt."

He articulated an important principle I've tried to follow all my life. Of course, David was talking not only about providing financial help but also about being there for others in good and bad times and giving what you can, when you can. This was a philosophy Uncle Jose had consistently demonstrated, going back to the days when we had nothing to eat and he made sure that we had food on the table. When Uncle Jose heard about the burglary, he and my wonderful aunt Amelia surprised us by sending a check for one hundred dollars. Their generosity was humbling yet infinitely appreciated.

Thanks to everyone's help, we moved into an apartment in the lovely, safe area of Brookline Village, about a ten-minute walk from the medical school. Our new home was in a large house that had been turned into six charming and spacious units. Our extended family grew even more once we befriended the other tenants, including a Cuban and African-American couple. Our gatherings looked like the United Nations, complete with international feasts we made together and a fantastic stew of music from different cultures.

Life was grand! Once we settled into our new place, Anna and I decided that instead of planning a costly wedding that our families couldn't afford to attend, we might as well be daring and elope. However, when I told Ed Kravitz about our planned elopement, he offered to throw us a party in his home in Cambridge instead. Though I objected that his offer was far too generous, Ed waved away my worry, assuring me it would be a simple event. All that mattered to him was for Anna to have the celebration she wanted. Ed and his wife, Kathryn, had adored Anna from the moment they met her and had already made us part of the family, inviting us to their home for holidays and showing the utmost concern about our well-being.

So that was how, quite on the spur of the moment, we decided to tie the knot and ended up having a dream wedding that cost us all of one hundred dollars—for the license and fees to be married by a justice of the peace. On the afternoon of February 18, 1996, after we returned from our quick jaunt across state lines to Maine (where the fees were lower than in Massachusetts) to make our union official, we arrived at the Kravitzes for an intimate yet unforgettable party held in our honor. Wells Messersmith played the violin brilliantly; Ethan Basch, a writer, displayed his mastery at the piano; and Ed's daughter-in-law, Majie Zeller, an opera singer, sang "Ave Maria," bringing down the house.

With classical music in the background, a sumptuous buffet, the clinking of champagne glasses, and heartfelt toasts to our future, Anna and I agreed that ours was the nicest wedding we had ever attended—full of love and connection. Since the Kravitzes were Jewish and our friends came from diverse backgrounds, we decided to include a mix of customs, which made the day even more special. One of the highlights was when I stomped on the wine glass—a Jewish custom that Ed had told us about, a reminder of the hardships that may come in life but that the bonds of marriage can overcome.

We missed having members of our family from California there but felt their love and presence. In the middle of the festivities, in fact, I had a moment when I strongly felt the presence of Tata Juan, Nana Maria, and my grandfather Jesus. While listening to the rousing toasts to our future children—should we be so blessed as to have them—I flashed on the fiftieth wedding anniversary party held for Tata and Nana nineteen years earlier, when I was nine years old. I pictured them, husband and wife, toward the end of their lives, celebrating with all their grown children and their spouses and their dozens of grandchildren of every age. Now Anna and I stood here celebrating the official beginning of our lives together.

The celebration surpassed anything we could have imagined, as close to perfect as possible. We did regret not having the time or the means to take a real honeymoon. And at this writing, over a decade and a half later, Anna continues to remind me that she is still waiting for one!

.   .   .

In hindsight, I have to laugh when comparing the pressure that accompanied the bustling pace of medical school to that of the blistering, nonstop action of residency. I got glimpses of what lay ahead, particularly in my third year of medical school, when my eyes were opened to how much responsibility is heaped on residents—especially in busy university hospital settings where the attending physicians are the generals to many foot soldiers and need their seconds in command to lead the fight in the trenches. The person who gave me the closest view of this stage of a doctor's training was Esteban González Burchard, who had come to Harvard for his residency in internal medicine.

Dr. Burchard was excited that I was leaning toward neurosurgery. He knew that I was encountering skepticism from some, including people who thought I was pushing too hard and becoming involved in too many areas. His message to me was to continue to distinguish myself, trust my instincts, and ignore the doubters.

But Esteban also warned me that neurosurgical residencies were among the most brutal in medicine. Although neuroscience had come into its own in recent years, it historically had been a subspecialty within other departments. Thus, while most top university hospitals might have several residents in each of their better-funded departments, many could support only one spot each year for an incoming resident in brain surgery. While I understood these concerns in theory, since I wasn't yet in the trenches, in the crosshairs of constant incoming crises, I anticipated that such challenges were up my alley.

In fact, all I could say to Esteban was something along the lines of "Count me in. Let's rock 'n' roll!"

Esteban laughed but still encouraged me to weigh my decision carefully.

But the bug had bitten me. My decision was confirmed one dramatic night in the emergency room when I was on call at Mass General Hospital and was able to watch a neurosurgical resident in action.

A young patient of college age was brought in comatose following a terrible car accident in which the vehicle had been totaled. The atmosphere in most big-city emergency rooms is invariably intense, with heightened pressure on personnel to withstand an unrelenting pace. And whenever a patient is brought in barely clinging to life, this pressure can turn into chaos. The resident I observed that night allowed none of the chaos to affect his judgment and didn't panic at the patient's slim odds. Instead, he sprang into action, moving with athletic agility and making the necessary decisions on the fly.

Within minutes, he secured a monitor that gauged the pressure in the brain. As the nurses worked with him, he called the attending doctor, our professor, for guidance and for the go-ahead to move the patient into the OR immediately to save his life. Under the resident's leadership, all of us on the team moved at optimal speed, arriving in the operating room in a seamless series of steps that we all understood—no need for discussion, hesitation, or frantic uncertainty.

Without any training in this area, I could have felt as lost as if someone had pulled me out of the tomato fields and pushed me into the OR. But because of the resident's clear, precise direction, I could rely on my reflexes and the general medical knowledge I had absorbed to contribute to the team's effort. Although there was no indication to suggest that this patient could be saved, that in no way deterred any of us from working at full throttle, summoning the best of our abilities. As I supported the resident's work to evacuate the hematoma—the bleeding inside the patient's skull—I was infused by his calm, focus, energy, and determination.

This seemingly impossible case of a young college student, brought in comatose, was my first encounter with the part of neurosurgery that is akin to going into combat, requiring the physician to perform like a sword fighter, in the mold of a true samurai. That's what the resident epitomized in the OR, demonstrating that every move counts toward life or death—every stroke, every word, every flicker of your eyelash. I watched him harness his own energy and everyone else's, moving expeditiously from start to finish. By the time the attending surgeon joined us, the patient was out of danger.

The next morning, our patient woke up with little more than a headache, and three days later, he went home to resume his life.

How could I measure this awe-inspiring experience of seeing someone who was still in training take charge, instill calm and order, and then save a life? There was no party, no backslapping, no attempt to claim the mantle of glory. We were all just doing our jobs. We had a purpose; we responded.

On other occasions, I learned that not everyone can handle the pressure as that particular resident managed to do. And I saw that not every emergency, no matter how much you do for your patient, has the kind of victorious outcome we witnessed in the ER that night. Yet this experience revealed the innate power that is in every patient, no matter the diagnosis or prognosis—the will to survive, to fight for one's life. Indeed, at a time when I was becoming conscious of my own journey, I began to recognize that one of my jobs as a physician was to get to know the unique journey that every patient travels. And in each patient's distinct story could be found this miraculous capacity to rise above the odds and become a hero in the life-and-death battles he or she faced.

The case that most influenced these understandings—and that helped seal my decision about the kind of medicine I wanted to practice and the kind of physician I wanted to be—wasn't part of my formal education but was an experience I shared with a friend, Neil Ghiso, a fellow Harvard Medical School student. Handsome, brilliant, and a star in everything he did, Neil had been a bartender before deciding to pursue medicine and was a wonderful listener as well as a connoisseur of stories. He was certain to be a great physician in whatever discipline he selected. But during our holiday break in late 1997, Neil called me from his home in Michigan with noticeable fear and concern in his voice as he explained that he needed to ask me for a favor.

"Of course," I said.

Neil told me that during his flight back to Michigan, he had blacked out and knew enough when he gained consciousness to conclude that he had experienced a seizure. He didn't need to be told that a brain tumor could have been the cause, and an MRI in Michigan had indeed shown a tumor.

"How can I help?" was my immediate response.

Neil wanted to return to Harvard so that he could keep up with his studies, regardless of the course his disease was going to take. He asked if I would set up appointments with a few neurosurgeons in the area. The only explanation for why he chose me for this favor—which I considered an honor—was his comment, "Alfredo, you always have the inside scoop." Though I didn't necessarily have the connections, I was able to arrange appointments for him right away. Waiting for his return to Boston, I spent a long time trying to understand how this diagnosis could be possible. There had been no clues, no symptoms, no premonitions. Or had there been? Most of all, I asked myself, Why Neil? No answers followed as to *why* Neil, or *why* anyone. Indeed, the question of why would cause me great anguish on behalf of my patients through the years to come. The most apt description of what it's like to be dealt the blow of a devastating diagnosis was put to me later by my patient Don Rottman. Don equated it to driving alone on a highway in the middle of a desert with the air-conditioning on—everything quiet, cool, and serene—and seeing another car come out of nowhere. "You are T-boned" as it slams into you. And your whole world collapses.

When I accompanied Neil to the appointments, which were at two top medical centers, both the specialists he saw came up with the same diagnosis, yet they delivered the message in entirely different ways. One of the doctors presented a grim scenario, citing statistics that suggested that little could be done to alter Neil's prognosis. The other doctor covered the same ground but did so with hope, discussing various ways to address the tumor and describing options that would enable Neil to take an active part in his treatment.

Neil chose the doctor who offered hope and then defied the odds by living longer than the doctor with the statistics had predicted. The experience was a crash course in why a physician must offer patients hope and positive communication. I watched Neil go through most of the stages of what seemed to be the most devastating disease possible because it afflicts what I believe is the most beautiful organ of our body—the organ that controls the functions that allow us to thrive and enjoy life, to love each other, to reason, to retain the memories that make our lives meaningful, and to be different from one another. He met every new development with courage, rarely succumbing to hopelessness—even when he had to take time off from medical school to deal with the effects of chemotherapy and radiation.

Neil returned to complete medical school the year after I graduated and was chosen by his peers to speak at graduation. Though I couldn't attend—held back in California by my own health and other concerns—I later read a portion of his remarks that I know inspired everyone. Neil talked about the importance of the mentorship of our teachers: "We are all really just the next chapter in a long, long story." He said that we needed to honor this gift by in turn becoming mentors and by teaching the next generation of medical professionals to give patient care "the same degree of respect that we give the MRI, or surgery, or medical science in general."

A little less than two years later, in February 2002, almost five years after he had been diagnosed, Neil Ghiso died at the age of thirty-one. His family established a foundation in his name to promote the education of medical students in compassionate care—the legacy Neil left to all of us.

In my memory, Neil lives on, larger than life, part of what I do and an inspiration to continue trying to be better at what I do. Very often, I bring to mind the images of the two doctors he consulted—one full of numbers and discouraging statistics, the other full of hope and seeking to engage Neil's love of life and desire to fight the disease.

Not by accident, when I later had to select my area of specialization as a neurosurgeon/scientist, I chose to focus on the removal and treatment of brain tumors—and to take the battle into the laboratory, where it ultimately must be fought if we are to achieve a cure. The larger the team grows, the more intensely I feel Neil Ghiso's presence with us in the trenches, cheering us on.

.   .   .

"You should change your name," said one of my more outspoken classmates in the middle of a study group one evening. "Alfredo Quiñones is a terrible name for a doctor," he continued, pronouncing it badly. His point? "Nobody can pronounce it!"

"Really?" I asked, feeling my usual insecurity. But in a sign of my growing confidence, I did challenge him. "So what did you have in mind?"

"Anthony Quinn was Mexican, and he changed his name from Antonio Quiñones." Pause. "You should change your name to Alfred Quinn."

Dr. Alfred Quinn? Fortunately, no one concurred, and we turned back to our studying. But the remark made me conclude that instead of hiding my background—by Americanizing my name or giving in to self-consciousness—I should go in the opposite direction and show pride in my heritage by making my name Alfredo Quiñones-Hinojosa. Even harder to pronounce! The longer, hyphenated name, soon made official, was not only a way to honor my mother and her family, as is the custom in Mexico, but led to my most popular nickname—Dr. Q.

Not that my insecurities were gone yet, but the ability to celebrate where I came from fed my growing sense of legitimacy—both in my field of endeavor and my hope to make a contribution to society. That was why—in late 1997 when I was doing my Howard Hughes fellowship during my fourth year of medical school—I decided that if I was going to raise children in the greatest country in the world, I needed to make my commitment official.

When I went downtown to the Office of Immigration at the Federal Building, I brought a hefty medical textbook with me, figuring that I was in for a long day of waiting, filling out paperwork, and cutting through other red tape. Having heard about my parents' prolonged ordeal to become full citizens, I assumed the application process would be similar for me and that I might be returning for more days of waiting after this one.

Because of the California immigration laws that existed when my family and I first came to the United States as undocumented workers, we soon qualified for green cards and achieved legal status that made us eligible for full citizenship. Requirements included proof of residency in the United States for a minimum of five years and proof that the applicant was a person of moral character, embraced the principles embodied in the U.S. Constitution, and possessed basic English skills, as well as knowledge of the history and government of the United States.

Of course, my parents met all of those requirements. And yet, over the past five years, they'd experienced one bureaucratic hurdle after another—lost paperwork on the part of the government, a change in personnel causing them to start over again, and generally dismissive treatment. I had no reason to expect my experience was going to be any different.

After receiving a number—112—I took a seat in a massive room with hundreds of other applicants. With me were sealed letters of recommendation written by two professors, in the event that I had trouble or came up short on any of the paperwork. Moments after an official at the front of the room began barking numbers and names, another court officer entered through a side door and spoke in a sotto voce whisper, calling, "Alfredo Quiñones-Hinojosa?"

Had I done something wrong? Before I had time to respond, she called my name again. I stood up, gathered my things, and headed toward her.

"How do you do?" the cheerful official asked brightly, shaking my hand. "Come with me."

Fearful that something terrible was going to happen, I followed her through the side door, at which point she informed me that I was going to meet one of the top immigration officials in Boston.

One of the *top* officials? *Ay, Dios mío,* I almost said aloud, certain the boom was about to be lowered.

My legal status was not in question, I knew. Any repercussions or fines stemming from illegal entry into the country had been dealt with when I obtained my green card and documentation in California. Still, my encounters with immigration services had never been pleasant.

The corridor we walked down seemed to go on forever. Finally, my guide led me into an office, where I met a woman who spoke with a fine, crisp pronunciation as she reviewed my application and the two letters of recommendation.

When the top immigration official finished her review, she looked up, stared hard into my eyes, and said, "I have only one question."

"Yes?"

"How did you do it? How did you go from being an illegal migrant farm worker, ten years ago, to being a Harvard medical student with glowing recommendations from world-renowned scientists and professors?"

Ten years? I hadn't thought of that before. But I'd arrived in 1987, ten years earlier. I didn't know what to say. Not sure whether it was a test question, part of the interview, I hesitated a moment and then answered, "Well, I had good luck, I suppose."

"Good luck?"

"I was in the right place at the right time on a few occasions. I've been very fortunate and very privileged to join the American dream."

As she scrutinized me, digesting my answer, I wasn't sure whether I had given a right or wrong response. Then she glanced at the paperwork and added, "I also notice that you have not taken the American history test." Apparently, I'd been fast-tracked to the interview without the required test. Before I could offer to take it, she continued, "But of course you studied American history in your undergraduate work, and now that you are a medical student at Harvard, I'm sure you are well versed in everything on the test."

With that, she stamped my paperwork, handed it to me, and said, "Congratulations. You've qualified to become a U.S. citizen."

Wow.

Leaving with relief and gratitude, my documents in hand, I had mixed feelings about the fact that I'd completed in one sitting a process my parents had spent five years struggling to get through and had only recently completed. I was stunned by the difference in treatment. Justice, as embodied in the Constitution, was supposed to be blind. The thought that there might be one set of criteria for more desirable candidates—the more educated, skilled, and specialized—and another for applicants who were poor, unskilled, and uneducated was unsettling.

At the same time, I was overjoyed and grateful to be welcomed to my adopted homeland! And I wouldn't have been able to make this leap if not for my parents—who deserved so much credit for whatever measure of success I could claim.

At the citizenship ceremony, held in the 250-year-old Faneuil Hall, where many of America's founding fathers had first gathered to discuss independence, my dominant emotions were pride and appreciation. Anna came with me to celebrate, and as we took our seats among the five hundred or so others in the grand hall, the two of us beamed at each other and gazed around, imagining all the American history that had taken place here. The officiating judge had invited a friend of his to deliver the keynote speech to welcome all of us new citizens to the United States. This gentleman told a rousing story of his great-grandfather's arrival in the United States in the late 1800s, with a dream to make a better life for himself and his family. Thanks to generations of struggle and sacrifice, our speaker's family had endowed him with the opportunity to attend an elite prep school and to complete his undergraduate degree and an MBA at Harvard. Now a successful businessman, he ended his speech by telling us how Harvard had inspired him and by assuring us that the road to the American dream was through education.

As I listened to every word of the forty-five-minute speech, I marveled that what had taken his family multiple generations to accomplish, I had been given the chance to attain with Kaliman-like speed! Finally I understood why the question about my ten-year trajectory had come up in my immigration interview. Memories of those years sped before my eyes—memories of arriving with no money, no knowledge of English, nothing; of working the fields and eating tomatoes, raw corn, and broccoli; of living in my leaky little trailer that I called a palace; of shoveling sulfur, scraping fish lard from tankers, and welding railway cars, nearly dying in the process. Every part of my education explained how someone like me could go from harvest to Harvard, meet and marry the woman of my dreams, and be contemplating the next steps of training in a medical career.

And on that day, with Anna taking photographs of her husband—me—standing solemnly to pledge allegiance to the United States of America, I realized not just what this wonderful country had allowed me to do, taking me in with its arms wide open, but also how much more I hoped to achieve and give back.

EIGHT In the Land of Giants

Toward the end of my fourth year of medical school, after wrapping up my research fellowship year, I met a patient whose story changed mine.

A fifty-two-year-old man who had been at the peak of his career, with a loving, devoted family, this patient came to Harvard afflicted by a disease that had eluded diagnosis by many brilliant physicians. After being in excellent general health, he had suffered the sudden onset of back pain and weakness in his right leg that was causing him difficulty walking. As the senior medical student on the team—a step down from the resident, overseen by the attending physician—I followed his case closely, not only during the examinations and surgery but also in the lab where biopsies were eventually performed, interacting with him and his family at every stage of his case.

Initially, we were as mystified by his symptoms as others had been. The patient's legs were swollen and covered by little brown spots, and his reflexes were poor—a mix of information that yielded no obvious diagnosis. After a battery of tests, a lesion of the sciatic nerve behind his leg was discovered that extended to below his knee and that proved, after surgery, to be a very dangerous and malignant lymphoma. Further tests revealed no other lesions, so we proceeded with a treatment plan that would entail four months of chemotherapy followed by a course of radiation. After finishing up chemo, before radiation began, he suddenly returned to us with his symptoms resuming in full force, now further aggravated by increasingly intense pain. We watched his journey take a drastic turn for the worse as his truly heroic battle began with his mystery disease, subsequently diagnosed as neurolymphomatosis—a horrific cancer of the peripheral nerve. Very few previously reported cases could be found, and his affliction, frighteningly, wasn't following those patterns either. In medicine, we call an anomalous, rare disease like his a zebra.

After he had responded well to more chemotherapy, the last downward spiral came at the next visit when we saw he was unable to move the right side of his face—an indication that the cancer was most likely invading his whole body. Yet every test turned out to be negative for any kind of systemic progression and further invasion of cancer. According to everything we knew, there was no direct connection between his symptoms and a cause. But there had to be. The plan was to continue with more chemo rather than radiation as we tried to unravel this frightening, unpredictable disease. But our patient was given little time for answers before another onslaught of symptoms occurred, the likes of which I had never witnessed.

The pain in his neck, still not traceable to a cause, became so horrific that he lay awake for days and nights. He was in tears, desperate for relief from the pain, which spread throughout his body and which not even morphine could assuage. The initial tumor had invaded most of the nerves of his body, forcing him onto a road of intense physical, mental, and spiritual pain—with a destination that offered little hope.

I can clearly remember sitting with the patient, holding his hand and watching the fight going on inside of him. One of the many lessons I learned from following his case, checking in with him several times a day at the hospital, was that physicians must be mindful that family members suffer their own agony when they see a loved one suddenly ravaged by a monstrous disease.

When the patient's pain worsened and his organs began to shut down, clearly signaling the approach of death, I learned that there is no right or wrong thing to say or do when visiting a family and a patient in a critical state. In the awkward moments I spent with the family members, who had endured sixteen months watching their loved one battle his disease, I learned to offer comfort by doing what was in my heart. Sometimes I struggled to say something meaningful and deep only to learn that silence can be as powerful as words. The connection is what matters— whether in the form of a hug or a pause to hold a patient or a family member and allow the tears to flow. Or comfort might be shared in a light moment of humor and energy or in the offer of a positive message for the day.

The time I spent with this patient's family laid the foundation that I continue to build on today and that I draw on in encouraging my residents and students to offer compassionate care in their work. It also helped me appreciate the opportunity that the clinician or scientist has to be an advocate, a champion. To do so, I believed that if we could study what happened to this patient to cause his illness, our discoveries could alleviate the suffering of others in the future.

By this point in medical school, I had published three papers based on my laboratory research, but telling this patient's story would be my first clinical paper ("Solitary Sciatic Lymphoma as an Initial Manifestation of Diffuse Neurolymphomatosis"). As the lead author with four members of our team writing with me, I had to make sense, clinically speaking, of what had happened. And I had a more personal reason: I needed a way to deal with the pain of losing someone—something I suspect I'll never fully learn to do.

At the outset, I didn't understand that the paper was my way of immortalizing this patient—giving his life lasting meaning and letting his family know that he didn't die in vain. It was so important to get it right that I wrote no fewer than thirty-eight drafts of that paper.

The case was a rite of passage—a test to determine whether I grasped the reality of my chosen path and to see if perhaps I wanted to reconsider. But writing about the patient also inspired me to have the courage to move past my own misgivings. Practicing medicine isn't about the sure bet, I told myself. It's about taking on a disease like brain cancer, a terrifying dragon, fighting it with every tool at your disposal—as a surgeon, a scientist, a patient advocate—and not succumbing to fear even when your tools seem inadequate for the job, especially in the risky business of unraveling mystery diseases.

·   ·   ·

Then again, I wasn't in the fight alone—given my expanding team of fellow students who continued to "be on the payroll," as we joked when the group showed up for movie-watching nights and potluck feasts. Anna observed that building the entourage was a throwback to my childhood days of enlisting my siblings and cousins to participate in my projects. She also pointed out that some of my younger colleagues, like Frank Acosta, were in fact like siblings.

Mexican-American, Frank had grown up in East Los Angeles in a neighborhood where too many of his peers dropped out of high school and were drawn into gangs and drugs. Frank made up his mind early on to go a different way, and his parents worked hard to send him to a private Catholic high school, where he excelled academically. From there, he continued on to Harvard for his undergraduate degree and medical school. Three years behind me in the program, Frank was brilliant and always willing to join me on an adventure whenever I began stirring the pot with interesting possibilities.

So when I procured research hours at Mass General—even though it meant a thirty-minute bus ride at five in the morning—Frank was game. Not much came out of that project, but we made great use of the commute, getting to know each other, studying, and grabbing a few minutes of sleep. Knowing how to sleep and eat on an "as-needed" basis is an essential survival skill for a physician. The other lesson we learned, as Frank later remarked, was that even research endeavors that don't produce specific findings or groundbreaking discoveries can pay off in unexpected ways. Sometimes you simply have to take the ride, just to do it—and the reason will come later.

Along those lines, I'd begun to realize that whenever I found myself struggling over a decision, if I hung in long enough, clarity would eventually prevail. Or so I told myself when, with only a year to go in med school, I suddenly started having nightmares like the ones I used to have as a child. This time, however, I wasn't a superhero who lost my powers just when I needed to save my loved ones from being devoured by mudslides or infernos. These dreams were much more real, casting me into debt and starvation and tapping into my fears of not making the grade. In one nightmare, I not only failed as a neurosurgeon but had to go back to Mexico in a state of shame and embarrassment; yet when I arrived home, I was not readmitted to the teaching system. In my waking hours, I'd occasionally catch myself wondering, What if the message of these dreams was true? What if I had been wrong to leave teaching or to pretend that I could, in effect, rise above my station? The voices saying "you can't" and "who do you think you are?" were my own. Some of the anxiety haunting my sleep was reflective of the life-and-death struggles I was observing every day. Some stemmed from my concern about my family members back in California and my inability to do much to help them. The Stockton neighborhood had continued to deteriorate, and the violence hit close to home when my brother Jorge's best friend was murdered. The youth had been killed within steps of his home, in front of his family, at close range. My family was living in this environment while I walked the hallways of the magnificent Harvard Medical School.

But the main reason I was worrying, even in sleep, was probably the news I received one night in the spring of 1998, after walking home from Mass General on a gorgeous May evening. Summer had come early to Boston, and it was very hot, even after sunset. In jeans and a green T-shirt, as I distinctly recall, I allowed myself to slow to an uncharacteristic stroll so that I could enjoy the sights of the city and watch the rowers out on the Charles River. The water was lit by the reflection of glowing lamplights and a yellow moon, its surface sparkling playfully as if to promise excitement in the making.

When I got home, Anna was also in a wonderful mood, but she attributed her joy not to the beautiful weather but to something else. In her hand was a home pregnancy test she had just taken. She handed it to me, and I looked closely. The blue plus sign was boldly delineated. Positive! *Holy guacamole!* We were going to have a baby.

We were ecstatic. But everything changed the instant I became an expectant father. As someone who had been taking serious risks for most of my life, I had avoided spending too much time worrying about future uncertainties. But now, with pending fatherhood, I had a new sense of responsibility. Happy and nervous at the same time, I felt the weighty duty to become a good provider—along with the fear of reliving the poverty and hunger my family had suffered. Then I began to worry that incurring more debt to become a brain surgeon was unfair and to wonder if I should choose a specialization that wouldn't require another ten years before I could earn a decent living.

By December 1998, with a few weeks to go before the baby's arrival, my nightmares stopped as abruptly as they had returned a year earlier. Looking back, I believe my psyche was preparing me for fatherhood and future challenges by letting me live out the horror-movie version of my fears in dream form. This process allowed me to make the conscious choice to stop worrying about everything that could go wrong and, in keeping with my true nature, to embrace the possibility of everything that could go *right*. Now I simply had to muster the courage and money to travel to the Bay Area to interview for the neurosurgical internship and residency position at the University of California, San Francisco. Having been turned down there for medical school, I was now back as a contender, hoping to seize the prize that many other top candidates from around the world wanted as much as I did. To return to the West Coast and train with the giants of the field would be a dream come true—and an incredible long shot. But if I didn't go for it, how could I live up to the credo that every man—and woman—is the architect of his or her own destiny?

When I arrived in San Francisco for my interview, I couldn't help but be intimidated. In the world of medicine, UCSF was sacred ground, housing the medical school and the sprawling historic complex of the San Francisco General Hospital in the rougher part of town and the more modern Moffitt Hospital in a more affluent neighborhood. The neuro-surgery department had been brought to renown by its first chair, Dr. Charlie B. Wilson, who was still there and whose influence as a brain surgeon was legendary. So too was Wilson's story—how he was raised in a tiny farming community in the Ozarks, the son of a full-blooded Cherokee mother and an Irish pharmacist father; how despite his slight build, he was accepted to Tulane on a football and academic scholarship, which he supplemented by working nights in the French Quarter, playing piano. But none of the lore about Dr. Wilson prepared me for meeting him in person. With his dark crew cut, high cheekbones, and blazing black eyes, he had the intensity of a Cherokee warrior, and his gaze seemed to bore holes into others when he spoke with them.

But Dr. Wilson's scrutiny didn't unnerve me. That moment arrived when I was introduced to Dr. Mitch Berger, the head of the department and the individual destined to be perhaps my most influential mentor. A visionary, Dr. Berger was regarded as an extremely tough taskmaster; his very name was known to stir fear in the hearts of many an unseasoned resident.

Standing next to the striking, robust, six-foot-three Mitch Berger, with his mane of sandy white hair and larger-than-life presence, I had no doubt that he was Superman! As Dr. Berger sat among his fellow attending physicians during my interview, seemingly just one of the group, his bearing let me know who was in charge. Afterwards, when he extended his hand to shake mine, its size and strength amazed me—equivalent to both my hands! Everything about him was huge: his work ethic, his focus, his talents, and his capacity for caring about patients, the quality I would learn to admire most about Dr. Berger.

Another future mentor I met on this trip, a Jedi master of neurosurgery, was Dr. Michael Lawton. A motivator and a role model, Dr. Lawton was well known for inspiring with patience and equanimity, never raising his voice in the operating room, as some did. Instead, Dr. Lawton would simply say, "Quiet, please," and all would be silent. In our interview, I was so eager to hear more about Dr. Lawton's approach to neurosurgical technique—which he had been taught in his stellar training and had further refined—I had to bite my thumb to keep calm. Dr. Lawton was among the first to identify this habit as a sign that I was onto something big. As time would tell, training with Dr. Lawton would shape how I do surgery today, particularly my use of the specialized instruments and equipment that allow me never to take my hands away from the patient—including a special astronaut's chair and a microscope controlled by the feet and the mouth. Moreover, Dr. Lawton was always accessible, always interested in encouraging me to develop the neurosurgeon's full portfolio—in the OR, in the laboratory, in the classroom, and at the patient's bedside.

Dr. Nick Barbaro, who was doing groundbreaking work in functional neurosurgery, was another champion at UCSF. He noticed my propensity for team building even during those couple of days of interviewing and began referring to my ubiquitous entourage as "Q, Inc." Dr. Barbaro, I learned later, had his own methodology for assessing candidates for the one or two positions that became available each year. Because there was no audition process for the would-be brain surgeon, he looked for clues to the applicant's level of dexterity. Dr. Barbaro had learned that he could tell a lot by how meticulously a candidate tied his or her shoes.

Aha! This test would normally have been a cinch for me. I learned to tie my shoes in infancy, after all. But no one had warned me about this part of the interview. In fact, because Anna and I had no money in the family budget for new shoes, I had to wear an old pair that were a size too small—the same pair I had worn for my medical school interviews five years earlier! After two grueling days of meeting professors and residents, my feet were killing me that day, and the only remedy was to untie the laces!

My dangling shoelaces could well have ended my journey at UCSF right then. What kind of an aspiring brain surgeon wouldn't even tie his shoes? Fortunately, instead of working against me, the untied shoes somehow convinced Dr. Barbaro that I was a jewel in the rough in need of refinement. Another important mentor, Dr. Michael McDermott, later reported that he thought my decision to untie my laces showed me to be very practical.

I left San Francisco with high hopes but no firm answer. My former ambivalence had been replaced by the desire to learn from the faculty I had just met, benefiting from their diverse journeys and areas of expertise. Though Anna and I had to wait for the verdict, we were in the highest spirits. And our joy was doubled when we welcomed our beautiful daughter, Gabriella, into the world. Three weeks later, the official word arrived that I had matched at UCSF! We breathed one celebratory sigh of relief and then started the daunting task of finding affordable housing in San Francisco.

I was ready to rock the world! But I cannot say that I'd finally banished the feelings of insecurity and shame that had messed me up since the TA's remark back in Berkeley. That moment came five months later, in June, when I delivered the commencement speech for the graduating class of Harvard Medical School. That triumph was also an exorcism. All the accumulated fear that someone would hear my accent and stigmatize and stereotype me vanished. I was an American citizen *and* from Mexico, and proud to say so!

And that was how, at age thirty-one, I lived up to the nickname of "Doc" that I'd been given in my teens. Selected by a vote of my class to give the commencement speech—the toughest ten minutes of my public-speaking experiences to date—I not only banished my insecurities but finally acknowledged in public that a brush with death had been pivotal in bringing me to this day.

In the speech, described by the graduating committee as a "Field of Dreams" address, I offered my story as an example of the hopes and striving we had shared as a class. I drew applause merely for stating the obvious: "I have learned if our minds can conceive a dream and our hearts can feel it, the dream will be much easier to achieve."

During the applause, I took a moment to look into the audience and spot the beaming, tearful faces of several members of my family, who were sitting very close to the front. Along with Anna—holding an exuberant Gabbie in her arms—most of my siblings were there, as was my Aunt Marta, and, of course, Sostenes and Flavia, my parents. Papá was already crying openly, but Mamá's eyes shone only with pride.

Then, gazing around at my fellow graduates and their families, I offered my thoughts on our next steps, observing that, as a runner, "I've found that a race does not end at the finish line; rather, each time you reach the end, a new race begins." Success, I suggested, would be determined less by our individual gifts and more by the teamwork that our studies together had helped to inspire. And this was true for each of us as we parted ways and went on into the fields of our choosing.

The ceremony was one of the most magical experiences of my life, and the best part was sharing it with my wife and daughter and my family members who had traveled across the country to celebrate with me. I will never forget the array of emotions on their faces—happiness, hope, excitement, surprise, maybe even sadness as they recalled past loss and struggle and as they contemplated the present and the future. But once the formal graduation had concluded, the whole family crowded around and couldn't stop hugging and kissing me and smiling, like I'd just won a heavyweight championship.

The following day we were still smiling, even though we had to get up early to tackle the huge job of packing all our worldly belongings into our rented moving truck—behind which we'd be towing our road-weary but indispensable red pickup, Pepe, for the trek from Boston to San Francisco. Fortunately, many members of "Q, Inc." were on hand to help. Several of them ridiculed me for dragging the truck back with us, calling it an "eyesore" and "junk heap." Oh, ye of little faith. Pepe would not only last through five years of residency and a postdoc year but would eventually be adopted by my father. At this writing, it's still clocking miles!

Before we'd finished loading up, a reporter from the *Boston Globe* stopped by to ask some questions for a piece the paper would run on me in a few weeks, complete with my photo on the front page. I was truly living *la vida loca!* Frank Acosta warned me, "Don't let all this fame and fortune go to your head!"

"Oh, yeah, 'fortune,'" I laughed, already not sure how Anna and I would make ends meet on the subsistence salary paid to interns. But for the moment I set those concerns aside to enjoy the victory send-off we were given as we said good-bye to Harvard and friends, amid cries of "Bon voyage!" and promises to stay in touch.

With five-month-old Gabbie in her car seat, securely wedged and belted in between me and Anna, gazing up at the two of us with a cherubic smile, we set off together on the next leg of our journey. Doing a last loop of the neighborhood, we drove past the medical school buildings, past Vanderbilt Hall, and then alongside the Charles River before I steered us out of town, away from Boston and everyone there who had become family to us. When we hit the freeway, Anna peered over her shoulder for a final glimpse of everything we were leaving behind. She reminded me of that first winter when she had to drive Pepe on the treacherous snow-packed roads, slipping and sliding the whole way to her teaching job in the suburbs. Anna had not only survived the adjustment process but was soon at home, loving her students and colleagues, and enjoying the freedom to explore the city on her own and with me, and most recently savoring her time as a new mom. As she reminisced, I glanced in the rear-view mirror, watching Boston fade rapidly into the past.

A feeling of incredible lightness carried us the whole way to San Francisco. For the first time in a long while, I had only one job to do and that was to drive the three of us safely from one side of the country to the other. We could laugh, talk, sing, or share the quiet while watching the changing scenery of the heartland pass by. Over and over, I marveled at the beauty of the country that I could now call my own.

The joy of our trip west was still with me when I reported for my first day of work at San Francisco General Hospital and when a few days later, I was summoned to the emergency room during my first night on call. By the time I reached the trauma staging area, I had descended from the clouds   hitting the ground just in time to see that the real climb was still ahead of me.

·   ·   ·

The first months of my internship brought ups and downs. On the plus side, within a few weeks of my arrival, I'd managed to gain my footing after the first drastic leap from the ivory tower to the battleground of a neurosurgeon in training. Navigating this new terrain was made easier by remembering lessons learned as a seasonal migrant worker—how it was possible to rise to a top position at one job only to be knocked down to start over from the bottom at the next. Besides, I reminded myself, if I could move irrigation lines barefoot in winter and shovel sulfur and fish lard, then I could handle the trials of internship.

On the downside, the first few brutal weeks of training were child's play compared to the trial by fire I was about to face. I would have been well warned to take the advice that Mickey (Burgess Meredith) gave Rocky as he began his training: "You're gonna eat lightnin' and you're gonna crap thunder!" As in a war, the only way to cope during residency was to look to the team, your fellow soldiers, to be there for you—and vice versa. This band of brothers and sisters were, first and foremost, my fellow residents. Being in the trenches together, we developed bonds to last lifetimes. Over the course of six years—with an estimated six to seven thousand brain surgeries that we were to cover collectively—I spent more hours with my co-residents than with my own family, after all!

We held each other up, in a constant state of high alert, on the cusp of life and death, working together in the middle of the night, helping to make decisions while in the midst of combating disease or injury in someone's brain, and confronting unpredictability in its most real sense.

We came to see ourselves as members of the Special Forces. Yes, we took orders from the generals, the attending physicians. But as chief or lower-level residents, we made many of the immediate decisions, often determining the ultimate outcome for patients on the verge of dying or addressing the aftermath of the deaths that did occur. We were also often responsible for communicating with family members of those patients.

One break I was able to catch during this first year of my residency was that as an intern, I was not yet in the harsh spotlight of training directly under the attending surgeons. Rather, the pecking order put me under the supervision of higher-level residents who were tasked with getting me up to speed on the fundamentals and preparing me for the more grueling training to follow. To my lasting fortune, during this period I was under the watchful eyes of Dr. Geoffrey Manley and Dr. George Edward Vates IV, two senior residents who quickly became my staunchest allies and closest friends.

Like me, Geoff Manley had an unlikely story. From Louisville, Kentucky—home of my hero Muhammad Ali—Geoff had been a high school dropout turned auto mechanic, with his own business, before a conversation with a customer changed his life. The man, who turned out to be a professor, told him, "Look, you're a really bright guy, and I don't think you'll be happy being a grease monkey the rest of your life." Not only did that comment set the gears in motion for Geoff to complete his high school equivalency degree and attend college classes at night, but when he looked for a way to support himself, Geoff wound up working in the professor's lab. Bingo! He proceeded to win scholarships and science grants that eventually landed him at Cornell, in the Ivy League, where he completed both a medical degree and a PhD.

About seven years older than I, Dr. Manley was the chief resident when I came in and was subsequently made an attending professor specializing in neurotrauma. A role model in many ways, he had an intense work ethic that matched mine. As he pointed out once, our need to compete with ourselves rather than with others was a shared pathology.

With a background very different from mine or Geoff Manley's, Ed Vates came from an affluent, highly educated family with a long line of doctors, and his father was a prominent neurologist. Like Geoff, he had gone to Cornell Medical School. Whenever a crisis erupted, Ed knew how to create calm within the storm; he was pure grace under fire. He was also one of the most down-to-earth, caring, and compassionate human beings you could hope to meet.

Two months into my first year, with Manley and Vates looking out for me, I was thriving. Hungry to learn and do more, I'd put in extra hours in the OR whenever possible. In turn, attending professors were beginning to request my presence there. Even with the pace cranking up after Labor Day, I had acclimated sufficiently to the demands to assume that the breaking-in process was behind me and that I could expect smooth sailing from there on.

Such was my naivety. Also wrong, as I would later discover, was the assumption that after the first year, I would no longer work a hundred-plus hours per week. But because of our expectation of a lighter workload by the following summer, Anna and I began thinking about having another child. Since I was home so rarely, only to sleep a few hours, we resolved to take advantage of every opportunity to pursue that goal. I remember joking that this task was easier said than done as I headed off for work on the day I was scheduled to go along on a rotation with residents in the orthopedic department.

When Anna and Gabbie saw me off that morning just before dawn,

I was caught off-guard by an unfamiliar sense of foreboding. Driving in for my shift, I pushed away a sudden fear that I would never see the two of them again. And by the time I arrived at the hospital, parked the truck, and jogged up the steps to the nurse's station to check in, I'd forgotten any such dark thoughts and was in great spirits. "Good morning, my ladies," I greeted a group of nurses, quickly adding, "and my gentlemen!"

"Good morning, Dr. Q!" I heard in response.

This was the moment when I first detected a higher than usual level of tension, which I again attributed to the larger number of emergencies that the neurosurgical trauma team had been seeing. But after a few minutes, the intense working atmosphere seemed no different than normal.

However, when I started the orthopedic rotation in the HIV-AIDS ward that afternoon, my earlier sense of foreboding returned. For reasons soon to be apparent, I would mentally revisit this scene many times, futilely wishing to rewrite it.

There was that instant of hesitation when I could have said no and not followed the orthopedic resident into the room of the patient we knew to have full-blown AIDS and hepatitis C. But instead of announcing my fear, I soldiered on, maintaining a respectful and professional demeanor. I remember the first sight of the patient—probably in his late twenties but with the appearance of an eighty-year-old, wasted into a shell of a human being, yellowed and bony with dark track marks on much of his skin. I remember feeling rather than seeing his pain and desperation, which seemed to color the air.

The closer I came to the patient, the louder his eyes spoke about the ravages taking place inside of him. The eyes, often described as the windows to the soul, are also doors to the brain, especially in patients with brain problems. This patient's eyes were bloodshot and his pupils were large; his gaze was fixed and glassy. In taking further stock, I noted that his feet were cold to the touch and that his lips were a grayish blue color. His jaw hung open, and he breathed through his mouth in rapid, shallow, labored breaths. He showed no response to voice or touch, as though his pain was so great he could no longer attend to anything outside of him.

Then there was the smell of death that had hit me when we entered the room. A sickening, haunting smell, it's not like the smell of urine or stool or putrefaction or sulfur. Nothing can mask it. I remember thinking of the smell that coated my hair and clothes and skin when I worked at the Port of Stockton scraping fish lard, and this was worse—because it came with the sight of a human being preparing to die.

I contemplated the fragility of life and the grotesque way in which this young patient was dying. By this stage of my journey, I had concluded that we all come to this world only for a short breath anyway. And yet, as I saw in this patient's last struggles, we all seek ways to exhale and inhale as slowly as possible in order to prolong our experience of life.

I keenly remember the moment when the resident announced that we were going to try to alleviate the buildup of fluids in the patient's knee by "milking" the area with a hollow-bore needle. I thought I saw the patient's eyes widen at the sight of the huge, forceful hypodermic but wasn't sure. Again, I ignored a bad feeling. However, when the resident asked me to help by putting pressure on the knee so that more fluid could be extracted, I knew at once this wasn't right. This was not a vague premonition, it was a strong gut reaction. Between the patient's fragile, brittle bones and the power of the needle, I thought that adding pressure would be dangerous. But lacking the valor to say no—in spite of my misgivings—I went along with the request, aware that I might pay for it. Another huge lesson! From this point on, I always listened to my instincts—even if it meant refusing a request from a person in seniority and getting into trouble for it. Certainly, this lesson came at a great cost, its impact closing in on me in only minutes to come during my walk down the dark hall to the exam room with hospital personnel waiting for me. Because of a slight shudder from the resident while draining more fluid, instead of withdrawing and securing this drainage full of contaminated blood and knee fluids, the resident's hands slipped in trying to move it away.

This was the sequence of events I had to describe to the hospital administrators in the exam room, explaining how the needle stuck me and then retracted, as if driven by a malevolent force, and then hit the senior resident's arm with more of a scratch. Demonstrating how it had moved initially, I pointed out that neither the gloves nor other precautions had helped when the contaminated needle buried itself in the upper part of my hand, near the wrist, stabbing deep into my veins.

When I stumbled out of the exam room, after hearing hospital representatives' description of the intensified triple therapy I'd undergo for the next month, the shock began to wear off and panic set in. The senior resident, after being scratched by the needle, was going to be given the triple therapy too, but because the fluid had already been discharged into the veins of my hand, this step was more of a precaution in the resident's case. One of the most difficult pieces of information to process was an administrator's description of a previous case in which someone had been stuck by a contaminated needle. After a full year of testing negative for contracting the virus, the person had tested positive and come down with full-blown AIDS. How long until I met a similar fate, lying in a hospital bed with the smell of death around me, staring at my loved ones with the same haunted look I had just seen in the eyes of the AIDS patient? Changing that image at once, I brought the faces of Anna and our baby into focus and simply tried to breathe—to inhale and exhale slowly.

How was I going to tell Anna?

Even though I was on my feet, walking slowly to the stairwell to make a phone call, inside I was flattened, back again at the bottom of the tank, helpless, without oxygen. The difference between then and this day was very simple: now I had a child. That changed everything.

Accidents happen, I reminded myself, and called home. When Anna answered the phone, she was in a happy mood, and I tried to work up to my news as calmly as possible. "Listen, sweetie, I don't want you to worry, but we're going to have to put our plans to have another baby on hold for a little bit."

"Alfredo, what is it?" She could hear that something was very wrong.

After describing the incident without any sugar coating, I told her about the plan of treatment. "You know me," I added, trying to comfort both of us, "I'm a fighter. You're a fighter. We'll get through this."

Anna said nothing. She later admitted that her heart stopped, as she felt certain in that moment that I was infected and had been given a death sentence. I couldn't tell if she was crying or not.

We made a pact to take this crisis one step at a time, preparing ourselves for the roller-coaster ride to come, which would include testing every couple of months for the next year. We reminded each other of our wedding ceremony, when we followed the Jewish custom of stomping on the wine glass, a preview of the hardships that are part of life—as we were now experiencing—but that the bonds of marriage could help us to withstand.

As word spread quickly, I was aware that Anna, my parents, siblings, relatives, and friends were in shock. Barely three months earlier everyone had been celebrating my graduation from medical school. We had all been caught up in the excitement that came with reaching that mountaintop—my match at UCSF and the fanfare over the honors and publications, not to mention the lengthy article about my personal story that had come out recently in the *Boston Globe.* To watch me drop so suddenly from those heights was devastating enough; worse, they had to grapple with the reality that they might lose me. Rarely would they put those fears into words during the coming year, but I knew they were terrified. Anna had to contend not only with the knowledge that I might die but also the possibility that she would contract the virus from me and follow me to the grave, leaving Gabbie an orphan.

Meanwhile, Anna had to stand by while I dealt with the unpleasant side effects of the triple-therapy drugs—vomiting, diarrhea, weakness, and exhaustion. For my part, aside from knowing that the medications weren't even guaranteed to work, I continued to be the low man on the totem pole at work and wasn't in a position to ask for time off or to request more lenient hours or special treatment. The system was such, in my estimation, that any complaints could derail me.

My colleagues did their best to appear optimistic, but I remember Esteban Burchard's face when he first heard what had happened—his expression conveying, *No, this can't be true!* He was at UCSF during this period, and I was grateful for his powerful brand of moral support. Not letting on how worried he was, Esteban later admitted that he was undone by the news. While I thought of him as my hero and role model, he saw me as the guy on the team who raised everyone else's game, always up for a challenge and so fast on my feet that nothing could hinder me. Now everything, even my life, was in jeopardy. Esteban also understood why I couldn't complain or take time off. There was an unwritten code of conduct for neurosurgery residents, especially with our Special Forces mentality, that discouraged complaints or requests for special treatment that could be interpreted as signs of weakness. Still, he was concerned that nobody in an official capacity seemed to care, nor did anyone in authority offer practical solutions to ease the physical and psychological symptoms while I maintained the crazy hours required for my training. In general, the situation would improve for residents in later years. Perhaps my case helped toward that end.

The only solution was to draw sustenance from my stint as a boxer. Was I going to give up before the final bell? No. Was I going to shirk my responsibilities as the winter holiday season approached and I would be needed for longer shifts to handle the expected jump in the number of patients coming into the hospital? Of course not. I had to stay standing and keep swinging, through every shift, every rotation, with every passing hour—not just to keep from getting knocked out but to preserve my chance to fight for the ultimate prize. Instead of resisting the demands of the job, I chose to embrace them more fully. Rather than weakening, I would get stronger.

Ironically, the tougher I was, the more requests I received to be in the OR—and the longer I needed to remain still, often for hours at a time. But with the vomiting and severe diarrhea I was experiencing during the first thirty days, I knew I would need to make many urgent trips to the bathroom. The solution? Before and during those thirty-six-hour shifts, I stopped eating and even kept my water intake minimal. If this idea was crazy, well, I had been known to attempt Kaliman-like maneuvers before, so why not? Anna understood me well enough to accept those terms. If the only way not to miss a beat on the job was to go without eating and drinking, then that was something within my control. At least I could hold my head high on a day-to-day basis. Not surprisingly, I began to drop weight precipitously—twenty pounds during the first month when I took the triple therapy and another five pounds over the months to come. The question we both battled then was, "Oh my God, is this from not eating, or is this HIV/AIDS?" To stave off panic and keep fear in check, I turned to the path of last resort: magic.

By that, I don't mean magic in the traditional sense or that I embraced the sort of magical thinking that can be a form of denial. Magic is my synonym for a remedy, when all else fails to give relief, that's found in ordinary or extreme settings—a mixture of humor, resilience, faith, imagination, and even stubbornness. I found that magic around me, mainly in the stories of my colleagues and the journeys of the patients I was caring for.

At the time, I felt too lousy to realize that this process was going to make me a better physician. The experience of living with a potential death sentence and taking medications that made me so sick I wondered if doing so was worth it (and, again, there was no guarantee the experimental triple therapy would work) was not taught at any level of training. But now I had firsthand knowledge. This education was also a kind of magic that was changing me, helping me to become mentally stronger—in spite of the battle going on inside my body.

When the first test results came back negative in the weeks after I completed the full course of medication, the news was enough for me to reclaim some of my sense of humor—always an important coping mechanism. One day a patient with a mild traumatic brain injury came in disoriented, sick from malnutrition, and afflicted with other issues from having lived on the streets. We needed to clean him up and get him on an IV, but he refused to let anyone touch him. Geoff Manley, in the room with me at the time (and responsible for reporting this episode to Ed Vates later), asked me to try again.

I attempted to coax our patient into cooperating. "Sir, you're going to feel better after all this, I promise you."

"Oh yeah, how do you know?"

I told him that I was a doctor, and we all specialized in taking care of patients like him and were trained to do the right things.

"Well, how do I know you won't screw up?"

Using some light humor, I said, "Don't worry, I know what I'm doing. I went to Harvard Medical School!"

"Oh yeah?" he replied. "Harvard, huh? But did you *graduate*?"

As much as this patient allowed me to laugh at myself, Geoff Manley and Ed Vates, graduates of Cornell Medical School, laughed harder.

The two of them, along with Esteban Burchard, did their best to keep tabs on me and buoy my spirits. But I knew that deep down they were as scared as I was. Geoff had survived something similar some years earlier—when less was known about HIV. His odds might not have been as damning, but he gave me hope, especially when the round of tests I took in June—nine months after the needle stick—also came back negative.

That was great news—only three months to go. The bad news was that while Anna and I had hoped for a less insane schedule now that I'd completed my internship and could start my second year of residency, the opposite turned out to be true. My first year had been only a warm-up!

On top of the long hours required of residents, the second year placed us under a whole new layer of pressure as our higher-ups placed greater demands on us and scrutinized our every move. Everything was on the line. For the most part, the chief resident or more senior residents were the ones responsible for bringing in the patient and doing the prep work with the anesthesiologist, usually assisting the attending surgeon and helping to open up the skull (based on the attending's map). Once the main surgical goals were met, residents would then step in to handle the closing. The closing included the tasks of taking out the tubes, other cleanup jobs of the brain before sewing or stapling everything closed, and then waking the patient in post-op—all part of what is often referred to as "taking the patient out."

These were the procedures that I was being trained to perform as a second-year resident. We were expected to have completed the first-year internship at the San Francisco General and Moffitt hospitals, as I had. Now most of the action took place on the UCSF Parnassus campus at Moffitt Hospital, where the attending professors did the majority of their surgeries. After that, the program was structured to prepare those who were ready to return to the front lines back at San Francisco General.

So while this second year was an incredible opportunity to soak up everything we could from the surgeons who ruled the operating rooms at Moffitt, by design it was intended to weed out anyone who didn't have the fire in the belly to handle the pressure. This was where the ability to screen out distracting thoughts—including worries about my mortality—was indispensable.

Many of the attending surgeons exhibited this capacity, a power of focus, to an astounding degree. Dr. Charlie B. Wilson was a master of it. Early in my training, whenever I wanted to observe him in the operating room I arrived well ahead of time, as he was known sometimes to lock the door to avoid all possible disturbances. There was never any music being played in the OR, as other surgeons sometimes liked to have. Dr. Wilson had his own internal music. No one was allowed to speak, and cell phones had to be on mute. No matter how many people were in the operating room, you could hear a pin drop.

Whenever the opportunity arose, I would look through the extra viewing lenses of the microscope to observe what Dr. Wilson saw as he looked through the main eyes of the huge overhead microscope, while using both hands to manipulate his instruments in the patient's brain and moving with fluidity and grace. His performance was art. This was how Picasso must have painted, I imagined, or how Mozart must have composed. Effortlessly. Barely breathing to ensure that I wouldn't commit the unthinkable by bumping the microscope, I never stayed near the action for long, instead standing in the back until my services were needed.

Finally, when he was wrapping up, he would break the silence and turn around to ask the nurses, "Who is taking the patient out?"

The most senior surgical nurse would name the resident who had been assigned this honor. As my training progressed, I would increasingly hear the senior surgical nurse answer, "Dr. Quiñones." Dr. Wilson would then turn again and lift an eyebrow to acknowledge me. As he left the operating arena and proceeded to scrub out, I would be responsible for taking his patient out. The first time that he had asked me to do this job—following a transphenoidal surgery to remove a brain tumor through the nose—he had apparently been pleased with my performance, because he started requesting me after that.

One day, as a surgery wore into its last stages, everyone in total focus along with Dr. Wilson, a medical student under my supervision crossed in front of me and bumped the microscope that Dr. Wilson was using to guide his knife. This type of blunder was potentially disastrous: one slip of the knife can nick the carotid artery and kill the patient. When the microscope was bumped, Dr. Wilson's reflexes prevented any such disaster as he froze momentarily before lifting his eyes and whipping around. The med student had managed to hide himself behind a table. And who was standing in front of the microscope? Me.

Dr. Wilson fixed me in his gaze with his intense black eyes. Clearly,

I was doomed. But then again, maybe not, because when he was finishing up, Dr. Wilson turned to his senior nurse and said, "Make sure that Alberto takes my patient out."

What a relief. I don't know whether he suspected that someone else had bumped the microscope. I never told him who had done it, nor did anyone else, as far as I know. Whether Dr. Wilson figured out that I was taking the heat for someone else or whether he decided to let it go isn't clear. All I knew at the time was that his hyperfocus on his patient had seemingly caused him to forget my first name and call me Alberto—not Alfredo. On that occasion, I didn't mind having a certain amount of anonymity to keep me out of the spotlight!

Two weeks later, I was surprised to be invited to his house for a special luncheon. When the appointed day arrived, I nervously knocked on the door to his grand home in San Francisco, and when it opened, I was greeted by Dr. Charlie Wilson himself. Smiling congenially and speaking in a charming voice, he said, "Hello, Alfredo, I'm so pleased you could join us."

Not only had he recalled my name, but when he introduced me to his wife, he gave her a detailed biography of me. Even though I had enjoyed my short-lived anonymity and was happy not to be connected to any missteps in the OR, I was honored that he had taken the time to find out more about my story. The message he sent was one of encouragement and confidence in me.

In the event that any of these moments of glory might go to my head, my training under Dr. Mitch Berger, the ultimate perfectionist, kept me from getting ahead of myself. No one could escape his all-seeing eyes. Once when a medical student touched a table that was designated as sterile, thus contaminating it (even though it was far from the patient), all Dr. Berger had to do was turn his head slightly, steel his eyes, and employ his kinetic powers to make the person bounce back against the wall. Crazy! Thank goodness that I wasn't in the line of fire that time. Imagine, however, the horror for anyone who committed the unthinkable of bumping the microscope during another surgery and seeing his eyes blaze. That person once was me!

Sometimes I imagined that Nana Maria had chosen to put Dr. Berger in my path as the one mentor who could challenge me to go further than I dreamed possible while setting the boundaries to keep me human in the process. Indeed, a perfectionist is exactly who you want training you as a brain surgeon. Dr. Berger wasn't concerned with trivial issues; he was a perfectionist about the key elements that contribute to a positive outcome for the patient. From the instant that he walked through the door to meet a patient, he was on his game. At one time he had considered playing for the National Football League, having played football at Harvard, and he brought the intensity of the competitive athlete to his job. Given that he also talked like Marlon Brando in *The Godfather,* those of us who trained under him came to see every surgery in his OR as the equivalent of a Super Bowl game, and we wanted nothing more than to help him win.

On one of the first days of my second year of residency, Dr. Berger had three surgeries scheduled to remove brain tumors, which would keep us working until about midnight. As the first case was finishing up in one room, the second surgery would start in another. With senior residents handling the setting-up stages in the second room, Dr. Berger could then focus confidently on the patient in front of him.

During a break when a member of the pathology team came in to collect tissue, Dr. Berger had a question about a patient scheduled for surgery the next day. "Alfredo, did you do the additional CT scan of our patient for tomorrow?"

Eager to contribute, I responded by offering an observation that I had made after looking at other films of the patient's tumors. When I finished my comments, Dr. Berger slid his magnifying goggles up to his forehead to look at me. Then in his Marlon Brando way, not modulating his tone, he said, "I asked you a very simple question. It was a yes or no question."

"No," I replied.

Lesson learned!

.   .   .

During this time, with the distractions of my work, I sometimes had an easier time dealing with the still-looming AIDS scare than Anna did. On

some days, the only outlet for her fear and frustration was her journal—
which she later shared with me as a reminder of how tough it was to
endure the mounting pressure.

On July 3, for instance, after I'd been gone two days and hadn't
checked in with her, she wrote, *Didn't hear from him all day. Got worried,
paged him at 11:30 P.M.—Nurse returned my call. AQ came home at 1:45 A.M.*

The next day continued similarly: *On call again, he got about 3 hours
sleep in the last few days. I talk to him maybe one time per day for 2–5 min.
Gabbie & I spent fourth of July home reading/playing alone.*

Intermixed with notes of what she had made for dinner in the hope
that I'd be home to eat (*Fried chicken, mashed potatoes, salad*) were comments that when I was home, I had no energy to eat and would grab
cereal at most, then collapse in bed, then wake to go to work for four
operations that day—only to return with aching feet, preoccupied and
exhausted.

Of course, my heart broke when many years later I read of her pain
in such stark terms—her loneliness and concern that I would fall asleep
driving home or her worries about Gabbie's growing clinginess with
her and reluctance to come to me when I was home. At the same time, I
am grateful that never once did Anna withhold her unconditional love
for me or ask me to rethink the direction I had taken. She also gave me
space to express how lousy and scared I felt when things were especially
tough, and she was there to listen when I simply needed to talk.

Around late summer or so, Anna observed that I had reached my
lowest point. Besides anxiety over the final blood tests that were coming
up and a caseload that felt like one terrible outcome after another, I was
ready to crash any minute from no sleep and little food.

The snap came one day not with Anna but with the wife of a patient
with brain cancer whom we had sent home with hospice care. Our neurosurgical team had been on his case through two surgeries, but we had
exhausted all means of arresting this malevolent killer that was devour-
ing his brain. I had taken the lead in arranging hospice care so that he
could return home for his last days. Instead of giving myself credit for
handling those details, I should have known that in addition to treating
the patient who was dying, a physician's job description also meant tak-

ing care of family members, especially this patient's wife, who was as entitled to compassion as the patient was.

My rundown state was no excuse, but when the wife of our patient called to complain about the hospice workers, I felt there was nothing to do for her. My comments of "I see" and "Yes, I understand" didn't alleviate her pain either.

"Stop saying 'I see,'" she said. "Is that all you can do?"

"Well, what do you want me to do? I mean, he's going to die," I replied, speaking words that I regretted instantly.

After a stunned moment of silence, she burst into tears and began to sob. What an idiot I was. How could I have been so self-centered, so oblivious to her pain and her loss and to everything that she had been through? My insensitivity was inexcusable. I took a deep breath, apologized, and tried to repair some of the emotional distress by offering to place more phone calls on their behalf. She accepted my offer, in the process teaching me that effective communication is often in the delivery.

I still cringe when I think about that phone call, and I've strived every day since then not to repeat the mistake. As humbling as the experience was, it helped me become a better physician in the long run; and in the short run, a better patient.

As a physician, I knew from watching others grapple with a disease with seemingly impossible odds how important it is to offer tangible hope. As a patient, I now lived the reality. My long year of waiting to see if I'd contracted AIDS helped me understand why some patients are able to grasp on to hope and others aren't. Over and over, I saw that those who felt invisible—left to cope with their disease alone, with no one in their corner to fight for them—were those who gave in to despair. Because I had witnessed the struggles of fellow migrant workers and others who had reason to feel faceless and voiceless, without legal representation or access to medical services, I understood how hopelessness can overwhelm anyone. Still, I was not prepared for the sight of a patient brought into the emergency room after having become so desperate, without family members to support him and without access to mental health services, that in attempting suicide he had taken a shotgun to his face. He was literally faceless.

Miraculously, he not only survived what he had done to himself, but everyone involved in his care, myself included, painstakingly accompanied him through many surgeries to give him a new face. He wasn't invisible to us. Though the journey that brought him to us was tragic, he transformed as the result of the care and the hope that he received from his extended hospital family. In turn, he helped give all of us hope, especially me.

When I mentioned this inspiring case to Dr. Burchard as the two of us passed each other in the hall one day, he listened with interest but could see something else was on my mind.

"There's a phone call from the lab," I began, and then confided that I was on my way to find out the results of the final blood tests that would tell me whether I had cheated death a second time or not. To pump both of us up, I assured him that if everything went as we hoped—as soon as I was given an all clear, if I was so blessed—nothing would stop me after that.

But Esteban, like Geoff and Ed, saw through my pretended optimism. The three of them later admitted to being gravely concerned.

My walk down the hall to take the phone call that would deliver the final verdict was as surreal as the one a year earlier just after the needle had sunk into my hand. Once again, I thought of going into the patient's room, smelling the smell of death and seeing his eyes staring into the void. Once again, I felt as if I were in a dark tunnel, walking toward a light that could be either my rescue or my doom.

As I turned the corner, my heart fluttered as fast as hummingbirds' wings, and my palms were wet. With many steps to go before I reached the door and walked over to the phone, I was sure that I would collapse in fear before I got there. When I finally picked up the phone and put the receiver to my ear, I heard little the technician said other than the word "Negative."

At that point, I took the first full breath I'd allowed myself in a year. Then I called Anna to tell her that it was time for us to get busy on baby number two. This time, I could tell without a doubt that she was crying. So was I!

NINE

Question the Rules and
When Possible Make Your Own

What is a miracle?

In medicine, we see healing as a kind of miracle, but is it the only kind? I certainly felt that I'd experienced a miracle when I received a clean bill of health after the year long AIDS scare, and I felt even more blessed a short time later when Anna told me that we had conceived our second child. My thirty-third birthday in 2001—with me alive and thriving and my family healthy and growing—was as miraculous a celebration as I could hope for.

Around me I saw everyday miracles, similar to mine, whenever a dreaded diagnosis was eluded or a patient was saved from the jaws of death and was able to walk out of the hospital on his or her own two feet. But what about those patients who didn't survive their trauma or devastating affliction? Were their lives any less miraculous for what they had accomplished in the time allotted to them and how they lived their final days? Was their ability to touch others—the legacy they left for the living—perhaps the greatest miracle of all?

As a midlevel resident, early in my surgical residency and training at UCSF, I met the answer in the form of a little girl named Maria who was brought into the pediatric department at Moffitt Hospital with what turned out to be a spinal cord tumor. From everything that our Spanish-speaking hospital social workers could learn, this five-year-old girl, apparently from South America, had been abandoned. She was very small for her age but brought a ferocious warrior spirit to her battle with the tumor that had made her paraplegic. Unable to move or to regulate her urination and other bodily functions, she endured horrific pain when her bladder burst and she had to be rushed into surgery. When she recovered from this operation, she had to undergo another surgery to remove the tumor on her spinal cord.

Throughout the weeks that she was with us, looked after by three teams reporting to Pediatric Service—pediatric surgery, intensive care, and neurosurgery—I thought often of my baby sister, Maricela. A strange sense of déjà vu haunted me, as I thought about the fact that my sister had never received the medical care that could have saved her and remembered my mother crying over the tiny casket amid an atmosphere of sadness that I couldn't understand. These memories added to the heartbreak of Maria's case and my anguish in watching her undergo her difficult journey with no family at her bedside to comfort her.

Whenever possible between cases, I stopped in at her room and sat holding her hand and talking to her in Spanish. As a physician, I knew by now not to underestimate the healing power of touch. Dr. Mitch Berger was incredible in this respect—as though the force and heat of his hand on a patient's shoulder or forehead was transferable to that person. Now I wanted to believe that healing energy could save Maria. But even while we made her more comfortable, the tests revealed another tumor, this time in her brain. The options for treatment ranged from putting her through more surgeries coupled with chemotherapy and radiation to starting with chemo to see if we could buy her some time. But how merciful would it be to extend her life only to find that we had prolonged her suffering?

What I remember most about Maria was the way she looked at me with her big brown eyes—questioning, asking why. Hers were the eyes of a very old soul, and I felt she knew that there wasn't much time left for her. Maria also seemed to be comforting me. Not in words. Her look and actions told us that she trusted us to take care of her and to choose the right treatment. Maybe it was my projection, but I felt she was asking that we not allow her to die anonymously and that we make sure she was remembered when she left this world.

On the day that Maria arrived at the hospital, I went home and poured out my heart to Anna. We ran together to look in on our daughter asleep in her bed, two and a half years old, healthy, safe, and loved, and we felt incredibly lucky. All the problems and worries about money, the long hours at work, the lack of time to see each other were suddenly irrelevant.

When I returned from work a day and a half later, Anna and Gabbie met me at the door to propose a plan. The two had gone out to buy some small gifts for Maria and wanted to take them to her in the hospital. I was touched to the point of tears. We had no money, and every dime that came in went to rent and the scant groceries we could budget for; we couldn't afford to eat at even the cheapest restaurants. But somehow Anna had worked some budgeting magic to buy these gifts. I tried to explain to Gabbie an unfortunate glitch in this unselfish plan: "What a beautiful thing you have done with your mom. I'm so proud of you. But you know what? There are rules against children coming into the hospital as visitors."

Her face fell. How could I go along with such a foolish policy, Gabbie seemed to ask. Anna shrugged, agreeing.

"Okay," I said, realizing that I was no match for these two very powerful women. "The nurses like me. Let me see if they'll make an exception."

Anna was familiar with my need to question the rules occasionally. Certainly we knew that many institutional rules and regulations were in place for a reason. But if I was going to survive the crucible of my residency, I had to allow myself to question those rules that didn't serve the best interests of either the patients or those in their service. In such cases, other, more compassionate rules needed to come into play.

Having been selected by the nursing staff to receive the Most Valuable Intern award during my first year, I hoped to work my charm. When I arrived at the pediatric nursing station the next day, I made a sweeping bow and greeted the mix of staff with my familiar phrase, "How are you today, my ladies? And my gentlemen?"

Instead of asking whether or not my wife and daughter could be allowed in, I asked what would be the best time for them to visit Maria. They were hesitant to allow the visit at first, but when Anna and Gabbie showed up with their arms full of toys and stuffed animals, the nurses waved us into Maria's room. Anna and I watched as Gabbie made herself at home and began to present the gifts to Maria. My wife and I still have a difficult time putting into words what it was like to see the two little girls interact. The contrast in their lives and their futures couldn't have been more stark. Yet, in the important ways, they were not at all different, and they became friends in an instant.

In the month that we followed her care, Maria did very well from a combination of surgery and medication that lessened her worst symptoms. But none of these measures were enough to kill the cancer and stop its spread, and we knew that she would not grow up to dream the dreams and live the life that we all want for our children. Yet in her short time with us, this little girl had become a star for everyone at the hospital and for my family.

When she died, Maria was no longer in our care and was with a children's agency, which filed a report so that we could close out the case and the paperwork. When I learned that her fight was finished, I needed to step outside the hospital for air—something I didn't do very often. I stepped into a picture-postcard San Francisco day in spring—with a blue, cloudless sky and the sun reflecting off the windows and spires of this great city on the bay. The weather didn't recognize the somberness of the occasion. There was nothing I could do to make sense of a life cut so short. Because of the understandings we had gained from Maria's case, we improved our approach to the resection of spinal cord tumors. Within the year, two girls—ages three and twelve—came in with spinal cord tumors and benefited from this improved resection approach. Both girls did beautifully and left our care with significantly fewer physical challenges than we were used to seeing. We all considered this outcome a miracle for them and their families. Writing about our findings in a paper that went through many revisions, I thought of the greatest miracle, Maria, the little girl alone in the world who had left such a powerful mark. When the published article arrived, I held it up like a trophy, thinking, *Maria, this one's for you.*

.   .   .

Having survived the first two years of training, I approached my third year with some expectations that the "eating lightning and crapping thunder" part was over and that the workload would be lighter. Wrong! I had simply been building up to the championship bout. Now I would find out whether I could silence those who had said "you can't" and "who do you think you are?"

As in the last of the *Rocky* films, this part of my training wouldn't be about how powerfully I could deliver knockout blows but about how much I could withstand. As Rocky tells his son, "It ain't about how hard you hit, it's about how hard you can get hit . . . how much you can take and keep moving forward." This would be my challenge: after being hit, and hit again and again, would I be strong enough to stay in the fight?

Did I question the rules of this game? All the time. Because I wasn't the typical neurosurgical resident, I was sometimes considered to be going against the grain. When others insisted that I was spreading myself too thin by doing research, working in laboratories, and training in the OR, I tended to push back even more. For example, I resisted the rule against moonlighting. For many of the residents who were from affluent backgrounds, the need to support themselves and their families during their training didn't present a hardship. For some of us who had no other forms of income, questioning the rule became a necessity, so I opted to supplement our finances on the weekends by working extra hours in out-of-the-way community hospitals. Geoff Manley, also married with children, had been in my place before and referred to these as "power weekends."

Such outside work was frowned upon by the higher-ups for good reasons. But for me, moonlighting was the only way to afford the San Francisco cost of living and to put food on the table for my family. So I would drive out to my second job Friday night and stay through six o'clock on Monday morning, then return to UCSF to escalating hours and responsibilities.

Another form of rule breaking for me was to refuse to let the pressure dampen my enthusiasm, curiosity, and fascination with the wonders of the human brain. Every day brought new reasons to be astonished by the brain's capabilities, which science has only begun to understand. I increasingly understood why Santiago Ramón y Cajal argued that before we seek to understand the universe, we must first study and unravel the mysteries of the brain. We need to be astronauts of inner space.

One memorable surgery during this period dramatized how adaptive and resilient our brains are. I was part of a team that removed an incredibly large brain tumor—almost six centimeters in diameter—from a patient's frontal lobe. Having seen the size of this tumor and knowing the risk that the patient could incur collateral damage from this type of surgery, I was in awe when I saw the patient wake up in the recovery room fully cognizant—a light in his eyes and a smile of relief that he was home, safe and sound. He was perfect! He could have gotten up and walked out of the hospital right then. When he did go home two days later, with no alteration other than the disappearance of a tomato-sized growth that could have robbed him of himself, he was an inspiring example of how much a brain can endure and how well it can bounce back from even the most severe hits.

There was so much to learn about how to harness the brain's natural ability to protect itself and fend off disease. Trying to consume the vast knowledge and expertise around me was like trying to drink from a fire hydrant. Too much! So the challenge was to find a way to figuratively purse my lips and sip at the flow. For me, the trick was to simplify everything at first and then gradually take in information in bigger gulps. This unconventional approach also helped me come up with a focus for the research groups I was forming with fellow residents and med students and enabled me to take the lead in collaborative writing projects with our professors. The groups were a way to learn by teaching each other. These atypical research teams evolved thanks to the leadership of Dr. Berger and to the vision of a handful of us, and eventually they became a more regular part of training.

As always, remembering that I was part of a team helped cushion the many sobering blows that seemed to come from every direction. Many of my fellow residents had been through similar trials by fire and come out the other side. In a joke that got old fast, we reminded each other that they didn't call it brain surgery for nothing. And we all saw gifted individuals fall by the wayside. One second-year resident failed to don the appropriate scrubs in a particular professor's operating room and then committed the worse blunder of making small talk with another resident while the professor was in the middle of handling someone's brain. After the operation, the resident approached me and asked if I thought he was in serious trouble.

"No, no," I tried to say, not very convincingly, "everyone makes mistakes. Keep working hard." When he walked away, I turned to Nader Sanai, a medical student who would go on to focus on brain tumors as a neurosurgeon and scientist, and said, "We'd better get the jam. That hombre is toast."

Having made other mistakes as well, the resident in question had been showing signs that the mental and physical pressures of training had clouded his judgment. Indeed, not too much later, he left the program. By design, every step forward in this weeding-out process, like training for the Special Forces, pitted us against an obstacle intended to make us question whether we had what it took to perform the unnatural job of brain surgery. After all, there is nothing natural in invading the inner sanctum of the cranium. Opening up the portals to other parts of the body is much less invasive. But to reach the brain, we must either drill through the hard casing of the powerfully protective human skull or find other secret passageways or side doors that will take us into the brain. Once we're in, the greater test is to perform our mission and navigate back, causing the least amount of collateral damage.

Unnatural though this job might be, I saw some correlations with my past jobs that helped me master the necessary skills—from working on car engines as a child to welding and opening up the lids of pressurized railway cars. But the most powerful motivator was the thrilling sense of adventure in learning to map the surgical journey. Early on, I began mentally plotting the course of each brain surgery, starting with the moment I met the patient in the examining room. I learned this technique from the attending surgeons, like Dr. Berger, as they artfully developed a battle plan before stepping in the operating room—the do-or-die arena, where no movement could be left to chance.

The stronger and more confident I became in my abilities, the more exacting Dr. Berger became, making me wonder if he was trying to push me to my breaking point. Yet I now realize that there was a method behind his tests, if only to show me that I could go further than I thought possible. While I was bearing the brunt of the taskmaster side of Dr. Berger, every one of his patients was the beneficiary of his most devoted, compassionate healing side.

I learned a valuable lesson in compassion when I accompanied Dr. Berger to Moffitt Hospital to evaluate a pre-op patient who had been transferred in for surgery from the top-security prison ward at San Francisco General. Inmates who needed life-saving procedures were brought to Moffitt and housed in a separate ward, where some of them were handcuffed to the bedposts and each room had armed guards stationed outside. We called the convicts "jailbirds"—as they called themselves—in recognition of their temporary escape from the penitentiary to receive treatment. Dr. Berger's patient that day was a massive, muscular fellow covered in tattoos of swastikas, white-supremacist symbols, and obscene messages, including the words "Suck this!" tattooed on his abdomen along with an arrow pointing to his genitals.

Being Jewish, Mitch Berger could have been excused for losing his usual caring bedside manner with this prisoner with the swastikas. Instead, in that meeting and in the OR, Dr. Berger granted the patient the same dignity, respect, and impeccable care that he gave to every other patient.

I saw this grace time and again in different contexts. He treated every patient the same—from the most famous to the most underserved—regardless of the diagnosis or prognosis. His example lives on every day in the practice I have built. And yet, for years I puzzled over how difficult my training had been under him. Eventually, I came to understand that Dr. Berger knew our field would never take me seriously unless I had been seriously challenged—passing tests that showed I was the real thing. If I drove myself, he would drive me harder. If a task was done well, it could be done better. If I did not perform at the top of my game, others might assume that I'd received special consideration because of my status as a Mexican immigrant. No matter how interested people might be in my story—a magic fable of a migrant farm worker who lifted himself up through education—did patients really want a former tomato picker removing tumors from their brains?

With Hispanic-Americans counting for nearly half the population of California, I was the first Mexican-American to be trained at UCSF's neurosurgery program, and Dr. Berger understood that many eyes would be watching to see how well I did. He understood that a rapid rise into the spotlight would be distracting and even dangerous for me. He also probably anticipated that people would make assumptions about me based on my ethnicity—and, yes, raise the common questions about whether I was smart enough or hardworking enough. Just as prominent African-American neurosurgeons of earlier eras had been able to break down barriers so that others could follow, he saw that I had similar potential—but only if I proved myself at the highest level of ability. He never said any of these things to me directly. However, I knew something of his heart from the fact that earlier in his career, Dr. Berger had instituted a program to teach inner-city kids about medicine—bringing them into classes at the Children's Hospital at the University of Washington where he was the chief of Pediatric Neurosurgical Oncology. His quest was to train a new generation of neuroscientists who would come from all walks of life.

For all my analysis of Dr. Berger's ultimately benevolent motives, not until I had gone on to another institution and become a faculty member in charge of training residents myself could I speak to him without my voice rising an octave or two! But by then, I had benefited so much from what he taught me that I was delighted when our paths crossed at a conference—and said so. Dr. Berger smiled and told me how proud he was of me. And then, after we'd talked a while about his work and mine, he leaned in to me and with his familiar Brando intonation, said, "You know, Alfredo, the moment that I decided to take you on, I knew you would be a leader and be able to do things that none of us could have accomplished." Then he looked me square in the eyes, placed his hand on my shoulder, and added, "I know I was tough on you."

.   .   .

Early in my third year of residency, Anna, Gabbie, and I welcomed the latest addition to the home team—David! We lovingly dubbed him "the Big D," even though he was born prematurely and was very small. But David had such an active, energetic, and mischievous personality that we knew we were in for some interesting adventures. Before long, he started living up to his nickname and began to grow like crazy—eventually to be on the tall side, taking after Anna's side of the family. In his relentless curiosity, the Big D took after me, as my parents were quick to point out, recognizing many of the traits they had seen in me in my developmental years.

To my regret, I had to hear about most of the Big D's antics from Anna because I spent most of my time back in the trenches at San Francisco General. Anna held down the fort somehow, now dealing with both a preschooler and an active baby. Once I added moonlighting hours, I was seldom home to see my children growing up.

Trying to keep a positive outlook, I'd remind myself that my weekend work enabled me to practice as a general emergency room physician—implementing the training that I'd received at UCSF while caring for patients who wouldn't otherwise have had access to the level of care available at a major big city hospital. But I was well aware of the cost of gaining this additional expertise. On the weekends, the patient load at the community hospital was as heavy as that at San Francisco General. On some nights, we'd have a waiting room full of patients, which might include a crazed meth addict tearing down partitions in the ER or a six-hundred–pound man unable to breathe and in need of a tracheotomy—the latter requiring a desperate struggle to get him on a breathing tube and a machine so that he didn't die in our midst.

Though I handled these crises at work, I was falling down on my most important job, that of a father. Probably the most painful exchange that I have ever had with a family member took place during this period. One Sunday night when Gabbie was going on three years old and hadn't seen me all week, I made it home for a few hours' rest and immediately collapsed on the couch. I had just fallen asleep when she climbed up and wanted to play with me.

"Oh, honey," I said, barely awake, "Daddy can't play with you now. He needs to sleep. We'll play a little later, okay?"

Gabbie's smiling little face suddenly darkened. She shrugged, as if giving up on me, and said, "You better just go back to your house now."

Her assumption that I lived at the hospital was in some ways more painful than the difficult time after the needle stick. But her reaction was a wake-up call. Though I wasn't very successful at cutting back on my work hours, I at least became more conscious of the impact of my absence on my family. And when I was at my most exhausted and my most overwhelmed, I could revive instantly by thinking of the sacrifices Anna and the kids were making so that I could keep going.

Just as I gained strength from my family's love, I continued to draw inspiration from the resilience of patients who were as much a part of the teaching staff at UCSF as the professors were. Our patients taught us not only how powerful it is to engage their fighting spirit but also how amazingly the brain can respond and adapt to trauma—lessons I had increasing opportunities to learn toward the end of my third year when I took on chief resident duties in our trauma service.

One revealing case was that of a young man in his early twenties—whom I'll call Jonathan—who had immersed himself in a lifestyle of drugs and partying until a terrible motorcycle accident left him in a coma and under our care. After two extensive surgeries to relieve the pressure in his brain and three months of care in the ICU after he awoke from the coma, something seemed to have changed in his wiring. By every measure, he had suffered a fatal accident and we had brought him back from the dead, but he returned as a different person. His family observed that the trauma seemed to have rebooted his energies, restoring his passion for life. Once he had recovered sufficiently, Jonathan enrolled in college and never looked back. Periodically, I received uplifting letters from him and his family about the happy, healthy productive life he now enjoyed. Jonathan's personal reinvention in some ways reminded me of the new drive and focus I experienced after surviving the ordeal in the tank. Perhaps our brains become supercharged by such experiences of survival—proving that what doesn't kill you indeed makes you stronger.

Another case, that of a taxi driver who was brought in because he had blacked out after picking up a group of teenagers, led me to a similar conclusion. A charming and well-educated man who had immigrated to the United States and was driving the cab to put his children through college, he remembered only that the teenagers were arguing and that he had felt a sudden sting in the back of his neck. Though he reported no dizziness, ringing in his ears, blurred vision, or hearing loss and had no symptoms other than a headache and nausea, an X-ray soon revealed a bullet lodged in his skull! He had been caught in the cross fire of a gun battle waged in the back of his cab. In surgery, I worked with Dr. Manley, now an attending neurosurgeon on his way to becoming chief of the neurotrauma division, to extract the .38-caliber bullet without any fragmentation. But although removal of the bullet should have provided a happy end to the story, the patient's condition worsened significantly after the surgery. In the brain's effort to protect itself from the trauma of the gunshot, a secondary and equally life-threatening condition had arisen. Known as transverse sinus thrombosis—a fairly uncommon situation in which a blood clot forms in the blood vessels that drain the blood from the brain back to the heart—it could have killed him at any moment. Suspended on the fine line between life and death for the next week, he finally responded to the anticoagulants—blood thinners— we'd given him to prevent the blood clot from expanding throughout the brain.

A short while after giving our intrepid taxi driver a clean bill of health and watching him return to his life with renewed energy and passion, an eight-year-old girl came to us who was able to benefit directly from his case. The story was that a television had crashed into her head (we weren't able to learn whether this was an accident or not). After blacking out and quickly regaining consciousness, she primarily complained of a headache, coupled with nausea and vomiting. Following the same clues we had pursued with the taxi driver, we discovered a serious skull fracture and determined that she too was at risk of death from a transverse sinus thrombosis. Again, we were able to avert the crisis and treat her successfully to prevent a fatal blood clot. In turn, I was able to write about the two cases in a paper published in the *Journal of Trauma*.

The medical moral of both stories was that in so-called freak accidents in which the head is bumped or struck, even when the patient doesn't report extreme symptoms, it's important to look further and to use multiple imaging techniques to find any lurking problems. Because of this potential for hidden trauma, anyone who sustains a head injury should check with a physician and be seen if necessary.

I give this advice not only as a physician but also as a father who experienced a family emergency when David was about four months shy of his second birthday. As I was reviewing the postsurgery orders for a patient one day at Moffitt Hospital, I received a call from the emergency room and was surprised to hear Anna's voice when I picked up the phone.

She started out calmly, explaining that she was downstairs. Then the tears followed as my cell phone reception began breaking up.

"What's wrong?" I asked loudly. "Can you hear me?"

"David . . . ," I heard her say. And then I heard "emergency room" and "hit his head." I ran to a window to get better reception and listened as she explained that David had fallen out of the shopping cart while she was grocery shopping with the two kids and had hit his head and gone unconscious. Now she and the children were in the emergency room.

My heart almost burst out of my chest as I grabbed a railing for balance, fear ripping through my veins. In my professional role, I had been mastering the skill of calm in the midst of chaos. But not this day. The main reason I worked so hard was to protect and provide for my family, and now I was hearing that my son had hit his head hard enough to black out. As I flew down the hall, the first person I called was Dr. Ed Vates.

"I'm right behind you," he said as soon as I told him what was going on. He let me know that he would get someone to cover for me and would meet me downstairs. He understood at once that at this moment, I was foremost a father and a husband and that I wanted him to take charge of all medical questions.

In full panic, I raced down the four flights of stairs to the ER and rushed into the back entrance. I found David lying in a hospital bed, with Anna at his side, crying. Four-year-old Gabbie looked as distraught as Anna was.

When Dr. Vates arrived, I said, "I need you to take over his care."

Within minutes, he assessed the damage as a skull fracture but found no brain trauma. He would order more tests as a precaution, but David was going to be fine.

"Did you hear that, Big D?" I asked my son, as I picked my heart up off the floor and began to breathe normally again.

David smiled broadly, seemingly unfazed by the drama. Anna and I embraced him and Gabbie in a group hug, and I didn't want to let go. As I reluctantly started to pull away to return to work, Ed put a hand on my shoulder to stop me.

"Forget it," he said. "Take a few hours off."

I knew that this offer would mean a double shift for him and probably for a second person as well, but Ed waved away my protests. Sometimes, he told me, we physicians had to take a break from our responsibility for others' life and death and put on our hats as parents or family members. "This is one of those times, Alfredo," he said. Anna looked supremely grateful that she wouldn't have to shoulder this one by herself, at least for an hour or two.

Soon enough, I would have to return to the war, but for the next couple of hours, I was on liberty leave, made sweeter by the fact that the Big D was out of danger. As I recall, the celebration of our relief involved ice cream.

David immediately returned to his mischievous ways, undertaking experiments like drawing on the walls with crayons, using beds as trampolines, and performing other fairly safe but annoying antics. But at some point we noticed that he was developing a disconcerting habit of eating dirt, seeming to prefer it to food.

At first we thought this behavior was just odd. But then it became worrisome. What was up? Other symptoms confirmed our suspicions that David's desire to put sand and dirt in his mouth was not boyish curiosity—especially when he became painfully constipated, with poop as hard as rocks. When Anna found him crying from the pain, we knew we were confronting a medical mystery. Anna did her own research, leading to the correct observation that David was anemic, which in turn led to a doctor's visit and full work-up. The diagnosis was pica syndrome. In David's case, because of the anemia, his body was craving iron so much he was putting dirt in his mouth to save himself and, in the process, had developed lead poisoning. Considering that we had moved from the lower-income housing in the Presidio near the hospital to a more modern and therefore non-lead-painted suburban neighborhood near San Mateo specifically to avoid that kind of toxicity, we didn't understand how this could be possible. Our move had been occasioned by frightening stories about lead poisoning among children and adults as a result of the paint in the Presidio's older apartments. But when I filled out the paperwork to rent in San Mateo, I was willing to take on a much longer commute for two specific reasons. First, the apartment building had a playground for the children. Second, the landlord assured me that there was no history or possibility of using leaded paint in the apartments. She had insisted that the building was free of all environmental hazards.

Anna immediately had the health department come out to run tests, which revealed that the parking area—the ground floor of the building— was covered in leaded paint. The foot traffic in and out of the garage had apparently spread leaded paint chips to the playground where David had been putting dirt in his mouth. Our supposedly lead-free environment was anything but, and we felt betrayed by the rental agents.

Now we had a very sick little boy. Having already suffered through my AIDS scare, Anna now had to stand by while David was taped down naked to the X-ray table to determine if he had ingested anything with lead in it and then take him for monthly blood tests for the first few months and every three months thereafter. And given that I was gone for days on end, she had to do this alone, while trying to keep a sense of normalcy for David and Gabbie. One of the most frustrating challenges for her was to get David to eat normally again. Although it is thought that the best treatment for lead poisoning is a proper, healthy diet, David understandably didn't want to eat because of the pain of constipation. Ultimately, because David was too small for chelation (the use of chemicals that bind with heavy metals in the body), four years would pass before all the lead would leach out of his body.

Meanwhile, we moved again, this time to a small house in the southern part of San Francisco, with a tiny yard of our own. Though our new home was a great improvement, worry about my family's welfare—and about the burden Anna had to carry on her own—was fairly constant. My colleagues sometimes pointed out that for many of us in the fast lanes of our field, the unspoken rule was that the pressures of training would inevitably place strains on marriages and threaten family stability. While I questioned that rule and attempted to create my own, I was being somewhat unrealistic. But one day, I promised myself, our lives would be easier. Maybe not perfect, but easier. I hoped we would all look back at this period and understand why the climb had been so steep and see that our travails had been worth the journey. And when we arrived at that place, together as a family, the medal of honor would belong to Anna.

TEN Brainstorm

"We've got officers down! Officers down!" The words crackled through the static on the emergency room's police radio late on Wednesday, June 12, 2002.

At one time I might have felt like I was caught up in an action movie or a TV drama. But, in fact, these dramatic words were real and marked the beginning of my fourth year at UCSF, now as a chief resident at the Trauma Center. Long gone was the night when I nearly passed out at the sight of a trauma victim with a light shining through the hole in his head. By now I was so well trained in my work with neurotrauma, that earlier in the day I'd persuaded Dr. Manley to go home for some rest after the nonstop incoming cases we'd been seeing all week. We had both endured three days largely without sleep, grabbing only a couple of hours of shut-eye in closet-sized hospital offices. As the attending surgeon, Geoff wanted to know why he should go home for a break if I, second in command as chief resident, was going to stay. Wasn't I as tired as he was?

"No, my hombre, you know me, I'm just warming up. Besides, I'm younger than you!" I teased my slightly older colleague.

With another attending surgeon en route to take over for Dr. Manley, I took charge and marshaled our forces, making sure that every able body was standing by at battle stations, ready for not one but four officers to be transported in. In our professional calling to treat the sick and wounded, many of whom were brought to us by police officers, there was an unwritten code that any time we treated people in law enforcement and were unable to save them, they would die in our arms. They were our brothers and sisters. Many of them knew me by name, or I should say, as "Q"—and I knew many of them personally as well. All of us working in the hospital saw them as heroes putting themselves in the line of fire—dealing with a kind of reality on the street that we knew little about. They, in turn, saw us as soldiers on a front line of another sort.

On this night, our two worlds were about to intersect in profound and powerful ways. For those of us on duty in the trauma ward, a rash of crime-related and traumatic injuries had begun early on Monday and then moved up to warp speed by the time we heard the police radio come to life again on Wednesday night. This week stood in stark contrast to the previous one, which had been relatively quiet, like an eerie calm before the storm. The weather for the first week in June had seemed more like that in Mexicali—hot and dry, overly still—than like typical San Francisco weather. Something was up, lurking around the corners.

Indeed, everything had cranked up on Monday the tenth and then exploded by Tuesday the eleventh. That morning, the first case that Dr. Manley and I saw in surgery was an assault victim whose head had been bashed in, causing a massive amount of bleeding in the right side of the brain. His situation was dire, but we emerged optimistically in time to get to the day's second case—a scheduled replacement of a bone flap removed months earlier from the skull of a patient who had been in a car accident and whose brain had swollen up like a mushroom as if trying to escape out of his skull. In this third surgery for this patient, we could see that removing the bone flap had been effective, allowing the brain to swell and ultimately to recede. We replaced the bone flap, moving expeditiously, encouraged by the signs. So far, so good.

But the next two cases were daunting. The first case was an aneurysm—a huge bulging vessel in the patient's brain that had to be repaired, much like a land mine must be defused while the clock is ticking. Next was a man of about thirty-three who, after suffering a trauma of the spine, had developed bleeding in the brain and required an urgent trip to the OR.

In the midst of these concurrent cases, we were alerted that the paramedics were bringing in a woman who had been the victim of a horrific domestic violence assault. Unlike many of the patients whose names and stories we never knew or were not allowed to give out, this patient's name, Maggie, would appear later in the news, part of a larger drama unfolding that week in San Francisco.

That Tuesday, Maggie—described in the news as an elegant, tall African-American woman in her midthirties—had returned to the apartment where she was living with her boyfriend, a man in his late twenties who weighed more than three hundred pounds, to find him threatening her grandmother. Before she could intervene, her boyfriend had grabbed a VCR and smashed it against Maggie's head—first on the back of her skull and against the side—and then, wielding a knife, had begun stabbing her and continued to the point that she was choking on her own blood. Still conscious, she felt him jump on her back and grab her neck, as his hand reached for her face, gouged out one of her eyes, and attempted to gouge out the other. When she eventually managed to call 911, she was holding one of the eyeballs in her hand, saying he had dropped it while fleeing the scene.

Maggie had to be sent to the intensive care unit before we could get her to the OR for plastic surgery. The one eye that had remained in the socket was going to be saved. But there was no hope for the other eye.

A manhunt began for her assailant. His name, as confirmed by the police and news sources later on, was Monte Haney, a young man with a long criminal record. For the next eighteen hours, he became the most wanted man in San Francisco.

After Dr. Manley went home on Tuesday night—and Maggie had been stabilized in the ICU a short time later—the pace intensified, delivering an array of crises that took us through the night, into Wednesday morning, afternoon, and then the evening. Two of the cases required lengthy surgeries. One was a patient with subdural hematomas on both sides of the brain, already in very poor condition. The other was a patient who had been pistol-whipped. Here again the surgery of choice was to remove the left side bone to uncover the brain and evacuate a bleed.

Once we finished up in the OR, I went back to the emergency room to review some X-rays and see the patients in less critical condition who were waiting for me. At this point, now late on Wednesday night, I heard the police radio announcing that there were officers down.

Later I was able to reconstruct the night's events by putting together details I learned from the paramedics on the scene before the officers were brought in and from published accounts. The citywide search for Monte Haney had led to San Francisco's Mission District, not too far from the hospital, where he was spotted by a policewoman, who had called her precinct office. A dispatch for backup was sent out, notifying patrol cars in the area to respond code 3—with lights and sirens. Two patrol cars raced at high speed from different directions, neither aware of the other, as they closed in on the intersection of 17th and Dolores Streets.

Inside one of the two marked cars were police officer Jon Cook, thirty-eight years old, and another officer. Officer Cook had come in earlier in the evening and learned that due to a scheduling mix-up, he wasn't on the night's lineup. His boss told him, "Take the night off," and Officer Cook replied, "No, I'm here. I want to work." He insisted that he wanted to go fight crime and, as the officers often said, "catch some bad guys."

Officer Nick Ferrando, twenty-five years old, and his partner were in the second patrol car, just as intent on capturing and arresting the man who had gouged out the eye of the patient we were closely watching in our ICU.

It was there at 17th and Dolores Streets that these lives and stories would intersect. The suspect was eventually apprehended. In the meantime, the two patrol cars had collided with such speed and force that one had flipped over the other. As Officer Ferrando's car veered away, it smashed into a light pole, causing the pole to topple onto the car, crushing it on one side and causing Nick Ferrando to be ejected through the front side window and fly headfirst into a brick building.

Officer Jon Cook was pronounced dead on the scene. I later learned that he was the first openly gay police officer in San Francisco to die in the line of duty. Both the fellow officer in Cook's car and Nick Ferrando's partner sustained injuries but were expected to survive. But the report by the paramedics bringing Officer Ferrando in told us that he was essentially dead on arrival; the technical assessment was that he was comatose at a Glasgow Coma Scale 3, which could be considered a formality in preparation for pronouncing him dead. Besides causing the massive head trauma, the crash had shattered both his femurs.

Even before the two ambulances arrived and the four policemen were carried in through our doors, we knew how to marshal our forces—with a death to certify, two officers to be cared for by the emergency room crew, and Nick Ferrando requiring lightning-fast action by me and the rest of the neurosurgery team. With Nick showing barely any brain function, our first step was to get him medications that could significantly reduce the brain swelling while rushing him to the CT scanner. Time and space vanished as I stepped out of the darkened room where he lay motionless during the CT scan. Watching him through a window, I scanned the readouts on the computer screens next to me as the captured images of the brain passed like a movie in slow motion on the monitor in front of me. Behind me was a blue wall of police officers, pressing in to watch my every move. With several higher-ups also standing by and adding to the pressure, I managed to convey a sense of calm and to transform the adrenaline pumping through my body into fine, precise decisions. At first glance, everything looked as disastrous as expected— signs of massive brain trauma, nothing hopeful. But as I looked more closely at Nick, I thought I saw the tiniest flicker of movement in one of his fingers. Yes, as I focused more intently, I saw the finger move ever so slightly.

A flicker of hope! I can still recall the jolt of adrenaline this sign of life gave me. If we could rush Nick Ferrando into surgery and remove a bone flap to give his brain room to swell, we stood an outside chance of preventing fatal brain damage. As I led the way and wheeled his gurney into the OR, all of us on the neurosurgical team lived lifetimes in each second. A powerful combination of chaos and elegance, the journey into the OR was a race against the clock, requiring us to take every possible measure to minimize the brain swelling as we moved.

Breathing heavily yet energized, I heard the pounding of my heart as a form of music, and I used its beat to keep me focused and—like the conductor of an orchestra—to direct the many jobs we now had to perform. I took inspiration from the way in which Gus had orchestrated all the maneuvers necessary to save my life when I lay at the bottom of the tanker. This time, Nick was the one fighting deep within his psyche and soul to remain with us, and I felt tied to his struggle.

Ready to move the second he was on the operating table, we were in surgery until the early hours of Thursday. When I joined my senior attending physician to talk to Nick's family members after the surgery, I told them the truth about their young son and brother: "I am not sure we will pull him through this, but we are going to do our best for him and you shouldn't give up hope."

We still had four more surgeries to complete that night. When Geoff Manley arrived on Thursday morning, we continued our efforts to save Nick Ferrando's life, taking him into the OR again so that we could attach a device to the side of the head to monitor the pressure in his brain, which was dangerously high. When the orthopedic team later took Nick back to the OR for repair of his leg fractures, we had to be at his bedside, monitoring him 24/7 because of his comatose state. Our work was far from done.

For the next six weeks, I was part of the team that monitored his condition minute by minute. Either standing or sitting by his side, sometimes taking his hand and calling his name, I kept up the watch for signs of life and awareness as he lay comatose. Hours blended into days and days blended into weeks, with no indications that he could hear the voices of his family members or any of the physicians, nurses, and caregivers who continually talked to him. At the same time, we had no indication that he couldn't hear us.

Then, on a day like any other day, I stopped by to check the readings from the monitors and took his hand, greeting him as usual with "Nick! Hey buddy, squeeze my hand, Nick. Okay buddy? Just squeeze my hand. Let me know you're in there, Nick."

As suddenly and drastically as a disaster can strike, something incredible happened. On this day like any other day, he squeezed my hand, and his eyes fluttered open. Blinking rapidly, he then opened his eyes wide and looked at me, as if to question why this man he didn't know was holding his hand! My joy was boundless, as I welcomed him home, back from his long, strange time away.

The next time I saw Officer Nick Ferrando, about two months later, he appeared in my office—walking and talking. This time, after weeks of physical rehabilitation and some speech therapy, he seemed almost to remember me, as if in a part of his psyche we had already met. We talked like old friends as he told me about the rapid progress he was making and said he couldn't wait to get back on the force and go catch bad guys.

Within four months, around Christmastime, Nick returned for the last of several neurosurgeries to have the piece of his skull bone replaced, and subsequently he went back to a desk job within the police department. Within two years, Officer Nick Ferrando returned to the field—where he is today.

Within the year that Nick returned to work, a series of ceremonies and presentations took place honoring the work done by Dr. Manley and me, along with that of the entire trauma service. A most treasured acknowledgment was the plaque I received from the police department bearing a quote by Vince Lombardi: "The quality of a person's life is in direct proportion to their commitment to excellence, regardless of their chosen field of endeavor."

Though greatly honored, I felt the awards and commendations belonged not just to everyone on the various teams that had provided support to Nick, but to the leadership of our mentors who had been training those of us on the front lines. Nick's case had put to the test everything I'd learned to date, and having the triumphant outcome that it did was a needed validation at that time that the struggles of training were paying off. I also liked the idea that those of us who battled disease and injury were going after bad guys too—an observation that would shape important decisions that were on my horizon.

In addition to receiving the plaque and the commendations, I was given a business card that had the direct office phone number of one of the police force higher-ups, along with a personal note on the back that read: "Any courtesy that you can extend to Dr. Quiñones will be highly appreciated."

Sticking it in my wallet for safekeeping, I did not have occasion to show the card until years later when I was pulled over for going forty-five miles per hour in a thirty-five-mile-per-hour zone in Yosemite. When I handed the officer my driver's license, I decided to give the card a try too. The officer glanced at it, went back to his patrol car, made a phone call, and then returned to me, handing everything right back.

"Thank you," he said, "we're so lucky to have doctors like you. Please continue your wonderful work."

·   ·   ·

One patient—whom I will recall by his initials, JO—crossed my path at a pivotal time when I was deliberating about what direction to take after my six years of residency were over. When Dr. Mitch Berger brought me in on his case, I had little idea that this young man's journey would change my worldview.

A first-generation Mexican-American, JO was the son of migrant farmworkers who had first settled in Salinas. Twenty-one years old, living in Oakland, he was a shining star—a good-looking, brilliant engineering student at the University of California, Berkeley. Full of promise and great prospects, he was the pride and joy of his family. He had also been healthy throughout his life, until he suddenly presented with a full-blown seizure. Like many patients diagnosed with brain tumors, JO had no inkling that anything was wrong until the seizure hit him, at which point he was taken to a hospital, where a large mass was discovered in his brain. From there, his case had been transferred to us. Dr. Berger wanted me to participate so that I could be a liaison with JO's family members, who spoke only Spanish.

Through different types of imaging and analysis of a tumor's general shape, location, and involvement with nearby brain structures, we can make educated guesses about what we're likely to find when we open a brain in surgery. Our review of JO's films showed us that we were probably dealing with one of the more menacing beasts that come to live and grow in the brain: a glioblastoma multiforme, or GBM. But until a biopsy of the tumor confirmed our suspicions and gave us other information, we wouldn't be able to measure its dangerous properties or know how best to fight it.

As JO showed no speech loss, Dr. Berger opted to perform an awake craniotomy, the same procedure Dr. Peter Black had invited me to observe the first time I saw brain surgery back in medical school. Assisting Dr. Berger with surgery as he asked JO questions in English and Spanish, I was also able to help translate. As JO answered, we would touch his brain with electrodes and find where the control centers were located for identifying words and pictures. We needed to avoid these areas— as well as those that controlled memory, sight, smell, logic, and motor control—while still battling the tumor. Dr. Berger removed the tumor with such tactical skill that JO came out of surgery with his capacities intact, returned to the state he had been in before the tumor had been discovered.

Now the hard part began. The likelihood that this kind of malignancy would recur was high, and we feared that the question was not *if* but *when*. We could buy time by ordering postsurgical radiation and chemotherapy, yet how could I explain the bleak prognosis without further devastating JO and his parents? JO's parents reminded me of mine—for obvious reasons. Their son and I were different in that he had come here as a child, but he embodied for his parents the same hopes and possibilities that I did for mine.

What could you say to parents in danger of losing their pride and joy, parents who had devoted so much hard labor, sweat, and tears to make a better life for their son, to help him attain the American dream? I couldn't lie to them and suggest that everything was going to be okay. I could only tell them that we would stand by them and their son no matter what happened and that we weren't going to give up.

The brain tumor came back about six months later, sooner than we expected. Its reappearance was a blow to their morale, squeezing out their hope that the earlier surgery would be a one-shot battle. I assisted Dr. Berger in a second surgery. But now with JO understanding that he was fighting for his life, everyone's spirits plummeted. His family members knew where the road was going to end, and it was breaking everyone's hearts.

Over the next year, JO hung in there, going through one more surgery. This last battle followed the same pattern but with diminishing returns; time was running out, and the enemy was gaining strength. When JO came in for one of his last appointments, his face reflected his exhaustion. He was not yet twenty-three, but he was broken. He was the same courageous and strong person, a young man of true character. But his looks were being taken from him, as every part of his body began giving out and giving up, robbing him of his youth. He was still mentally sharp and knew he was going to die.

JO asked how much longer he had to live.

A block in my speech center left me without words. I honestly didn't know.

With his mother and sister sitting at his side helplessly, JO looked at me, his eyes full of tears, as I took his hand in mine. We sat in silence, tears streaming down all our faces. It was our good-bye.

That night, driving home, I was not only brokenhearted, I was angry. At what or at whom, I wasn't sure. Maybe at myself. Maybe I expected too much from medicine. I had thought I would know more by now. I didn't expect to save the world, but I at least wanted to do my part. At that moment, I realized I had to expand my vision. I couldn't simply hope and dream about fighting brain cancer some day; I needed to take more focused action to defeat it. Sometimes a single patient can inspire such a moment of clarity. For me, that patient was this young man, who was about to change my direction and who, I wanted to believe, was going to leave a legacy that would change science.

Because of JO, and a new sense of urgency to seek treatments and a cure, I had to make research a more important part of my arsenal. Becoming a brain surgeon, alone, wasn't enough to battle the devastation of brain cancer. After all, as I told Anna when I got home, "Anybody can do brain surgery!"

"Anybody?"

"Not anybody," I agreed. "But you can do it if you are well trained. If you are methodical and you can remain calm and can remain focused, you can do it!" Building the argument from there, I explained why I needed to take my fight into the laboratory.

As I recall that point in our conversation, I broke down in tears again. After sitting with me in silence for several minutes, Anna finally spoke. "Alfredo, in working with brain cancer, you'll be specializing in an area in which many of your patients will die. Are you sure that out of everything you could pursue, this is where you want to go?" I would be asked this key question by many of my professors and by various institutions that would offer me appealing opportunities to pursue other paths in neuroscience. The only way to answer with certainty, again, was by discovering the weapons that research could provide. The one-pronged approach, clearly, wasn't going to cut it.

Combining research with neurosurgical training, the one-two punch— as Dr. Michael Lawton would have called it—was an approach that some residents avoided. Research was seen as slow-going, painstaking work and was nowhere near as immediately exhilarating as brain surgery. And researchers didn't enjoy the rock-star status that came with wielding the scalpel. But if the multipronged approach—doing what I liked to do—wasn't going to make me a rock star, so be it. I would still be able to rock 'n' roll! For those reasons, I decided to use my fifth year to do a postdoctoral fellowship in research at UCSF, with yet another mentor who arrived in time to bring me down to earth about what real research was going to entail. If I had fantasized that I would be struck by a brainstorm that would allow scientists to unravel the cause and cure for cancer, I lost this illusion quickly. At first, I even wondered if it was one of those "be-careful-what-you-wish-for" situations when I came under the mentorship of the brilliant Dr. Arturo Alvarez-Buylla.

Like Dr. Berger, Dr. Alvarez set the bar extremely high. He was a countryman, a native of Mexico, but had taken a much different journey from mine. His grandfather had been a governor in Spain and had been assassinated by the Franco regime, leaving Arturo's father to flee to Russia for his education before going to Mexico. Dr. Alvarez had studied in Mexico, Canada, and the United States, doing graduate work at Cornell before moving on to a post with the Rockefeller Foundation—where he was when Dr. Mitch Berger discovered him and saw the visionary stem-cell neurobiology research he was overseeing. At UCSF, he would develop such innovations as a device for mounting tissue sections and a computer-based mapping system for studying those tissue sections.

When I started my research, full of great expectations and ready to conquer the world, Dr. Alvarez didn't take long to assert that I wasn't ready. He wasn't in the least impressed that I was an up-and-coming hot-shot in the eyes of others. In the laboratory, such fanfare was incidental.

A straightforward, no-nonsense teacher, Dr. Alvarez also had great kindness in his heart—which I had seen in the way he had cared for his wife one day when he brought her into the emergency room with a severe infection in her finger from a dog bite.

Having seen that side of him, I found it easier not to take it personally when he challenged my work on every level. Meanwhile, I had to relearn lessons about patience, as well as face reminders that laboratory work doesn't offer the immediate results and drama of brain surgery—that heart-stopping moment when a patient wakes up or not or the post-op MRI that gives proof of your handiwork. Scientific research is much more plodding and requires a long-term vision—a sense of where your work should take you, not tomorrow or next month but over years of small daily discoveries.

Dr. Alvarez recognized my sincerity in wanting a day when we wouldn't need to operate to treat brain tumors. But he was fast to point out deficiencies in how I pursued lines of research. Whenever he found me searching out paper topics or comparing research ideas on the Internet, Dr. Alvarez would say, "Get away from the computer. You're not going to learn anything that way."

In hindsight, I realize he wanted me to work on the basics—to use my hands, my brain, and my creativity to explore the world, as Cajal would have wanted me to do. But, to no one's surprise, I still only moved in two speeds—fast and faster. So at the time, his constant admonitions that I was in too much of a hurry were maddening. If I dared to bring him data that I had not carefully analyzed—just ideas that I wanted to run by him—Dr. Alvarez would send me away, dismissing my thoughts as garbage!

After a while, I wondered whether going against the grain by pursuing a dual path of surgery and research was a mistake. Perhaps research wasn't for me. Frustrated and unsure, I felt I was staring into a void, fooling myself into thinking that I could make a difference.

Then one day in the lab Dr. Alvarez walked by when I was looking at a brain tissue sample under the microscope.

In his no-nonsense way, he asked, "What do you have?"

"I'm not sure yet," I answered honestly.

"You've been standing there for how long and you're not sure of what you've got? Open your eyes! You need to pay attention and keep your eyes open to what's right in front of you."

I had no idea that what I was about to observe was going to be almost as exciting as my first look at a human brain.

"Let me have a look," Dr. Alvarez said, and as I stepped away, he took over, looking through the eyepiece at the tissue sample from a patient's diseased brain. Within two seconds, Dr. Alvarez located what he wanted me to find and put his arrow on it, asking me now to have a look.

There, on the slide, was magnified movement! For the first time, I was seeing what Santiago Ramón y Cajal and his American contemporary, Harvey Cushing, had each written about—keys to the kingdom for any neuroscientist intent on unraveling the mysteries of the brain.

"Well?" asked Dr. Alvarez. "What do you see?"

What I saw was something like the starry night sky I had stared up at as a child, complete with the equivalent of a tiny speedy star in the midst of the others. Now I had a name to describe the fast-moving one, as I told Arturo Alvarez, in awe of the implications, "A migrating neuron!"

He nodded, as if to say, *You see?* We had just taken a quantum leap in identifying a single moving young neuron in a sea of cells in adult brain tissue—whose existence had been hypothesized before but had not been witnessed in this way. A door to another universe had been opened, multiplying the possibilities for exploration. In the months that followed, working under Dr. Alvarez's guidance, we confirmed the existence of stem cells in the human brain, which wasn't known before. We established that the areas in the brain where stem cells are found are organized very differently in humans than in rodents—also not known before.

Throughout this process, I often returned in my mind to that moment when Dr. Alvarez had asked me to take a look at the movement on the slide under the microscope and asked if I could see it.

Yes, I remember nodding in response, dazzled. My eyes were opened. I had seen the light.

.   .   .

"Why are you so driven?" my dear friend and colleague Dr. George Edward Vates IV once asked me. I asked myself this question more and more often as I entered my sixth year of residency and faced an even crazier obstacle course than anything I'd encountered in the preceding five years. As I made my dash toward the finish line, I was not only training as second in command to the generals but was also continuing the power weekends at the community hospital, writing papers, overseeing research, mentoring others, and trying to decide what I would do when my training days were over. Moreover, I was driven to be a better husband and father—probably the area where I was failing the most.

When Ed had originally asked me this question, I hadn't been able to articulate why it was so ingrained in me to make every second count and grab every opportunity to learn and improve. So I shrugged and joked, "Me, driven? What makes you say that?"

Though he laughed, I could see that he was serious. "Look," he said, "I'm speaking as your friend and as a physician." He had reviewed the lab work from my checkup. "Your cholesterol is high, and I'm concerned about hypertension in your future."

Dr. Vates didn't have to remind me that my father had undergone heart surgery for similar conditions about five years earlier. I knew Ed was right in saying, "You need to find some balance between what you do to care for others and caring for yourself." If I didn't, he warned, I'd be no good to anyone.

His words echoed in my mind as I started my last year—especially his advice to use my remaining time to focus on becoming the best brain surgeon possible and to prove to myself above all that I was battle ready.

In our earlier conversation, he had been most concerned about the moonlighting hours. But I had reminded my dear friend that the additional income was the only way we could get by. He understood that the typical resident's salary was barely enough to pay San Francisco rent for one person, let alone food and clothing for two adults and two children. And though neither one of us knew then, by the middle of my last year, Anna and I would have a third child on the way.

Ed had nodded thoughtfully, acknowledging that he understood, and then did something that I will never forget. He bolted from my office and returned shortly with a personal check made out to me. How could I accept this unbelievably generous gesture given the huge debt I already had for educational loans? Who knew when I would be able to repay him? We haggled for over a year. But finally, in this last year, Dr. Vates prevailed. By this point, I had dropped the hours on the weekends, as he had hoped, and had instituted changes in my regimen to improve my diet and get in some exercise. His loan enabled me to make the most of this last year of training—to prepare for the time when I would be able to run my own show. It was a gift of health and peace of mind, for which I will always be grateful. Some years later when I did repay the loan, I reiterated my feelings to him that some acts of kindness, like his, can never be fully repaid, especially when they're motivated by the desire to do something meaningful for someone else. Even though I have sought ways to live up to his example, I haven't yet. As I have said to Anna from time to time, "I will never be as good as Ed."

Though I didn't see it as clearly at the time, I came to the conclusion that mentors like Ed and Geoff were not only training me in the skills they had been taught but were teaching me to pass on my training. To that end, the team approach that I'd cultivated since childhood was more important than ever, and though I was tough in my expectations, everyone on the front lines with me knew I had their backs. But I did learn a lesson about how far this could go when I came to the defense of Dr. Frank Acosta after he determined that a patient's condition showed no cause for concern.

A younger colleague and longtime member of Q, Inc., whom I'd first met at Harvard, Frank was now a third-year resident at UCSF and continued to be like a younger brother to me. So when his decision about the patient was questioned, I felt justified in standing up for him—until I decided to have a look at the patient myself.

"Where is the patient?" I asked Frank and immediately saw that he didn't know. "Are you kidding me? You haven't seen the patient and I almost opened a can of you-know-what to defend you?"

"I carefully examined the CT and MRI scans and they were fine," Frank said sheepishly.

"We don't treat films! We treat patients," I reminded him. Although our subsequent examination of the patient confirmed his assessment, I was able to reinforce a lesson that I had learned early on and that I'm sure he would not forget. In fact, Dr. Acosta, now a neurosurgeon specializing in spine issues at Cedars-Sinai in Los Angeles, uses the story in his own teaching!

With my sturdy band of brothers and sisters, I was tempted to continue at the University of California, San Francisco, after my residency—where I was established and was already part of a talented team. Dr. Geoff Manley was doing incredible work in neurotrauma and would have loved for me to join him, even though he knew that I wanted to focus on brain tumors. But would that entail staying on at UCSF or involve a move to a setting that would give me greater autonomy? I imagined Tata Juan sitting across from me and knew that he would urge me to go where the road hadn't yet led.

Everyone had a different opinion about where that might be. The mentor who held the most sway was Dr. Michael Lawton. He told me to aim high. When I expressed my concern about having to establish myself all over again in a new program, Dr. Lawton pointed out, "From the time you arrived here, you've shown your greatest strength under hardship, and when given opportunity, you capitalize on it."

In a rare yet welcome pep talk, he reviewed the many publications I had under my belt, including the twenty to thirty papers on which we had collaborated. Dr. Lawton was certain that this work would be a strong foundation wherever I went—the academic presence, surgical talents in the operating arena, the stem cell studies I'd been doing, and the drive to bring the discoveries from the bench to the bedside. He believed that I'd gotten the best pearls from the important influences at UCSF and would be all the more attractive to other institutions as a result. Then he gave me a list of places where he thought I'd fit well, with Johns Hopkins at the top of the list. I took the suggestion to heart. He had gone to medical school at Hopkins, as had his grandfather.

Michael Lawton's advice was particularly meaningful because he would have loved for me to follow in his footsteps as a neurovascular specialist. In fact, I had been flown to the Mayo Clinic for an interview and was asked to consider an appealing position there—but in neurovascular surgery. Dr. Lawton knew that wasn't what I wanted to do. Perhaps the most decisive reason that I valued his input was my knowledge of his sister's losing battle with brain cancer. I could only imagine how excruciating it must have been for her brother, one of the most gifted neurosurgeons in the world, to have to stand by with time running out. Dr. Lawton's advice on where I should go mattered even more to me because he recognized that my mission was to change the odds of survival for people like his sister.

But I still had to answer the "Why Hopkins?" question. The consensus was that Johns Hopkins was the least likely setting for someone like me. But this was Dr. Lawton's point—that I would bring something different to the mix and thrive in the process.

Dr. Burchard seconded the motion, telling me, "Hopkins will challenge you, keep you on your toes. Otherwise, you'll get soft. And then someone will come along and take your job and your wife." Though he was joking, he knew the competitive side of me would respond!

But now I had to figure out why I should turn down other excellent offers and choose Hopkins—where I'd be starting as the fourth-string quarterback because the institution already had three world-class brain tumor neurosurgeons ahead of me. Going to Hopkins would be the equivalent of deciding to play for the New England Patriots with Tom Brady and two quarterbacks just like him already in line. I would have to start from the bottom again and prove myself.

Yet there were compelling reasons to take on this challenge. Two years earlier, I'd met one of the quarterbacks, Dr. Alessandro Olivi, who had sought me out at a conference to say, "When you're looking for a job, send me your *résumé*." From Italy, Alessandro Olivi is a kindred spirit—joyful, with a constancy of heart, passion for his work, and great respect for others. True to his word, Dr. Olivi brought me to the attention of the department head, Dr. Henry Brem, likewise a distinguished surgeon and scientist, also kind and personable, and they extended a warm invitation to me to join the department. Although I would start at the bottom, they made me feel that in terms of freedom to develop my own practice, expand my research interests, and teach in multiple related scientific disciplines, the sky was the limit.

Another plus was that Johns Hopkins, historically, was where modern Western medicine as it is practiced today had its beginning, where the concept of medical school had evolved, and where many pioneers of neuroscience had done groundbreaking work. Harvey Cushing, considered the father of neurosurgery, had been at Hopkins at the same time that Santiago Ramón y Cajal was in Spain—each contemplating the need for a system of classifying brain tumors. I loved the parallel between the two men and knew that a protégé of Dr. Cushing's, Percival Bailey, had gone to Paris to train under Cajal's disciples. When Bailey later returned to the United States, he approached Dr. Cushing and proposed a classification system for brain tumors based on criteria such as their location, composition and appearance, and rate of growth.

Another larger-than-life figure had worked under Cushing at Hopkins in the early 1900s, developing numerous surgical techniques that had altered neuroscience and the field of general surgery at the hospital. Dr. Walter Dandy had conceived the idea of the "brain team"—a patient-centered approach that coordinated the roles of the lead surgeon, residents, anesthesiologists, and nurses. He was a fascinating character known for his temper and his refusal to spend time away from work without his family. There were many stories about his children coming to visit him at Hopkins whenever they had free time.

Not only did the institution have an impressive history, but it continued to be at the cutting edge. Year after year, Johns Hopkins Hospital had been rated number one in the country by *U.S. News & World Report* and other organizations. The neurosurgery department was also rated number one, and the Johns Hopkins School of Medicine was close to the top as well.

I shared such particulars of my deliberations with my junior resident, Nader Sanai. On that occasion in March 2005, Nader and I were walking down the hall at Moffitt when I realized it was time to meet Anna and the kids outside the hospital for a quick hello. Pregnant with our third child, Anna had proposed the idea, noting that I could grab five minutes of fresh air while we showed Gabbie and David where I worked. By seeing me here, they'd know that I was fine and wouldn't worry about me when I was gone most of the time. Since Nader was a member of the extended family, I invited him to come along.

The plan was launched like clockwork. When Nader and I walked out the doors of the hospital, Anna, six-year-old Gabbie and three-and-a-half-year-old David were there to meet us. It was a blustery San Francisco spring day, not too sunny, not too cloudy—perfect for running around campus and blowing off some steam. The kids were excited, and Anna was in high spirits too.

"We brought you a present!" David said eagerly.

Gabbie rolled her eyes, telling her brother, "It was supposed to be a surprise!"

Anna smiled and presented the gift to me, a coffee mug with the words "World's Best Dad" on it.

As my eyes misted over, Gabbie mentioned that it wasn't even my birthday. David now rolled his eyes, saying, "That's because it was mommy's birthday."

Shock shot through me. I had forgotten my wife's birthday two days earlier. I was the biggest idiot in the world! As apologies and excuses poured from my lips, Anna stopped me. She simply shook her head and shot me a loving look. "Alfredo, I'm still here."

We hugged as I offered more apologies, and then, as always, it was time to get back to work. Racing with me back into the hospital, Nader gave me a disgusted look. That was all I needed to begin recruiting helpers to make sure that I didn't forget again and to set up reminders on several technical devices. Though my birthday record did not become perfect, I did much better after that.

But my improvement in that area wasn't going to resolve the dilemma that followed. After I made up my mind to leave the Bay Area and head to Hopkins, I found that Anna was adamantly against it. The timing was terrible for organizing a move to the other side of the country, to an unfamiliar city like Baltimore—with Anna still running the household on a shoestring and undergoing a very challenging pregnancy. After almost going into premature labor at twenty-seven weeks, she was on bed rest for the last trimester. Anna had also recently reconnected with her family in California and wanted our children to continue to be able to spend time with multiple generations of relatives on her side and mine. And with all the places we could have gone for the more rural, greener setting that she loved, plus access to great public schools, Baltimore wasn't on the top of her list.

After all the sacrifices Anna had made over the past eleven years, asking her for another leap of faith was no small consideration. But at the same time, when I visited Hopkins to see the lay of the land, I could feel the magic! Baltimore had its own richness—a history that went back to America's beginning as a true melting pot. It was second only to New York City in the number of immigrants it had taken in over the centuries. Parts of the city were rough and tumble, but on the whole, the spirit of the metropolis and of Hopkins made me feel at home. There was a pulse, a vibrant energy, and a future full of possibilities, even a feeling of destiny suggesting that this was where we were meant to go. We would have no guarantees that the days of struggles would be totally behind us. I could only promise to do everything in my power to make this move work and to plant us on a semblance of terra firma, where our children could grow up with a wonderful education and not have to move again—at least not right away. As I often tell anyone who wants to know my secrets for success, one essential is finding the right mate—as a friend, lover, traveling companion, and risk taker. Positive communication is vital. And so, after lengthy discussions, Anna once more took the leap to believe in me. As she balanced bed rest with child care and packing, still unhappy with the decision, I continued in the trenches for the last weeks of residency—determined to complete the remaining weeks of the six-year climb without any thoughts that I could have done more. The pressure was on!

As usual, everything happened at once. On June 19, 2005, a week before

I graduated from the residency program, our daughter Olivia arrived, managing, even as the tiny peanut she was, to quickly become the queen of the household. To express her displeasure with our other distractions, Olivia had a dramatic case of colic that complicated Anna's already difficult life. With all this turmoil, we decided that she and the kids would not attend my graduation festivities. Instead, I used the occasion as an opportunity to give due honor to my parents and my siblings, including my brother-in-law, Ramón, who was one reason I was alive to see this day.

Everyone in the extended Quiñones-Hinojosa family was jubilant. There was my father—the adventurer who had never stopped reminding me that each of us is the architect of our own destiny. And there was my mother—the ultimate survivor and dreamer who had taught me not to be afraid of adversity but to make something positive and powerful out of it.

All of my siblings had also been part of this journey, and each deserved to share in the victory—maybe none more than Gabriel, my best friend and closest companion the first half of my life. Together with our cousins, he and I had invented a place called Faraway—and here we were!

As I spoke, many of the nurses who had worked closely with me over the years wept and ran to hug my family! I don't know if any of the attending professors let their tears fall, but I heard a few manly and womanly sniffles. It was, without a doubt, a mountaintop moment for me. But before the reality could sink in, I had to grab a plane to Baltimore and find a place for us to live.

After I had looked at twenty-two houses in two areas that Anna had researched and that met her criteria, e-mailing her pictures of them throughout the day, I was just starting to think none of them were going to appeal to her when my cell phone rang. Anna was looking at a photo of the twenty-second house on the computer and declared immediately, "That's the one!"

And so I went back to San Francisco and said good-bye to Pepe the red pickup, as I watched my father happily drive off in the now almost eighteen-year-old truck. Then we loaded up our new minivan for its maiden cross-country voyage with my most important entourage.

A mix of emotions washed over us as we left the Bay Area. The jury was still out for Anna on our next destination. The past six years had been so grueling, and we had hung on to the thought that everything would be better once I started to earn a real living. But now, uprooted once more, we faced new uncertainties. Yet the spirit of adventure that had brought us this far was alive and well.

As we crossed the Bay Bridge to forge our way east, we started to laugh about the fact that we had a wonderful new house but no furniture. Anna thought we could camp in it for a little while. Then, with her interior design talents and budgeting know-how, we could buy quality furniture economically in the Amish country and at the many antique stores that covered the Northeast.

"Camping!" I said, excitedly. "Does that mean we could build fires and roast marshmallows?"

"Dad," Gabbie questioned, "did you ever go camping in your life?'

"Me? Go camping? I used to live in the wilderness, only eating what I could grow with my bare hands."

David piped up, "Were you a cowboy?"

"Yes!"

"Did you have a lot of gun battles?"

"Certainly!"

Anna said, "Not exactly."

No one bought the story that I could outrace a speeding bullet by riding around on a horse that was actually a three-wheeler motorcycle. But when I started telling the kids about how I'd come to this country in search of a better life, they listened just as intently. Even our tiny newcomer woke up from her nap and seemed content to hear the music of our voices as we drove through the heartland.

During the stretches when we weren't talking, I savored the silence and let my mind wander. The closer we came to our destination, the more vividly I thought of the past—remembering the twists and turns in the journey so far. Almost everything that had happened along the way suddenly appeared to have a purpose—showing me new connections, like puzzle pieces fitting together. Recurring questions about why certain events had to happen were starting to have answers—including the lessons from living with the fear of HIV infection and from being two minutes away from dying at the bottom of a railway tanker sixteen years earlier.

After promising never to talk about that day and managing to mostly avoid the memory, the time had come to rethink that decision. Until this point, I had referred to the main events of falling in the tank and waking up in the hospital in the abstract, but had never allowed myself to return to the scene of the accident. Other than the few words my father spoke to me about it afterwards, he too had avoided any references to the trauma. And though I did know that Ramón and Gus had played heroic roles in my rescue, neither of the two had ever recounted the details. Because they had acted out of selflessness, maybe they didn't want to detract from their intention by claiming credit. Another explanation for our collective reticence may have been a shared post-traumatic reaction and a shared superstition that speaking of the near-death experience might be a form of tempting fate. Perhaps this came from our cultural belief, reinforced by our Día de los Muertos celebrations, that after cheating death once, unless you can speak mockingly of it with rhymes and costumes, it's better to say nothing!

But the time had come to revoke my oath of silence, broach the subject with my father and Ramón, and open up the vault. Until I could face my fear of the past, I would remain in the dark about what had happened and would deny them the acknowledgment long overdue.

Behind the wheel of our new minivan—as I drove late into the second night of the trip with the rest of Family Q asleep around me—I realized that much of my thinking had been prompted by the fact that I had never thanked my relative Gustavo for his part in saving my life, and now it was too late.

A few months earlier, while I was traveling to various institutions and wrapping up my residency, I learned that Gus had died of brain trauma suffered in a motorcycle accident. After his many years of hard work, he had finally rewarded himself by buying a Harley-Davidson, the bike of his dreams, and on one of his first outings, he had been in a head-on collision that ended his life.

At the funeral, still sharp in my memory as I drove the minivan under the stars toward a new galaxy, I mourned over not being at the right place at the right time to operate on Gus. I would have fought with everything in me to give him what he had given me. Gus's graveside service had been held on a beautiful sunny day in Stockton, California, so much like the one in 1989 when he had taken command of the effort that saved me.

At the funeral, I had sat alone in the back, tears in my eyes and a knot in my throat, unable to talk to anyone. After the remembrances were over and all the mourners had paid their respects, I waited in my seat until the cemetery was nearly empty, trying to find a way to express my gratitude in honor of Gus's memory. My only consolation was that for everything that I wasn't able to do for him, I would fight that much harder for every patient to come under my care—with the same commitment that he had used in bringing me up from below.

Then I walked over to the grave, put a red rose on it, and left.

PART THREE Becoming Dr. Q

*First there is darkness. Then a beam from a bright white light illuminates the
overcast night. No, it's a pair of headlights—shining as if in a tunnel—that
momentarily blind me as they approach.*

*Shielding my eyes from the glare, I stand at the curb outside Boston's Logan
airport, where I've just stepped out into the freezing New England winter after
a red-eye flight from San Francisco. Within seconds, I realize that this ominous
image—which has become linked in my mind to terrible accidents—is merely the
approaching headlights from the town car that's been sent to drive me the ninety
minutes to Dartmouth. I exhale with relief, watching my breath disperse into the
night air, and wave to the driver.*

*As he pulls around to the curb, I take a second to question my decision about
making this trip. Two weeks earlier, when the Dartmouth faculty members*

extended the invitation for me to visit, I had debated the pros and cons. Asking for permission to leave UCSF for interviews at other institutions wasn't easy, especially because I had to find someone to cover my shift for me. Plus, I already had two appealing offers on the table. But something told me I needed to at least pay a visit to Dartmouth's campus and community, which I'd heard was ideal for raising a family. I was willing to rethink my decision to go to Hopkins if I thought Anna and the kids would be happier at Dartmouth.

Anna appreciated my logic but tried to talk me out of the trip. With my crazy workload, she felt that the twenty-four-hour turnaround wouldn't be worth the exhaustion. But after further discussion, we agreed that if I didn't go have a look, we might regret it later on.

And something else seemed to compel me to take the trip, although I couldn't put my finger on it. Whatever that "something" was, it still hadn't revealed itself to me by the time I leapt into the back of the town car and we headed out onto the open highway.

"A little nippy?" the congenial driver jokes as he turns up the heat in the car.

With a glance out the window, I detect storm clouds above us, leaving just a sliver of a moon. In these early hours of the morning, the town car is the only vehicle on the road, and our headlights offer the only relief from the darkness.

While I'm eager to arrive at the motel to sleep for a few hours before starting an early day, I'm thankful that the driver isn't trying to race through the mist and darkness. But instead of closing my eyes to rest, I decide to open my laptop and use the time to catch up on work.

Suddenly, out of the corner of my eye, I spot a pair of pale beams, the head-lights of another car, coming up from behind on our right. The car is approaching so fast—about eighty miles per hour, I estimate—that I figure the driver is intent on passing us. Why the hurry, especially with limited visibility? A small wave of fear flutters through me. Before I can banish it or chastise myself for not wearing my seat belt, the other car has reached our side and grazed the town car's back end, near where I'm sitting.

All hell breaks loose. When we lurch to the left and start to spin out of control at a tremendous velocity, I realize that we've hit a patch of black ice. My laptop flies out of my hands, and I hurtle to the other side of the car—with my bags jumping up and down—everything defying gravity and centrifugal force at the same time. Grasping for any thought to keep myself from imagining the worst—

that after surviving two major brushes with death my luck has finally run out and the end has arrived for me and my driver here in the middle of nowhere—I see that things are about to go from bad to worse. Not only have we begun spinning, turning, and sliding into a spiral, but the ice has propelled the other car into an equal and opposite violent spiral. And the two cars are now careening at top speed toward one another.

Again, as earlier, I'm staring at the lights at the end of a tunnel, but this time they're the blazing headlights of the other car as it comes perilously close to ours. Straining to find hope in the face of disaster, as I have in the past, I can only come up with images of operating rooms and the tragic consequences of traumatic brain injury caused by automotive accidents.

Why did I push myself to take this trip, only to hit a patch of possibly fatal black ice? Why didn't I listen when Anna told me not to go? I had two job offers already. Why did I have to pursue this one too? What am I supposed to learn that the forces of nature seem hell-bent on teaching me?

Could the lesson be that no matter how much mastery any surgeon or scientist attains, there are moments when you can't fight nature—either on your own behalf or that of your patients? Maybe. Now that I've overcome most of the obstacles of my training, could this nightmare scenario be a final test that I need to pass before I can go on to mentor others, build a practice, and empower patients in their battles? Perhaps.

And without asking too much, might I also ask whether my driver could possibly have a degree of expertise in navigating these unpredictable patches of black ice?

As soon as I ask this practical question and think of the patients who place their faith in the hands of their physicians every day—the crash inches away—I know at last that the time has come to accept everything that I can't control. Everything. And to surrender.

No sooner do I surrender to forces bigger and more powerful than me than both cars instantaneously careen out of their icy twirling and come to an abrupt halt! What? How is this possible according to the laws of physics?

We emerge from our town car, as does the driver of the other car, speak to each other briefly, exchange information, everyone panting with relief and disbelief and the cold, and then return to our cars and carry on. Slowly, I might add!

The entire episode, including the visit the next day at Dartmouth, which, of course, didn't change my family's plans, was prominent in my thoughts on the eve of my start at Johns Hopkins.

The lessons that had been reinforced for me during this extremely close call, I suspected, were going to be guiding lights up ahead. But if there was a clearer explanation for why I had to face this test in the middle of nowhere, it remained a mystery.

But it wouldn't forever.

ELEVEN Hopkins

"Dr. Q, you're the attending neurosurgeon on call for this weekend, correct?" said the voice on the phone late on Friday, July 29, 2005.

Six years earlier, I had felt great trepidation hearing similar words on my first night on call as an intern at San Francisco General Hospital. Back then, the mere thought of examining a patient with a gunshot wound to the head had almost made me consider turning back as I walked down the stairs to the ER.

But this time, the question, asked by a staff member in the emergency room at the Johns Hopkins Hospital, was whether I was the *attending* neurosurgeon on call. Not the resident or surgeon in training, but the attending professor, the number one person in charge when any neurosurgical emergencies came in! This new role was incredibly exciting though slightly daunting, and I listened intently to the description of the symptoms of Mr. O, who needed to be seen right away.

Within minutes of hanging up, I sprinted down the grand hallway of Phipps, one of the oldest and most storied buildings on the Johns Hopkins Medical Campus. Having arrived only days earlier, I had planned to take all of August to settle into my new digs as an assistant professor of neurosurgery and oncology at the Johns Hopkins School of Medicine and then to build my surgical practice and, eventually, a research laboratory from there.

In my status as fourth-string quarterback in a department with three well-established and distinguished neurosurgeons, I had no illusions about how easy this was going to be. But then again, I was a veteran at arriving as low man on the totem pole and having to prove myself! Or so I told myself while dashing into the hospital, leaving the humid Baltimore evening air behind and entering the cool, air-conditioned hospital lobby as throngs of visitors and employees headed for the exits, all eager to get home for a restful summer weekend.

Hurrying down the corridor toward the stairs to the emergency room, I felt a surge of pride when I came upon a sight that would become a touchstone for me: large mounted posters lining both sides of the hallway that proclaimed Hopkins the number one hospital in the nation as rated by *U.S. News & World Report*. Not just in the current year, but year after year, poster after poster! Only time would tell whether I had what it took to hold my own at this institution. But in the meantime, I was confident that if my goal was to play a significant role in the search for a cure for brain cancer, I'd come to the right place.

Nevertheless, the sight of those posters that first night on call was also nerve-wracking. Not that being scared was all bad. As Cesar Chavez once said, "If you're not frightened that you might fail, you'll never do the job. If you're frightened, you'll work like crazy!"

With the echo of those words firing me up, I went to meet Mr. O and his family. For any attending surgeon taking on a first official case, it's always preferable to start with a relatively simple, clear-cut operation—just as boxers begin with the easier fights and work up to the championship rounds. As it turned out, once I'd examined Mr. O, I was starting with a championship fight—an extremely difficult case.

Mr. O was a janitor at the University of Maryland, getting ready to retire, whose children had brought him in when he suddenly stopped talking, had a seizure, and became unable to move his right leg or arm.

When I asked him a question, he would struggle to answer but was only able to say "Sorry" repeatedly. Though he had no loss of comprehension and could understand abstract ideas, he was unable to coordinate his vocal cords and mouth to form words. Because the brain tumor we discovered in this visit had gone undetected for some time, it had become so large and destructive that it was not only bearing down on the part of his brain that controls speech and right-sided motor control but was causing so much swelling that the normal plumbing channels that irrigate the brain were backing up and overflowing. So, aside from addressing the tumor, I knew that within the next twenty-four hours, we first needed to operate to fix his brain's plumbing system. We would then take out the tumor.

We scheduled the two stages of the operation for early the next morning, knowing that we would need many hours to complete the surgery. I discussed the particulars with Mr. O and his family, outlining the risks, discussing his fears, and laying out the potentially negative outcomes that are the realities of neurosurgery—from the chance that neurological deficits would remain even after successful surgery to the risk that he wouldn't wake up. But Mr. O and I agreed, in a pact that set a powerful precedent for me from then on, that when I met him in the OR in a little more than twelve hours, we would go in together as gladiators: he and I would combine our positive energy, working in partnership, each doing our best to achieve the best possible outcome.

"Deal?" I asked. With effort, he mouthed the word, "Deal," as his children nodded stoically.

No matter how many brain surgeries I had been involved in—opening, closing, or assisting the attending surgeon in every aspect of neurosurgery—everything changed for me on the morning of Saturday, July 30. Thanks to Dr. Henry Brem, chair of our department, I had quickly been able to assemble an outstanding group. As we were new to one another, I took extra time that early morning to prepare my team members for every step in the two stages of the surgery so that we could move like a SWAT team, as expeditiously as possible. Before everyone entered the operating room, I went in alone and visualized where each one of us needed to be, surveying the layout and assessing the instrumentation,

machines, surgical tools, and equipment. I had done this type of planning before in service of other attending surgeons, but now I was doing
it as the head of the team—a totally different experience.

Even though the second stage, the removal of the tumor, would be
the tougher of the two, the first stage proved to be the more memorable
because of the metamorphosis it caused in me. None of my mentors had
ever described to me their experience of walking into the OR for the
first time as the general in the war, no longer the second or third in
command. Maybe they hadn't described it because the moment is so
personal, a walk down the razor-sharp edge between confidence and
arrogance. As the attending surgeon, you must summon superpowers
on behalf of your patient, while never forgetting that you are human
and fallible. The challenge is to rally your highest levels of energy while
maintaining perfect calm and control—a combination that lets you bend
time and space so powerfully that you could dodge a speeding bullet—
like Keanu Reeves in *The Matrix!*

The change began that morning as I went to scrub at the sink just
outside the OR. I had felt the energizing effects of this ritual many times
during my training, but this time—and from here on—my senses took a
quantum leap in intensity as I scrubbed vigorously, up and down each
arm, getting the blood going, feeling my heart beating, and breathing
more rapidly. All distractions washed down the drain as I rinsed my
hands and arms and dried off with a sterilized towel. By the time I
entered the OR, put on sterile surgical gloves, and made sure Mr. O was
sterile-prepped, I was no longer the person I had been. My voice had
changed. When I caught a glimpse of my face on a monitor, I hardly recognized the intensity and urgency in my eyes. The minute I cut through
the skin, opened Mr. O's skull by drilling multiple small holes to remove
the bone flap, and then peeled back the dura, the velvet-textured covering of his brain, I saw time was of the essence. His brain was dancing
frantically. Because the tumor had blocked the drainage system, the fluid
that normally surrounds the brain was flooding the tissue; the brain
was bloating rapidly, mushrooming with pressure at a dangerous pace.
Making sure my resident kept suctioning the blood, I made a little hole
in the plumbing system and, as if popping a balloon, was able to redirect

the water flow around the tumor; the swelling immediately began to decrease. But we had a mess to mop up before we would successfully meet our surgical goals in this first stage.

Round one went to the Q Team. But round two was a dogfight. Because of the large size and entrenched nature of the tumor—which we would soon know was, as feared, a high-grade glioblastoma multiforme—and because it had rooted itself in the areas controlling speech and motor control, I knew that removing it was going to be a brutal, protracted process. If the tumor had been detected earlier (or symptoms had shown up), we could have opted for an awake craniotomy, which would have helped us map the brain ahead of time and use Mr. O's answers to questions during surgery to guide us safely along the right path. But with his speech already failing, he had to be asleep, and I had to move at microscopic increments, along a much more treacherous route. Another issue of concern was that because of the frequency of seizures—caused by the encroachment of the large tumor—there was an increased possibility that Mr. O. could seize during surgery, the tumor much like a hidden land mine exploding under the touch of the scalpel. The key quality needed at this moment, epitomized by my mentors, was what some call the eye of the tiger, an ability to bring hyperfocus to what really matters in the OR—the patient—and to unleash one's skills to bring the best possible outcome. For me, this translated into the need to move around the brain in a kind of neurosurgical dance that matched that of the patient's brain, to orchestrate all the other moving parts of the operation, to observe the big picture as well as the details, and to communicate without words to ensure that everyone on the team was in sync.

For the last two years of my training at UCSF, Dr. Michael Lawton had mentored me in the magical arts of what I refer to as the astronaut chair—or "the throne," as some call it. For long surgeries, which can go eight hours or longer, the chair can literally be a lifesaver. As you sit in the chair, tapping the left toes of your foot, you can control the zoom of the microscope in and out, and tap a special pedal for adjusting its magnification; in addition, the left foot can move the microscope side to side, left to right, and up or down at an angle. The dance requires partnering the left foot and the five functions it serves with—for example, the mouthpiece that moves the microscope in a circular motion, tilting it up or down. With the right foot, you control two panels that work with a miniwelding machine for closing off vessels and the like. Moving the right foot side to side engages another pedal that acts as an accelerator for suctioning very hard brain tumors. Meanwhile, as you sit in the chair, your hands are free to operate multiple controls for managing the intensity of the suction and the welding machines. The chair allows you to use all four extremities and your mouth to fully connect to your patient. One incremental surgical move might employ your whole body in the chair—as you adjust the microscope, manipulate the brain, create an open space, go in with the scalpel in your right hand, and then suction with the foot pedal and thumb force.

Astride the throne during the second stage of Mr. O's surgery, I thought about how powerful memory could be as a weapon in a life-or-death battle. Mr. O's survival memories had prepared him to fight the enemy; my memory kept selecting data from the past to guide me when all roads appeared blocked and to give me insights into what might be on the other side of a structure in his brain. Memories surfaced not just from training but also from working on car engines as a child, pulling weeds, driving tractors, shoveling sulfur and scraping fish lard, repairing and welding the lids of railway tankers—and figuring out how to hop all kinds of fences. Some of the pertinent data came from seeing Nana Maria energized by her work as a *curandera*, even after being on her feet all night, and imagining the way in which she lived, breathed, and became one with her patient. Some of it even came from stargazing up on our roof on hot nights and dreaming of traveling into the future in my astronaut chair.

Before closing, we did our janitorial work for Mr. O, making sure we welded shut any small bleeders, contained any other oozing passageways, and left behind medications to prevent swelling and promote healing—along with a cancer-fighting chemotherapy wafer that had been developed by our Hopkins department head, Dr. Henry Brem. With one last look around, I was satisfied with the resection of the tumor, which had allowed us to get everything we could see with our eyes and with the microscope, while keeping the thinnest of outlines of where it had been. This thin layer prevented us from touching any of the parts of his brain that controlled important functions and acted as a guide when we inserted medication to seal off the area, also performing as a firewall to keep the aggressive cancer from growing back in the same place.

Then came the ultimate test for Mr. O: waking him up. No matter how perfectly any surgery goes, success or failure is defined by whether patients wake up and how they wake up. No matter how many times I have gone to wake patients after surgery, I still feel anxiety until the moment that they open their eyes. The greatest test is whether they can follow simple commands, such as squeezing my hand or holding up two fingers. To my great satisfaction, Mr. O awoke easily—just from my hand on his shoulder as I called his name. Even better, he immediately greeted me, saying softly but surely, "Hi, Dr. Q."

When I asked how he felt, he answered without a moment's hesitation, "Good. When can I go home?" He could talk again! His right-sided movements were back too. While this was an optimal outcome and not a bad way to start out on a championship-type case at Hopkins, there were going to be more bouts for Mr. O. But what a heavyweight champion he turned out to be, battling with amazing fortitude for almost two more years.

He did so well at first, in fact, that I almost convinced myself that we had banished the GBM for good. Slowly and stubbornly, however, periodic seizures began, followed by the ebbing of his control over speech and muscle movements on the right side of his body. The last time I saw him in my office, Mr. O had something important he wanted to say, difficult though it was. With painstaking effort, he told me what the treasure of the last two years had meant to him. Soon it became clear that he was consoling me!

With my eyes watering, I sat looking at his droopy face, with his hair combed distinctly, wearing the Baltimore Ravens jacket that was his uniform, and I mourned for Mr. O. I wanted him to grow old, to see his grandchildren play, take them on hikes in the mountains, and then have them sit at his bedside in his final hours.

But he had made his peace. For most of his life, he had gone to work and acted out of duty to feed his children and send them to school, but he had been unable to see how much they appreciated him. The tumor was a gift, he seemed to be saying, that allowed him to experience how much he was loved and to express how he felt. He told me all this over the next thirty minutes—with every word spoken in parts. Now he knew that he had made a difference in his children's lives and that they would miss him and hold his memory in their hearts. And that made him the happiest he had ever been.

·   ·   ·

Coming in as the new kid on the block at Hopkins turned out to be an advantage for developing the kind of broad-based, multifaceted practice that I hoped to have. This was unfamiliar territory for me, as it can be for many starting faculty members at university hospitals, where the practical demands of establishing a clinical practice for seeing patients, scheduling surgeries, and being on call to cover a hospital's emergency neurosurgical needs all must be balanced with teaching responsibilities and overseeing the training of a department's residents. In the past, I had observed how established neurosurgeons *sustained* busy practices, but none of this demonstrated how to set up an office, hire staff, or let the public and the rest of the medical community know I was in business. Because these concerns were unfamiliar, I was forced to proceed carefully and slowly.

My colleagues began referring a range of surgical cases to me, from traumatic injuries and brain imperfections to brain and spine tumors and a host of other neurological concerns. In an era of ultraspecialization, this varied menu went against the grain. Never a bad thing in my opinion! It also gave me the opportunity to meet many more of the highly talented and devoted professionals across the Hopkins medical campus. Soon, thanks to a new rainbow of students, residents, and colleagues, Q, Inc. (aka the Q Team), was alive and kicking.

Early in my journey at Hopkins, I made the important decision to befriend my perpetual underdog status. In the past, I had allowed insecurities about my accent or background to make me feel that I wasn't going to measure up in the eyes of others. Those days, thankfully, were gone. Now I found that embracing who I was gave me confidence with the truth—that, of course, I had a strong accent and that, at heart, I was still a poor Mexican kid who came to this country with nothing and had a lot to prove. And that wasn't going to change—because in my view the worst thing that could happen was to let my guard down or to become complacent. I also knew that staying humble and staying hungry would keep me on my toes.

Now, as a self-assured underdog, when I walked into a room of Johns Hopkins's most renowned professors and world-famous neuroscientists and surgeons—all seemingly (but not really, of course) six feet three, light haired, and light eyed—instead of feeling embarrassed about my shorter stature, brown hair and brown eyes, and my impoverished background from a developing country, I started to think of these differences as a badge of honor.

Indeed, the principles and values instilled in me as a little boy were as relevant as ever. In fact, many of the people I sought out as mentors, as well as many of my colleagues, students, and patients, reminded me of important figures from my childhood. Although many of the people who had influenced me in my early life had been uneducated, they shared the quest for knowledge that I witnessed in the brilliant scientists and professors who populated Johns Hopkins University. Similarly, those who most inspired me as a child had endured hardships with the same courage and determination that I saw in my patients.

Those influences from my past were also reminders for me to acknowledge the great distance traveled to date. Anna and I had a lot to celebrate in our family life. Not many years earlier, when we had wanted to splurge and treat Gabbie to a trip to Burger King, we had been able to afford only one cheeseburger, which we wanted our toddler to enjoy. Those leaner days were behind us. We now had three beautiful, healthy children and no longer had to worry about putting food on the table or paying for a roof over our heads. The sacrifices were yielding real dividends, and we could focus on raising the kids in an environment in which they could flourish and grow to reach their potential.

In theory, I could say that the sacrifices were paying *only* dividends. But at this new stage of the journey, I had to acknowledge the dark side of being hyperdriven and overly goal oriented. For years, many of my closest friends and colleagues had warned me that I was in danger of neglecting other priorities. They didn't doubt my concern for the well-being of my loved ones but they pointed out that because my work was never done, there would always be someone or something outside of the family competing for my attention. They were right: at times my drive threatened to drive me rather than the other way around. This pathology is not rare among physicians, but it still takes a toll, especially on marriages. Anna and I simply had to agree not to ignore or sweep feelings under the rug, recognizing that we would pay a steep price if we did so.

Some of the members of the Q Team, residents and students, would come to me for relationship advice from time to time, asking in the process whether I would have done anything differently in trying to find the balance between work and family. My answer is twofold. First, yes, I've made many mistakes in achieving balance; and if I had it to do over, I would have cultivated a better habit of mindfulness about the everyday niceties—like remembering birthdays and anniversaries or making a point of calling home when an emergency brain surgery had me running to the OR and I would be late for dinner. Some of those basic measures are ones I'm still learning to take. But the second part of my answer is no, I wouldn't go back and rethink how I chose to focus my energies. I wouldn't advise myself or anyone else to tamp down even the loftiest dreams and goals.

Maybe I had once harbored the illusion that after my residency, I would have more time to enjoy hobbies and family while pacing myself in growing a new practice. Unfortunately, Anna and I discovered that getting started required as great an investment of time, if not more, as running a fully booked practice. Besides, if I had found free hours to play golf, I would have complained that the game does not move quickly enough for me! Nor have I ever been the sort to knock off early or run home immediately after clocking out.

Meanwhile, Anna didn't fall in love with our new life right away. More time had to pass before her routine with the kids and her connection to friends and neighbors would make her feel that we'd made the right decision. This period was rough going, with plenty of angst and frustration. One of Anna's ongoing complaints was about the anxiety of sitting up waiting for me to come home late at night, worrying that I'd fall asleep at the wheel and end up in a fiery crash. When work was especially stressful, I didn't want to hear that and would say so. Arguments ensued. Then Anna would stop complaining, which was worse. I was afraid I'd arrive home late at night to discover that she had packed up and returned to California with the kids.

Throughout these rough patches, we had two saving graces. First, we never doubted that we were the loves of each other's lives. Second, I never forgot that Anna's belief in me and constant support were the magical ingredients that would help me, and our family, turn dreams into realities. No matter how crazy my idea or vision, Anna would listen, contemplate the pros and cons, even close her eyes to mull it over, and then open them to look at me, revealing in her green sparkling eyes that she saw its possibilities too!

That was exactly how she had reacted when I described the multifaceted practice that I was going to build, even though I wasn't sure how. Anna's advice made perfect sense, as she nodded reassuringly and said, drawing on our mutual passion for movies, "If you build it, they will come."

.   .   .

After the first night of being on call at Hopkins and having to rush Mr. O into surgery that weekend, I anticipated that the next time I was on call, I was unlikely to have to perform another emergency operation as challenging as his had been. Wrong again! For my second case as a newcomer at Hopkins, instead of heading into the OR with a more controlled set of circumstances, I began with a nightmare scenario: a pregnant woman in her late thirties who had miscarried, setting off a violent domino effect. When she was brought into the OR, all her body's functions were readying to shut down, and she was on the verge of dying in my arms.

Twelve hours earlier, this healthy, lovely young woman—we'll call her SH—who had a bright and shining future, a career she loved, and a baby on the way, was stricken by a mysterious, unpredictable complication of eclampsia that caused her liver to work poorly, her blood to become as thin as water and lose its ability to clot, and then her body to miscarry. Like water rushing out of a burst dam, her bleeding appeared impossible to stop because of the loss of clotting ability. Every bloodstream, every tributary began to overflow, including those in her brain.

Surrounded by shouts of "Move, move!" I blasted orders for all troops to go to their battle stations as we transported her into the OR—seen by us as our own Roman Colosseum, where we were going to fight as if our own lives depended on it and if we lost our patient, she would die in our arms. Once we were all in place, even with our accumulated expertise, the atmosphere bristled with fear and uncertainty, as blood flowed from our patient's unconscious body, refusing to coagulate, soaking the table, and spilling onto the floor. To add to the chaos, phone calls from the deans of many Hopkins departments started coming in immediately. As I had learned, our patient's father was a prominent academic in the medical world, and everyone wanted updates. I knew very well from my training that no matter how nightmarish a case is, it can become dramatically worse when there is little order in the operating room, at which point the odds of achieving a positive outcome go from slim to none. Restoring order required almost a Kaliman maneuver; it was essential to assert an immediate sense of calm that was more powerful than the fear, not exactly with Kaliman's facility for mind control but something along those lines, so that we could proceed on a lifesaving surgical course. Restoring order was also going to entail opening up the skull and removing the bone to prevent her brain from imploding— exploding inward and assaulting her brain stem, at which point all life would end. Then we needed to get into her brain to stop the bleeding at the main site of the rupture—a process that could kill her before we could do anything to save her.

Feeling moderately encouraged after removing a bone flap from one side of SH's head, I peeled back the dura, hoping against hope that we had reached her brain in time. However, the situation immediately went from terrible to disastrous, as a fulminating volcano of blood spewed out.

Clearly, nature ruled the day at that moment. Currents of panic again seized the OR, with nurses, anesthesiologists, and brain-monitoring personnel trying to help but flailing against the flood. We needed to control the panic if we wanted our patient's chances of survival to increase, and I decided that if we could at least stabilize the systems that were shutting down, we could navigate the storm. Wanting every possible resource at our disposal, I called in Dr. Olivi, a world-renowned neurosurgeon, to assist with his experienced hands. In the meantime, as I gave the orders needed to keep everyone on track, I realized that this crisis was less about our heroics than about giving SH the means to be the hero, to be the miracle worker in her struggle to live. This subtle shift in my mental focus galvanized the team. In a matter of a few minutes, I was able to direct us out of the storm, from chaos to order. Now we could move expeditiously, administering a combination of blood-clotting medical products, in exact stages and with the right sequencing, to stop the explosion of blood.

By the time Dr. Olivi arrived, everything was under control. In his rich Italian accent, he used his personal nickname for me, asking, "How does it look, Alfredino? Are we going to get her out of the OR alive?"

At the beginning, I admitted to him, with the extent of her bleeding, I had seen no way to get her out alive. Now there was hope that we could. And with everyone's help, I was able to inform her family at the end of the surgery that though she was in a coma, we had stopped the bleeding and she was holding her own. But this calamity was far from over. Moving her to the neuro-intensive care unit, we left the bone flap off to allow her brain to push out, relieving any pressure that would permit further bleeds or explosions. But the team at the unit had its hands full with other issues, facing one crisis after another. SH's body was so traumatized that, although she was young, her heart began to fail, followed by her lungs and then her kidneys. She needed to have a tracheotomy and be on a respirator, and then to be attached to a dialysis machine and have a feeding tube inserted in her belly.

The family refused to give up on her. I was especially moved by her sister's continual presence and involvement. She never stopped believing that SH would come through as the ultimate hero. Right she was! Three months after being struck by the nightmarish syndrome, SH had stabilized to the point that she came out of her coma and could be taken

off the machines. We returned her to surgery to replace the bone flap
we had removed—the first step in her slow but magnificent recovery of
function and eventual return to an almost normal life.

SH's herculean struggle did not end when she left the hospital. She
required months of physical and speech therapy. But the remaining deficits—a limp and difficulty using one of her hands—have not prevented
her from returning to full-time work and to a rich life. She is an example
of why I feel privileged to be in this field.

Coming in rapid fire, these first two very difficult cases at Hopkins—
from a neurosurgical standpoint—served as rites of passage. They
altered my status as a fourth-string quarterback. Though I wasn't moving onto turf covered by the other three neurosurgeons, I wasn't going to
have to sit on the bench either—now that people were sending referrals
my way with heightened confidence.

Mr. O and SH, in different ways, taught me important lessons about
how to instill hope when all seems lost or impossible. They, along with
the growing number of patients who became part of my extended family,
also became part of the DNA for the practice as it evolved.

After all, if I didn't learn something from each patient about how to
provide better care, I would be missing valuable information. As I told
Anna on my cell phone during one of my late-night drives home after
many hours in the OR, though I couldn't build monuments to memorial-
ize patients, I could adopt aspects of day-to-day operations based on
what we learned from their journeys. Anna agreed with the positive
thrust of this approach—although she knew the subtext was the heart-
breaking case that had kept me late in the OR.

Even before we had gone into surgery for my new patient, a beautiful young model who had recently booked her first acting role in a
movie but hadn't shot it yet, I had been alarmed by the imaging of the
large tumor identified in the vicinity of her motor cortex, slightly above
the part controlling speech—and by her symptoms. Dragging her right
foot and too weak to lift her right arm, she also struggled to move the
right side of her face. We had determined that she had suffered a severe
stroke—actually *inside* the tumor, which had caused it to hemorrhage. I
had admitted her immediately.

If, as I feared, she had the highly aggressive form of brain cancer, surgery, followed by radiation and chemo, would only buy her time. How much I didn't know. There was a possibility that she would come through the surgery like a superstar and go on to do her movie role, and we were going to battle to make that happen. But when we had taken her into the OR and I saw the monster in her brain, I also knew it would return.

After Anna and I hung up, saying little about the surgery or the new patient, I drove on in silence. I recalled something Dr. Michael McDermott said toward the end of a long surgery at UCSF. Dr. McDermott—whose many gifts included an ability to develop strengths in others—was prone to powerful understatement. He and I, along with the rest of his team, had been in the OR for many hours and had just removed a gigantic brain tumor that was near the patient's eye and had been causing severe optical problems.

A neurosurgeon with many years' experience, Dr. McDermott had impeccably navigated the way in and out of the brain, and I was struck by the calm and control he'd maintained from beginning to end. When I took over to close, Dr. McDermott stood by, seemingly lost in thought. Both the MRI and CT scan for this patient told a discouraging story about the kind of tumor we could expect. We wouldn't be sure what type it was until we received the biopsy results, but its location and menacing appearance seemed to confirm the likelihood that, although the surgery would give the patient some relief and a little more time on earth, the tumor would come back in double strength, and probably sooner rather than later.

Not sure if that's what was on Dr. McDermott's mind or not, I turned to him after we were through and asked, "What are you thinking?"

"It never gets any easier," he revealed.

Conventional wisdom holds that the best coping method for physicians who battle deadly tumors is to learn to distance themselves—to create a wall between the job they must do and the reality of their patients' suffering. For all kinds of reasons, this approach didn't work for me, nor did it for Dr. McDermott. If anything, I wanted to tear down walls—or at least hop over them!—not build them. Disconnecting from my patients so that I would not feel their pain? This made no sense to me. How could I be a good physician if I denied my own humanity? Therefore, I understood why "It never gets easier."

That statement was in my mind when I arrived home to find Anna reading a murder mystery while she waited up for me. This wasn't her usual fare, but apparently it had caught her interest and was helping her stay awake and avoid worrying about me.

"You really don't have to wait up," I told her, not for the first time.

"I know, Alfredo," she said quietly and looked up at me.

Anna knew from our earlier conversation that I probably needed to go to sleep or to be alone and shed private tears. But she also knew that sometimes, as on this occasion, I might need to talk. Did I feel discouraged? Yes, I did. Searching for words, I haltingly told her that nobody can move forward without hope, not even somebody like me with a lot to prove. "Well," Anna asked, "what would give you hope?" I answered that giving my patients hope, empowering them somehow, would give me hope as well. Anna insisted that I was already doing this. But it wasn't enough, I argued, not with brain cancer, not when you're trying to stop a mass murderer with supernatural powers while you're still clueless about what went wrong to create the monster in the first place.

"What do you think needs to happen then, Alfredo?"

I explained that there was still so much research to be done before anyone could understand the origin of any brain tumor, let alone unravel the mysteries of the most lethal kinds. "The problem today is that we categorize tumors based on their appearance on a slide, with a system for understanding their pathology that uses technology devised a hundred years ago. This is how far behind we are." In the midst of my complaining, however, I had a hopeful thought. "But if we could understand at least one type of brain tumor and its origin, if we could figure out how a normal neural stem cell becomes an abnormal brain tumor stem cell— regardless of where it has come from in the brain—then we might be able to shift the balance of power." Thinking of the murder mystery Anna had been reading, I added, "We would then have some significant clues."

My wife nodded as she saw my wheels turning. Then we talked about my patient who had helped inspire this conversation.

Almost three years after that night, after the young model and actress shot her movie and did indeed live her life to the fullest, the killer returned with a vengeance. In rapid decline, she wanted another surgery, but it was not advisable.

I remember our last visit—how thin and frail she was as her mom wheeled her into the exam room. Remarkably, though, she still had the spark in her eye that had lit up the screen when she captured a dream that many others never attain. She had no regrets about how she had spent the time that had been given to her. Many who live to be ninety can't say the same thing.

When we hugged good-bye for the last time and I watched her and her mother go out into the cloudy winter day, I was reminded again who the real teachers were—here at Hopkins where I'd come to learn.

TWELVE

Gray Matter

I had a simple vision for my dream practice, based on my experience of reaching terra firma at the hospital where I woke up after being rescued from the tank. I wanted to create for my patients the same feeling of security that I had experienced. Because of the genuine concern and warmth of the doctor in the white coat, I had known that everything was going to be all right. Though he was obviously a stranger, there was a familiarity about him. Given his dark coloring and prominent nose and features, I assumed he was from an immigrant or minority background, perhaps Hispanic, Indian, or Middle Eastern, but his ethnicity wasn't the connection for me. Rather, his caring demeanor and meticulous attention to my case made me feel he could have been a member of my family—wanting the very best medical care for me, taking special precautions by keeping me overnight, setting up oxygen lines and intravenous infusions, and doing a thorough assessment before releasing me.

In addition to wanting patients to feel safe and grounded when they arrived in the modern, state-of-the-art clinic where my practice at Hopkins was based, I wanted them to feel that I would be a full partner in the journey to come—just as Nana Maria had been as a midwife. Next to helping a patient in childbirth, I couldn't imagine any act as intimate as touching the brain of another human being.

In thinking about my patients as part of my extended family—just as I did about the diverse assortment of staff, students, residents, nurses, technicians, and colleagues on the Q Team—I also envisioned a practice that was as welcoming and inclusive as the country that had given me terra firma on which to build a new life. With that thinking, I set an early policy that patients should have equal access to our office and to me at all times. The best way to do that, I decided, was to give out my cell phone number to patients, so that they or their family members could call me any time, and to make my schedule available on-line to staff, residents, students, and colleagues alike. Many of my associates thought this was nuts. But why? If I really wanted patients to be at the heart of the practice—in the OR, in the clinic, in the classroom, and, later, in the laboratory—this seemed like a perfectly reasonable measure to establish the atmosphere I envisioned of "mi casa es su casa."

Small hitch. While I could clearly visualize this welcoming, broad-based, richly diverse practice, the reality—as I had confided to my wife when she had advised that if I built it they would come—is that I had never built a practice before. Neither had my second in command, Raven Morris, the physician's assistant whom I was fortunate to bring onto my team early on.

In fact, the process was so new to both of us that when I was informed that a secretary was being assigned to me, I had to ask Raven, "What does a secretary do?"

Raven—who had opted to become a physician's assistant, even though she had the talent and tenacity to become a doctor and surgeon in her own right—didn't know either but wasted no time finding out. Once she did, we were excited to have someone to stay on top of the paperwork, schedule appointments, and field calls, because we could now devote the majority of our time to caring for patients. Aha! Instead of having to build the infrastructure and then wait for the patients to arrive, we could pursue a much more organic process—with the practice evolving in response to the varied needs of the patients and their families.

Because I had learned early in my training that tending to family members and loved ones is an important part of providing good patient care, we set up clinic hours that fit into people's lives and were sure to create a direct line of communication during surgery from me to the loved ones waiting for the life-or-death news of the patient's status.

When you're fighting for a patient to make it out of the OR alive, as was the case with a patient I'll call RD, having the family standing by can provide powerful energy. Without warning one day, RD was cut down by what we suspected was a ruptured aneurism. In his early fifties, moving toward the pinnacle of his professional career, RD was otherwise in peak health, happily married and the father of three children. But not long after arriving at work that morning, as he was conversing with colleagues, he had begun to shake with uncontrollable spasms before blacking out. Paramedics were summoned by a 911 call and when they arrived, finding him comatose, they intubated him, thereby saving his life, and then brought him into the hospital. Upon arrival, RD presented almost as poorly as had Nick Ferrando, whose only sign of life had been a twitching finger.

Any time a person is stricken with a brain aneurism—a bulge in a blood vessel that can rupture violently and fatally—the odds of survival aren't great. Generally, one-third of the people who have an aneurism die before they arrive at the hospital, another third die in the hospital despite heroic measures, and only one-third make it out alive. With the possibility that RD had the complication of a ruptured aneurism, I knew that he had a two-thirds chance of not making it. But if we didn't get to the root of the problem and turn it around, the odds were zero that he would regain consciousness. Because of my training under Dr. Michael Lawton, who specializes in these kinds of dangerous cases—a path that might have been my focus if I had stayed on at UCSF as his second in command—I knew the stakes very well.

I let RD's family know that the only hope of keeping him alive was to operate immediately, but if the problem was a ruptured aneurism, there was a 10 to 20 percent chance that another rupture would occur, exploding like a grenade during surgery. The family gave the go-ahead, and we proceeded with fast force.

The complications were such that I asked Dr. Olivi to work with me in the OR. Now that I had been road-tested with a few crises, the team knew me well enough to move with me—requiring few verbal commands on my part. The same utter stillness that I'd witnessed in the rooms where my mentors operated was now in place in my OR, with only the sounds of the monitoring equipment and the whirr of drills as I began the craniotomy—using a blade capable of cutting through skin down to the bone, carefully preserving every layer I removed, and then drilling a series of very small holes in the bone to enable me to remove part of it to make the opening, without putting pressure on the brain itself.

After lifting off the bone flap, the next step was to pull back the dura, which can be very tight, like the clutching petals of a Venus flytrap, and refuse to budge. Though time was of the essence, I had to be careful not to peel the dura back too speedily, which can disrupt the pressure in the brain and cause the heart rate to speed up or go crazy or even stop, in turn stopping the patient's breathing. None of these events occurred. Nor did we face the nightmare scenario in which the brain rises like dough with too much yeast—which can sometimes require you to use both hands to literally press the brain back down into the skull.

Finding only a thin layer of blood coating RD's gray, pulsing brain, I moved the microscope into place. Out of the corner of my eye, I could see everyone leaning in—Dr. Olivi, my chief resident, the nurses, the anesthesia team, the technicians monitoring the brain's electrical activity, students, and observers—to see how quickly we could diffuse any remaining explosive or bulging vessels. With no signs of trouble yet, everything quiet and almost eerily normal, in the instant that I spotted the point of rupture, the vessel exploded disastrously again, and blood spurted up like a geyser, splattering all over my mask, clouding my vision, threatening chaos. But everyone battled back, and order prevailed. Without my saying much, the nurses moved into action, cleaning up around us, and Dr. Olivi acted as my eyes and extra set of hands while working side by side with me until everything returned to normal. And then we were back on terra firma and could clip the aneurism and make sure we had no more trouble spots before mopping up and getting out.

Still in a coma, RD had come through the toughest part of the storm, and we hoped that he would rally once we moved him into the neuro-intensive care unit. For the first few days, he showed signs of improvement, spontaneously moving his arms and legs. But without warning, his vessels suddenly tightened, preventing blood flow through them, and whatever improvement we had seen was reversed. With everything his brain had been through since the first rupture when he collapsed at work, it began to shut down, along with the vital functions it controlled. Organ by organ, the rest of his body also began to shut down—his heart, his lungs, his liver, everything. We tried a range of medications to reverse this disastrous slide but watched helplessly as his condition deteriorated.

When we came to the place of no return, after a month, when all options had been exhausted and the results of his neurological exams were so dismal, I couldn't find a shred of good news to offer his family—except that I would be there for them and do whatever they wanted me to do. After multiple painful meetings, understanding that the chances that he would make a recovery were minimal, they requested that care be withdrawn. That day, I stayed with the family, and when they were ready, we went in together to the unit, RD's wife sitting on one side of the bed and I on the other. I held his hand and removed the feeding tube and then the breathing tube. The faces of his family members and particularly his wife were full of sorrow and grace. Within minutes, he slipped away, peacefully and silently.

This wasn't the first time I had been present at the time of a patient's death, although it was the first time I'd experienced such a loss in my role as the attending physician. And, of course, it wouldn't be the last. I agreed with Dr. Michael McDermott: it never gets easier. But as physicians who work in the field, straddling life and death, this is our reality. Every person who experiences the loss of a patient deals with it differently. For me, the sense of failure is hard to measure, a bitter, bitter pill to swallow after so many twists and turns in a patient's journey—when all the efforts to restore them to safety and health come to naught. But being with a patient to proffer care at the end, to extend such comfort as one human being can give to another, is also an honor and a gift. With RD, I remember, in those moments before and after he died, that I saw his light. I had seen this light with other dying patients before and would again. Whether it's in my imagination or in the way that the daylight fills the room at those particular times, I'm not sure, but I believe that the miraculous life force that's in all of us has a kind of light that can be witnessed at the time of death. There isn't a way to describe it any better than that, except to say that the light is larger than life, and perhaps it's there at the end of the passageway between this life and the next to let us glimpse the great hereafter, whatever it really is, at the moment when people go peacefully to sleep for good. Seeing that light and the look of peace in RD's face, I felt we had become close in the short month since he had come into my care, as a fellow soldier, and I was infinitely sad to watch him go.

Just as each of us has to travel our own path when mourning the loss of a loved one, every physician and health care worker has to find his or her own way of coping with a patient's death. The men and women of the nursing staff—who provide hands-on care to patients around the clock and who see the toll that a loved one's suffering takes on family members—know this well. I've often thought that if most of us who experience loss on a daily basis didn't have some form of post-traumatic stress disorder, there would be something wrong with us. So those of us who choose not to distance ourselves and not to compartmentalize our feelings need an outlet to process the experience—whether by a form of therapy, attendance at a patient's funeral, the creation of a personal grieving ritual, or all of the above. Something that helps me, and was meaningful with RD, is to do that which I almost never do—to slow down, take as long a break as I can, and maybe take a walk outside to look at the world the patient has left behind and appreciate the life that he or she lived.

There may be tears or not during this walk, but always I feel the knot in the back of my throat, and whether I'm outside or walking from the hospital back to my office along the basement route, everything seems quiet and empty, and the quality of the light in the atmosphere is dimmed somehow by the loss of that patient, that person, who is no longer part of my life and the world. As I decompress, the best way to rekindle my fire is to be humble, remembering that I'm not superhuman; like anyone else, I can only work harder and use my intellect and passion—and motivate my students to do so too—to try to make a difference for those who are suffering.

It is the habit of memory to lodge in our minds the cases that ended poorly rather than the successes. The reality is that of the almost three hundred surgeries I now do in a year, the majority go extremely well. And most of them, even if the war is eventually lost in cases of brain cancer, have better-than-expected outcomes. Still, we surgeons tend to remember where we fell short, when nature brought us and our patients to our knees. But I have never sought to numb the feelings of loss when a patient dies; my habit is to use these losses as ammunition for doing better and fighting harder—in memory of the patients who have not made it.

Strange as it may seem, the death of a patient reminds me how much I love what I do, lest I forget that not so many years ago I was picking tomatoes in the fields and now have the rare privilege of treating and handling the human brain. To merit the trust and faith of others, I have to also remember that what I do carries a great deal of responsibility. So along with my walks, my solution, today as much as in the early days of my practice, is to love all parts of what I do, even the most painful aspects of the job, and to search for the joy that can arise even in dark times.

·   ·   ·

By early 2006, a growing number of patients with brain tumors were being referred to me. Each case was different, challenging and compelling at the same time. Each patient's journey taught me new lessons or reinforced old ones.

One case, later featured on the front page of the *Baltimore Sun*, drove home the reality that even a tumor classified as benign can require all-out warfare. My patient, a twenty-six-year-old college graduate turned surfer, had been out of state when a surfing buddy noticed he was standing oddly on his surfboard. His parents insisted that he return home to Baltimore and be seen at Hopkins. When he came to me, imaging showed that his tumor, the size of a tennis ball, was stuck up against the left side of his brain, in the area that controls speech, tangled up in the veins and arteries like barbed wire. While I had my suspicions about what kind of tumor it was, not until we were on the inside and staring at the sea monster, all twisted in the blood vessels, was I fairly confident that it was benign—what's known as an epidermoid.

We had a rumble in the jungle, that tumor and I. Though it was probably benign as far as we knew then, it was extremely dangerous. One wrong micromove in an area of vascular weakness could cause a blood geyser to go off. But with my dream team on the job, we extricated the tumor and bid it "Adios." When I stepped out of the OR and sped down to the pathology department to take a look at the tumor tissue that had been flash-frozen to get an initial finding, sure enough, it was an epidermoid. Under a microscope, its appearance was a shimmering pearl white, splaying out all sorts of colors, like a rainbow. One hundred percent benign.

My patient's parents had been so certain that their son's case was going to have a positive outcome that they had agreed to have the *Baltimore Sun* chronicle his story. Fortunately, as we all celebrated when I discharged my patient with a clean bill of health, they turned out to be right!

Still, the pressure that the presence of reporters and photographers had added for everyone on my team was no small matter. When we gathered to review the case, I applauded my group's focus and composure, adding, "Whenever you see a patient leave after surgery without any collateral damage whatsoever, it doesn't get any better than that." Some of that was luck, especially with a benign tumor. Even so, I felt great pride in the tenacity of every person on my team, particularly because the pace of my schedule was starting to pick up significantly.

I remember those days very well—when I began to come into my own as a mentor and became more demanding of the team, of residents, students, and staff, and of everyone around me. Now and then I would unintentionally cross the line between mentor and tormentor—a professional liability perhaps—and feel disappointed in myself for not setting a better example. Whenever I was upset that we had let a patient down, even with something as small as not delivering a phone message or not being able to schedule an appointment for a patient, Raven would remind me that not everyone on staff could multitask and run nonstop on high octane.

I supposed that she was right. But I didn't see why they couldn't learn!

.   .   .

As simple as it sounds, I found over the first year of being in practice that as long as I asked myself at the beginning of every day how my team and I could better serve patients—and then take the relevant actions—both I and my patients won. Some days we came up with simple innovations as a result, time-saving measures that helped patients cut through red tape and get faster, more helpful answers to their questions. For instance, instead of conferring with patients' primary care physicians after the post-op exams—which usually entailed a series of phone calls to set up the appointments or follow-up treatments that patients needed—I began making calls from the exam room, with patients and their family members able to listen to my conversation with their other doctors and to ask questions and receive immediate answers.

In a teaching context, my students were amazed that I could coax (or badger) the top brain-mapping expert at Hopkins to drop by on short notice. They were convinced that I had magical powers. Which is a very good thing! Not just because I wanted to inspire my troops but also because I wanted them to believe that they too could do what's never been done—each one capable of a Kaliman maneuver. This kind of confidence was especially needed when I decided the time had come to shake up the status quo by establishing my own lab—to focus on improving our understanding of the causes of brain cancer, developing better treatments, and ultimately finding the cure.

Some saw my timing as the height of arrogance. They resented me for not waiting my turn and paying my dues, for trying to leap hurdles that others had taken the better part of their careers to do, and, judging by a few comments, for being foreign born, specifically Mexican born. At one time in my life, the implied question "who do you think you are?" would have bothered me. But no longer. I had to believe that the power of imagination—not mine so much as that of the young, brilliant scientists and physicians on my team—could do what others hadn't yet. So I welcomed the skepticism, knowing it would make me fight harder to figure out how to carry out my vision. I knew that one focus of my lab's research would be the connection between stem cells and brain cancer. But I hadn't yet conceived of the extent to which patients were going to participate as part of our team. At the same time, I was aware that a sense of great urgency needed to inform our focus—because lives were on the line. As I planted the seeds for such a lab while working day to day in the OR, teaching, and running my clinical practice, I had to remind myself not to expect overnight success and not to be thrown when patients did not immediately accept me.

One afternoon, for example, as our last patient for the day was leaving the clinic, I noticed that Raven was close to tears, and I pulled her aside to ask what was up. Though she hadn't planned to tell me, Raven admitted that one of our patients—someone suffering from a brain tumor—had asked, in so many words, if my degrees and awards on the wall were forged. After Raven calmly explained that they were real, the patient asked, "Is it true that the doctor is a dirty Mexican? Isn't there another surgeon I can see?"

Raven, who is Caucasian, is a self-assertive young woman, wife, and mother who can say a lot without words. She assured me that she hadn't lost her temper. But then she added "I don't think I hid my reaction. I'm offended."

Pained to see Raven upset, I offered her the same counsel that had helped me. "I know it's hurtful to hear those things," I conceded. "But remember our patients are really sick and many are depressed. They're not bad people."

The next time I saw that patient—or any other who made the standard remarks about my being lazy or not intelligent enough—my job was to win over his heart and mind by being the best physician I could be. By the time such patients were ready to leave, whether or not I would see them again in surgery or in a follow-up exam, Raven would watch in amazement as I walked them out of the room, joking, laughing, hugging—the best of friends.

"What's the secret?" she asked, after this had happened more than a few times. There was no secret. I simply looked for a connection, something the patient and I had in common—motorcycles, farming, railroad cars, Rocky Balboa, Spiderman, our children, our spouses, places we'd both visited or places we'd both like to go.

Occasionally, patients would apologize to Raven, acknowledging that they hadn't meant what they'd said. And many times, those patients and family members became my most vocal cheerleaders. So I believed that if we stuck to the Q Team mantra of "patients first," the terra firma that I was trying to build would be a place of equality and acceptance—where our differences would be much less important than the ways in which we were alike.

On this point, in fact, while grabbing a quick nap in my office one afternoon just before a radio interview, I dreamt that I was already on air and commenting on my philosophy when the interviewer asked, "Why do you love the brain so much?"

In my sleep, I knew the answer immediately. "No matter how different we are from one another—black, white, yellow, Jewish, Christian, rich, poor, educated or not—our brains are all the same, the same beautiful, noble gray color, the same shape and size. I love the small and large red rivers that run through everyone's brain like roads that show us the way to unravel the universe. I love how every single person's brain can dance just as magnificently as the next person's. I can't tell the difference between brains of patients of different races, religions, or classes, because they have all these features in common."

When I woke up and looked around my office at the many images of my patients' brains, it also struck me that despite our sameness, each of us has a distinctive interior road map—as unique to each of us as our fingerprints. In the early years of neuroscience, researchers and physicians learned generally where various human functions are usually controlled in the brain, but advances in technology have allowed us to map brains with electrical stimulation and to more precisely approximate in each individual where, for example, words are recognized, specific memories are stored, concepts are processed, objects are named, words are produced, and so on.

Knowing even the little that we do know, how could anyone *not* love the brain? How could anyone not believe that our brains are our least-used natural resource? I have never been shy about asking these questions or stating in public forums that before we give up on finding solutions to the most pressing problems facing humanity, such as a cure for cancer, we should roll up our sleeves and look for a solution in the place where all other advances have started—in our brains.

．　　．　　．

Unraveling the mystery of how brain tumors begin is complicated by their powers of stealth. Time and again, patients and their families ask, "How could this have happened?" and "Why weren't there any warning signs?" and "Would earlier detection have made a difference in my prognosis?" As a result, many of us in the field are beginning to discuss the advantages of early detection. We would like to think that there are warning signs that we can learn to identify and that, yes, if a patient learns those signs and discovers that a tumor is growing inside of his or her brain, stopping it early has the potential to improve the patient's chances at living longer and with a better quality of life. The hope is that in the near future we will be able to develop an affordable means of regular screening for brain tumors that can be as effective as early detection of breast cancer has been.

Interestingly, even patients who are themselves in the medical community often ignore telltale clues or write them off as being "all in my head" (pun intended). Dr. Olivi had such a patient, Dr. GD an ob-gyn and a surgeon—who had been referred to Hopkins from out of the country. Apparently, Dr. GD's partners had asked him to leave the practice because of bizarre changes in his personality. Previously a cheery, courteous, and polite gentleman, he now never smiled, was perpetually grumpy, and had been making increasingly inappropriate, rude remarks to patients and staff. Everyone assumed he was having serious psychological problems. Only when he started complaining that he wasn't able to taste food did the light dawn on someone in his circle. Since two-thirds of our sense of taste comes from smell and only one-third from the tongue, this symptom suggested that something wasn't right in the region of the brain housing the olfactory nerve centers.

An MRI revealed that Dr. GD had a grapefruit-size tumor above his nose, directly behind his eyes—what is referred to as a skull-based tumor. Again, though we would discover the tumor to be benign, its location spelled big danger. Dr. Olivi asked me to help with Dr. GD's case, and we conferred about the best approach. With a tumor in this location, we could not take the more common route from the top of the head into the brain and instead had to enter via the passageway above the eye. To do so, we needed to pull the face down first in order to remove the bone above the eye. Removing bones in this area, known as the orbital rim, put us directly behind the eyes and above the nose to get to the tumor, minimizing any risk of encroaching on areas of the brain that are the most eloquent—where senses like speech, smell, motor control, and more are located. Trained in this surgery by Dr. Michael McDermott at UCSF, I could feel an almost electric energy connecting all of us in the OR to Dr. GD's brain. Dr. Olivi and I and the rest of the team were able to get everything we came for, and when it was safely in the container for pathology, in a moment of relief and victory, I proclaimed, *"Hasta la vista, tumor!"*

After a brief stay to recuperate, Dr. GD walked out of the hospital, all smiles. When he returned to Hopkins a few months later, he reported that food tasted delicious again and that he was savoring the time he was spending with his family. He and his wife were having a second honeymoon. In fact, he had decided not to return to work but to remain retired. When we saw Dr. GD for a follow-up a year later, he was continuing to thrive. The strange trip into the dark side of his psyche had allowed him to see what mattered most to him.

There was a lesson there for me in his story, a reminder of Einstein's observation about valuing what really matters in life. The way I first heard the original quote may have been a variation of it, but it resonated just as powerfully: "Everything that can be counted does not necessarily count. And everything that counts cannot necessarily be counted." While I hadn't yet succeeded in building more hours into the day in order to strike the optimal balance between work and family, I was improving. And I certainly knew which people counted the most. I also knew that no matter how different we human beings are from one another, one of the most common bonds we share is the desire to be a good parent. Most of us would do everything in our power to ensure our children's well-being, even though we all have to live with the fact that not every force in the universe can be controlled. This reality played out for me in the stories of two mothers whose daughters were patients of mine. The two cases both involved accidents that represented their parents' worst nightmares, but they each had a different outcome.

During this period, my first winter in Baltimore, hospitals across the county had seen a rash of traumatic head injuries—such as that of nineteen-year-old Tiffany, who was brought in unconscious to an ER in our area after the car she was driving flipped over and smashed into a streetlight pole, shattering her skull. The team in that hospital had taken her to surgery and saved her life. As time went on, however, her mother asked that I take on the case. In the six months following her accident, Tiffany was found to have difficulty understanding and producing words; her cognitive abilities were intact, but therapy was needed to address the difficulty she was having with speech. She was progressing well. But meanwhile the surgical opening was not closing as it should have, and a dangerous infection had developed. We needed to remove the metal plate that had been used to provide covering for her brain and close up again to allow the infection to resolve before undertaking the next stage, which would entail reconstructing her skull and protecting her brain for good.

After I had scheduled the surgery, producers for the ABC series *Hopkins*—in which I had agreed to be followed and filmed for a couple of the episodes—approached me to ask if we could include Tiffany and her mom among the cases for the show.

The family had been through so much trauma already that I was initially resistant to the idea. No matter how unobtrusive the production people promised to be, I knew their presence would add another level of uncertainty and pressure. But Tiffany and her parents decided they wanted to take part in the filming, feeling that the benefits of sharing their story with other families would outweigh the risks.

I was still wary, knowing that if they had second thoughts once the filming began, it would be difficult to stop the cameras. But Tiffany believed that if she could muster the courage to participate, she might be able to save countless lives. Just after the cameras started to roll, I asked if she was nervous about the filming. "No," she said, taking time to shape the word. But as for whether or not she was nervous about the surgery itself, Tiffany paused and then smiled at the camera and at her mom, answering slowly and with effort, "I'm scared. . . . But I can do it."

Going into the OR to do the reconstructive work on her skull, I knew we would encounter some significant scar tissue from the previous surgeries. But I didn't expect to hit a geyser in the form of a loose blood vessel. Nor did I expect that I would be leaning over the geyser at the exact angle that would allow the spurting blood to come down over the rim of my magnifying glasses, under my eyebrow, and into my eye. My heart stopped. Tiffany had received many blood transfusions, and now some of this blood from multiple sources had splashed into my eye—on camera no less!

I asked my chief resident to step in so that I could go wash my eye and call the occupational safety office to request a blood test. Though the test results would later show that I was fine, the memory of the HIV needle stick was much too vivid for comfort. In the meantime, I was able to return to the surgery and finish the job. When Tiffany woke up, she beamed with pride. As concerned as Tiffany's mother was about her daughter, when I went to the waiting room to give her the news about the outcome, she found time to worry about me, having heard from the nurses about the bloodbath. "Are you all right?" I assured her that we were checking it out, and the first order of business was to celebrate how beautifully Tiffany had done.

Without question, a positive outcome like Tiffany's is the prayer of every parent whose child has been in an accident. Yet it must also be a reminder of the constant pulse of life and death and the myriad particulars that can affect our work as physicians—again, some controllable, others not.

Under the heading of things that can't be controlled belongs the story of the other mother and her daughter, a fourteen-year-old whom I'll call EM. An only child of adoring parents, EM was not yet of driving age, so the winter storms didn't pose the same threat to her as they had to

Tiffany. The danger for EM and kids of all ages came from hidden treacherous ice that had built up after a snow in the region had melted—right
before the temperature had suddenly dropped. Overnight, the previous
snow froze, but by morning a light layer of powdery snow had fallen on
top of the ice a quarter of an inch below. With school called off for the
day, EM excitedly went out with friends to go sledding. She jumped on
top of the pile of three or four girls and raced down a hill at such a high
velocity that the sled caught air. When the sled landed, EM was in the
back, and her head hit the ice like a watermelon going splat—leaving
blood and brain matter on the ground.

EM was brought into the ER by ambulance when I was on call, and
we moved her into the OR within minutes to remove a huge blood clot
underneath the brain. We saved her life, but the injury to her brain was
such that she was no longer there—a vegetable. For the next month, I
saw her daily and also talked to her mother in person or on the phone
each day. Nothing could alter the excruciating pain for her parents, made
worse by the fact that EM still looked like the beautiful young girl she
had always been—the happy child who had run out to play with her
friends. But from the moment her head hit the ground, her brain was
basically gone.

Together with her parents, I refused to accept the fact that she was
beyond rescue. Whenever I went in to see her in the ICU, I would gaze
at the photos all around her depicting her life up until the accident—pictures of her, happy and alive, thriving with her friends and in her school
activities. In sad contrast, she lay in her hospital bed with a tracheotomy
tube for breathing and a feeding tube in her abdomen. Immobile, she
had no light in her eyes, and nothing signaled brain activity as it had for
Nick Ferrando and SH and other patients who had recovered even when
all had seemed lost. Every day I convinced myself that the impossible
could happen for her. But I was wrong. After a year and a half of torture
for her parents, EM died.

As seasoned as I was from the death and devastation that was an
inevitable part of my daily work, the hopelessness of the situation made
me feel, irrational though it was, that I should have been able to do more.
In the wake of a senseless accident like EM's, I was both sad and angry

that I couldn't mount a crusade to advocate more for more research to fight a murderous disease, and that I had no way to let her parents know that her life was no less meaningful for having been cut short. But I did adamantly encourage others to make sure their kids wear helmets for outdoor sports involving speed, no matter how uncool this headgear might seem. Wear helmets!

Together, the journeys of EM and Tiffany sharpened my desire to do more in my field and more as a human being. Despite their different fates, their stories enhanced my appreciation for life—the joy of being fully alive and engaged in all that life brings. Each of my patients has shown me in his or her way that life is not all dark or all light. Truly it is both dark and light and comes in varying shades of gray—like the color of our beautiful brains.

Life is not static; neither is it golden for some and only full of shadows for others. It is tragic and miraculous, hilarious and terrifying, cruel and glorious, the full spectrum. And I wouldn't have it any other way.

THIRTEEN

Seeing the Light

"There's a Professor Schmidek on the line for you," the Hopkins hospital operator announced as I picked up the phone in my office one Sunday evening after finishing rounds.

"Did you say Schmidek, as in Dr. Henry Schmidek?" I asked, fairly certain that I didn't know anyone by that name—other than *the* Professor Schmidek whom I had met at Dartmouth a year earlier. A legendary figure of science and medicine, he was also the editor of *Schmidek and Sweet's Operative Neurosurgical Techniques*—the most widely used text in neurosurgery the world over. "Please, yes, thank you, put him through!"

A momentary flashback of my winter trip to New Hampshire reminded me of the heart-stopping slide on the black ice and my lingering question about why I'd been so compelled to make the trip. Already feeling the pull of Hopkins, I should have known that regardless of how impressed I was with Dartmouth, my direction wasn't going to change. Then again, I wouldn't have wanted to miss meeting Professor Schmidek and spending two memorable hours talking about everything from neuroscience to parenting.

Why he was calling me now, I had no idea, but I was nonetheless delighted to hear Dr. Schmidek's booming voice as he asked, "Alfredo, how are you doing?"

"Everything is going beautifully. Thank you! I hope all is well with you, Professor?"

"Well, very well."

Flattered that he had interrupted his busy schedule for a social call to check up on how I was enjoying Baltimore, I was surprised when he shifted the conversation, saying, "There is something that I want to talk to you about." He paused. "It will change your career. Do you have a few minutes?"

Of course I did!

Dr. Schmidek's naturally joyful manner of speaking took on a more serious tone. "Alfredo," he began, "this next edition of *Schmidek and Sweet's* will be my most ambitious and my last."

"But you're a young man," I replied, wondering why he was so certain that he would say everything there was to say in the five years or so it would take to prepare the next edition. New techniques in our field were emerging daily, and discoveries in the laboratory would also be changing the course of neurosurgery.

Dr. Schmidek didn't explain his reasoning other than to say he believed future editions would need to come from the next generation of experts. "Like you, your colleagues, residents and students," he proposed.

I was confused. The next generation could certainly contribute, but why would he step down as the editor after his sixth edition?

"Good," Dr. Schmidek said. "I look forward to working with you." My surprised silence prompted him to explain, "I'd like you to help me edit my next and last edition of *Schmidek and Sweet's.*"

I was dumbfounded, given the many more experienced and more prominent authorities he could have asked. Why me? But I sputtered something about what an honor this was and that I was thrilled even by the suggestion.

"Wonderful!" Dr. Schmidek said, and then signed off. "We'll be in touch."

For a moment after hanging up the phone I tried to convince myself this was no big deal. Who was I kidding? This was unbelievable! And when I mentally replayed the conversation a couple of times, I saw that besides the fact this opportunity would change my career, the mystery of why I had needed to take the trip to Dartmouth was now solved.

Everything made sense—even my emergence from the near wipeout on the ice. Not only had I been meant to meet Dr. Schmidek, but I needed to relearn old lessons from Tata Juan.

Now I understood why my grandfather chose the most difficult and, sometimes, indirect routes to drive up to the mountains; why he took us on treacherous roads that could have sent us crashing over the cliffs at any turn; why he stopped periodically to explore caves and look at other landmarks that weren't always of interest to an impatient little boy. Now I understood why our hikes took us off the main path and into the woods, yielding no immediate discovery other than a feeling of discomfort. Those detours and dangers were actually part of the journey, all part of the eventual victory of reaching the pinnacle, all preparation for teaching me to trust my own instincts in the future.

Professor Schmidek and I began working together soon after he first called, speaking by phone at least once a week and transmitting material to each other frequently—although I wasn't helping in any official capacity as a coeditor or contributor. In the fall of 2008, although Dr. Schmidek was spending the year at Oxford University in England, we kicked up the intensity a notch, aiming to complete a detailed outline of the vast work by Christmas time.

But in October everything changed when I heard the shocking news that Henry Schmidek had suddenly died as the result of a heart attack. He was only seventy-one years old. Our field had lost one of our most youthful, vibrant heroes. Saddened for his family, I also greatly regretted that he had been unable to complete the undertaking that had been so important to him. I assumed the project was in limbo, either canceled or in need of a new lead editor.

Then, a month after his death, I received a weekend phone call at home from Mary Schmidek, who wanted to discuss the future of the project that I had been working on with her husband.

"I understand," I said, assuming she was about to inform me that the work would be turned over to more established, experienced hands to finish editing.

On the contrary, Mary said that her husband, apparently sensing that he might not live to see the publication of his last and most ambitious edition, had wanted me to be the lead editor of the sixth edition of *Schmidek and Sweet's Operative Neurosurgical Techniques.*

Words failed me. Both the honor and the responsibility were humbling. Mary Schmidek assured me that her husband had very good instincts and recognized that I would approach the work with the same sense of passion and adventure that marked his life. She went on to describe the love of the outdoors that had occupied him throughout his life. In addition to setting national records in sailboat racing after only two years in competition and taking joy in fly-fishing, Dr. Schmidek had developed a recent fondness for driving his off-road vehicle at high speeds.

I realized then that there are many kinds of off-roading, some planned and others not. More than ever, I was grateful that I'd made the trip to Dartmouth four years earlier.

That evening, after Mary and I said good-bye, I went to the computer and opened the last file I'd sent to Dr. Schmidek, picking up the work where we had left off a month earlier. Slated for publication in early 2012, the sixth edition of *Schmidek and Sweet's Operative Neurosurgical Techniques* at this writing is close to being completed.

In the meantime, Anna and the kids decided to make a special dinner to celebrate my new assignment, which would involve some extra work at home over the next few years but would introduce all of us to new colleagues and friends from around the world. With contributions from leading neurosurgeons at all the top institutions in the United States and in other countries, the many volumes of this encyclopedic format would also connect me to leading research being done in the fight to cure brain cancer.

Looking around the table at my beloved family, I was thankful for everything, confident that I had lived up to my nickname of Lucky Quiñones. To be sure, the past three and a half years at Hopkins had posed new tests for us. In the first year or so, before the practice had begun to really rock 'n' roll, my long hours did not make Anna's adjustment to living in Baltimore any easier. And now that everything was moving at a much faster pace, the long hours only persisted, leaving her to continue holding down the fort, with three very active children (and a growing cat population).

But in certain respects, our labors were finally bearing fruit. Anna's creative and budgeting gifts were on display in our home, which was a dream come true for us. We were even talking about building a pool in the backyard, since all three of our kids took after their mother in being natural swimmers. Still, if we were to learn from Tata Juan's teachings, perhaps the time had come to venture away from old patterns. To that end, Anna proposed that we look at my schedule together, now that my practice was up to speed, and set at least one night a week when I would be home for dinner and put aside the better part of one day on the weekend for me to enjoy being a family man.

Sometimes a basic, small step works magic. Though the new schedule was far from perfect, Anna and I, to the shock of everyone, were even able to work in a date night every now and then. What a luxury to go out and savor dinner *and* a movie. We had come a long way to reach this point.

Now that the kids were older, I was delighted that they were able to visit Hopkins occasionally with Anna (following in the footsteps of Walter Dandy, whose kids famously roamed the halls of Hopkins in his day). Most of our visits in these years were easy to organize, except for the time I sent my wife an enthusiastic e-mail suggesting that she bring the children to a lunch I was throwing for the nursing staff and a few members of my team—including my two physician's assistants, Raven Morris and Jill Anderson, a terrific addition to our group. No sooner had I sent it off than Anna called me, "About this lunch on March tenth . . . um, you forgot, didn't you?"

Oh, crap! Her birthday is March 10! I had been doing so well, but now I had forgotten again. Back into the doghouse I went!

For many years, I think Anna and I both expected that we'd get to a place where there would be more time for us—a real separation between professional life and family life. By now we were both coming to terms with the reality that this was always going to be a work in progress. We knew that others struggled with this question of balance and that no one, to our knowledge, had an answer that we didn't.

Anna, of course, never used the demands on me as a reason to withhold her support or love, nor did any of this deter her from becoming increasingly involved with various aspects of my work at Hopkins—adding more responsibilities to her role as chief counsel in all my decisions. A few years back, Anna had begun an annual Thanksgiving tradition of preparing an incredible feast and hosting an open house for the students, residents, grad students, postdocs, and patients who made up our ever-expanding extended family. Among the regular attendees at our annual fiesta are the members of the team who do research in the laboratory that I was finally able to establish at the end of 2007. In fact, Anna deserves credit for an idea that became one of the secrets to the lab's success.

.   .   .

In the beginning, the Neurosurgery Brain Tumor Stem Cell Laboratory, soon to become known as "Dr. Q's Lab," had the tiniest of armies—just researcher Grettel Zamora, a recent graduate of Hopkins with a degree in biology, and I. The two-pronged challenge we set for ourselves was first, to connect the dots in our understanding of how brain tumor cells migrate through and invade normal brain tissue, and second, to develop therapies to halt the invasion and eventually eradicate the invaders.

In developing our approach, I drew inspiration from my hero, Santiago Ramón y Cajal, who stressed the value of simplicity in the work of the investigative scientist. Cajal also urged researchers not to be overly bound by established science or by the renowned geniuses who laid it down.

My lab was also influenced by the passion for research exemplified by another one of my heroes, Dr. Ed Kravitz. At any time, he could retire with a stunning body of work—including his studies of the primal neurological battlegrounds of different species. But he continues to break new ground, most recently exploring the inner workings of fruit flies and how their level of aggression affects how they live and die. Ed calls this project the Fruit Fly Fight Club.

Because of these influences, I have stayed with the simplest, albeit unorthodox, way of communicating the stakes of the battle against brain cancer. Let's say we were to make the explanation simple enough that even a little boy from the outskirts of a small town named Palaco in Mexico could understand the challenges. In previous descriptions, we have compared a cancerous brain tumor to a supernatural serial-killer dragon: if you cut off its head, it grows two more heads and summons more murderous cohorts to join the battle. The boy dragon slayer, my tale continues, started out with nothing more than a homemade stick with which to track and slay the dragon. But over time, as the dragon grew more powerful, the boy grew stronger too and developed a few smart weapons to add to his arsenal. And, in his most important move, the boy built a small but brilliant army to fight alongside him.

What, then, is the face of this dragon? We know that in the United States today over 600,000 individuals, including nearly 30,000 children, are living with a diagnosis of a primary brain or central nervous system tumor. Every day ten children—over 3,700 each year—are diagnosed with pediatric brain tumors. Approximately 75 percent of nonadult patients diagnosed with brain tumors are under the age of fifteen. Brain cancer is the deadliest form of childhood cancer, and even noncancerous tumors can be fatal, especially for children, if the tumor's location makes surgery or medical therapy difficult.

We also know there are more than 130 types of brain tumors, which can make diagnosing brain cancer a challenge. Gliomas—a range of low- to high-grade tumors—are the most common type of primary brain tumor. Some 124,000 people in the United States have malignant brain cancer, and each year nearly 14,000 individuals in the country die of the disease. Around the world, the number of brain cancer deaths each year is between 130,000 and 140,000. The disease is a mass murderer by any measure.

The worst killer among the glioma tumors, the high-grade glioblastoma multiforme (GBM), infiltrates the healthy brain with its deadly cells so as to make complete surgical removal nearly impossible, which in turn enables it to grow back in 99 percent of cases. Even with a combination of chemotherapy and radiation treatment, median survival remains at little over one year for patients with GBMs. We have learned that the tumor likely gains its first foothold in a specific population of cells that share traits with normal neural stem cells and brain tumor stem cells. The frightening discovery is that the cells that make the tumor cells can regenerate, are not stopped by current treatment, and can migrate long distances.

When Grettel and I began our work in the lab, our first step was to apply current knowledge about how normal stem cells in the brain migrate to our own observations of how tumor cells behave. The monumental challenges of the task we had set for ourselves immediately became apparent. The first painful realization was that with only the two of us, our efforts were going to take much longer than the time left for our patients with brain cancer. We needed to grow our army and diversify, pulling in brainpower in a variety of areas of expertise to cover all battle stations. But how to do that? How could I motivate more students from the school of medicine and from other scientific departments, along with residents, grad students, and postdocs, not only to do groundbreaking work in the lab but also to feel the same sense of urgency that we neurosurgeons have in the OR? How could I further motivate team members to give up one of their very busy nights and come to a weekly meeting to share findings—so that we could keep alive the collaboration and the competition? The biggest question of all was how I could convince these brilliant young minds from every corner of the world and every cross-section of society—as I envisioned—to believe that I had something meaningful to add to the conversation and the lab?

Anna gave me the answer. She reminded me of the very lean days of my residency, when a rare night on the town involved one cheeseburger for our daughter at a fast-food restaurant and none for us. Maybe some researchers would show up for meetings if I included refreshments on the agenda. I took her suggestion and ran with it, adding my own simple embellishments: first, establish a not-to-be missed Friday night meeting, set for the end of the week when researchers' brains are already tired and they're in need of a dinner break; second, feed them an appealing meal with ample servings. Then, when they're already tired and half asleep—postprandial and lulled into complacency by their full stomachs—they'll believe whatever I say and think I'm a genius!

Despite this clever plan, an almost insurmountable hurdle remained: funding. Money would be needed to launch the research, pay the researchers, and cover the considerable expenses of building the operation I had in mind. Not knowing how difficult this task would be, I applied for no fewer than a dozen grants—a prime case of ignorance being bliss. True to form, I figured that I might as well shoot high, so I went for the most-sought-after and most prestigious grantors, spending untold hours and effort filling out the applications. Even as optimistic as I was, I was astonished when seven of the twelve grants came through—from important sources such as the Howard Hughes Medical Institute, the Robert Wood Johnson Foundation, and the National Institutes of Health. With a growing team and now with funding, we soon realized that the availability of human brain tissue—especially brain tumor tissue—was severely limited. In surgery after surgery, after removing countless tumors, I had seen most of that tissue taken away for disposal; only a tiny amount ended up on a slide for pathology. My team and I came up with a simple solution. Why not offer patients the opportunity to donate any tissue taken interoperatively to our lab? To our delight, almost every patient not only consented to make this incalculably valuable contribution to our research, but did so with such enthusiasm that it inspired the formation of our lab's tissue bank. The bank includes cancer and noncancer specimens from adult and pediatric patients—tissue that would otherwise be discarded after operations. With over seven hundred specimens collected at this writing, our lab also has a bank of postmortem brain tissue.

Patients and their families continually tell us that being able to contribute to the tissue bank and to the lab's work makes them feel they are participating in history, which gives them hope and a sense of purpose and allows them to feel part of something even bigger than their own struggles.

So, with increased funding to build the infrastructure of the lab, and with the creation of the tissue bank, which is essential to developing cell cultures and cell lines for use in our experiments and those of other scientists doing vital research, how did it all work out? Well, before too long, we had almost two dozen fully invested members of the team. And in no time the Friday night meetings became standing-room-only affairs.

Open to the entire Hopkins community, the public at large, and the media, the meetings draw crowds in part because of what's on the menu—every cuisine from Chinese to Indian, from soul food to deli, Mexican, Italian, Peruvian, and more. I have to remind researchers that they should arrive early to go through the buffet line before it's all gone. But the real draw for the meetings is that we have featured guest speakers. Our stars are our patients—scientists in their own right—the ones who provide the needed sense of urgency for our research.

This view of patients' critical role was something I shared with my friend and longtime mentor Dr. Esteban González Burchard, who was on campus in mid-2008 as an invited distinguished professor and who made time in his schedule to attend a Friday night meeting.

As we jogged across the Hopkins campus toward the laboratory, Esteban said, "You know, Fredo, you are the only person I know who would spend all day in the OR on a Friday and then, when everyone else is knocking off early, you're throwing a meeting. That's commitment!" Then he added, "And crazy!"

Luckily, I replied, there were other crazy researchers willing to join me.

"How do you motivate your people to stay there late on Friday doing science? Not everyone is as driven as you."

The answer was simple. "I've been fortunate to live the American dream, to make the most of opportunities. If anybody wants to join my team and work hard, I will create that many more opportunities for them."

Esteban wondered if they were motivated by my decision to turn down the big money offered elsewhere and to embrace the freedom to pursue the goals I believed in. With a smile, he suggested, "They can relate to you as a guy who drives a Honda SUV instead of a BMW."

True, many of the researchers loved my stories about making the most out of what little I had, like the saga of my red pickup truck's customized hydraulic kit that let me raise and lower it to the music of Whitesnake! But I also had other devious ways of goading on the members of my team. For example, I was not above calling a lead researcher at 6:00 A.M. on a Sunday morning to check on the progress of his or her experiment. The conversation usually went like this:

Q TEAM RESEARCHER (*answering sleepily*): Hello?

ME: Good morning! Did I wake you?

Q TEAM RESEARCHER: Wake me? Uh no, I'm just here, uh, working.

Or,

ANOTHER Q TEAM RESEARCHER: Uh, no, I was just waiting for your call on a Sunday morning at six A.M.

And then we would discuss some excellent ideas I had for a paper that I was sure the researcher would want to write up. Motivation!

Esteban laughed. He was well aware that my style as a mentor had been influenced by the mentors who had motivated me—including him.

When he and I arrived in time for dinner before the meeting, he seemed to sense the energy, especially among the excited and nervous lab scientists who were scheduled to present their research that night. But not until I called the meeting to order and introduced our guest speakers, Ken and Betty Zabel, did I see the light go on in my dear colleague's eyes.

Ken, my patient who was battling brain cancer, began by telling everyone how encouraged he was to visit the lab and see the team's dedication.

"He's on the payroll!" I joked, causing Esteban to shake his head at the familiar line.

Ken and Betty laughed too. A large, gregarious, and deeply spiritual man in his early sixties, Ken explained that he was able to maintain his high spirits because he believed that everything that happened to him was part of a grand design. "God has a plan," Ken announced, and he told us that he believed that part of that plan was to contribute to the work of finding a cure for brain cancer.

With staples still showing on his bald head from his recent craniotomy, Ken then told us his story of achieving the American dream after building a successful business from the ground up. He and Betty had been married for twenty-five years—a second marriage for both of them. The two had combined their two sets of kids into one big family and had never stopped acting like newlyweds.

"I was so lucky to meet Betty," Ken recalled. "She was a beauty, and I was this big bald guy." On an up note, he added, he never had to change his hairstyle for brain surgery.

Betty interjected that their romance had been love at first sight, bald head and all. She also reported that Ken had always been careful about his health; he ate a nutritious diet, exercised, and for years had gotten annual checkups and screenings in the belief that he would live a long, healthy life. But one Friday afternoon when he was away on business, he had landed in the local hospital with strange symptoms.

Doctors told him his brain was riddled with cancer and that he needed to have surgery on Monday. But Ken felt he was being rushed into something that wasn't right. He recalled lying in his hospital bed in Florida holding his BlackBerry and feeling that the hand of God was directing him to surf the Internet to learn more about his options. While searching the top-rated hospitals in neurosurgery and seeking keywords about promising research in brain cancer, he clicked on a link that brought up a story about Johns Hopkins and "Dr. Q's Lab."

Ken called Baltimore directory assistance and eventually got through to a secretary in the neurosurgery department who then gave him my office number. In a voicemail message, he indicated that he was supposed to be my patient and that a copy of his MRI ought to already be there. He added that he needed to be seen right away.

Around the room at the lab meeting, I saw a lot of jaws drop and eyebrows rise. "What did you do then?" someone asked.

I jumped in, remembering that when I learned of the message from this Ken Zabel who lived in Florida and for whom I had no records, I didn't know what to think. But if films had been lost or a patient in need had been unable to see me, someone needed to address the situation. So I called him.

"I couldn't believe Dr. Q picked up the phone and called me," Ken told our group. In truth, he had not been sure that his ploy would work. Ken recalled, "No matter what happened, I just knew this was the guy I was supposed to see."

How could anyone turn down someone who made that kind of effort? If he could get himself to my office on Monday, I told him, I would be pleased to see him.

Ken Zabel's case was indeed very serious. Because he still had all of his verbal and cognitive faculties, we were able to do an awake craniotomy and buy him some time. As everyone at our lab meeting could witness, he had done beautifully. But at least one more tumor was lurking in a different region of his brain, and another surgery would likely be necessary. Worse, the serial killer that we knew GBM to be—and that we had seen under the microscope and in experiments with the tissue that Ken had donated to the lab—was by no means gone for good.

At this point, as Esteban looked around the room and saw how emotionally connected everyone was to the plight of this real-life patient sitting there with his wife, he simply nodded his head, showing that he now understood why I sought to engage my team's emotional energies.

But I don't think any of our guests were prepared for the heightened emotion that followed, when the night's presenters took turns reviewing their latest findings. The atmosphere during these weekly presentations often takes on the intensity of an episode of *CSI: Miami* or the medical series *House*—with each person in the room channeling his or her inner Sherlock Holmes. With the Zabels sitting in the room that night, the feeling of urgency was palpable, as if everyone sensed a murderer was about to strike and knew we needed to tap our full brainpower to help one another with ongoing investigations. This was not a time to offer happy talk to Ken and Betty. Our mandate was to deliver real discoveries and legitimate reasons for hope.

By the end of the meeting, after we had gotten into fairly complicated neuroscience, I expected our guests to be tired and ready to say good night. After three presentations—two in PowerPoint and a third in the form of a minidocumentary—I also thought our lab people would be eager to go home and start their weekends. Not so. I watched with something like paternal pride as all the researchers approached the Zabels and Dr. Burchard to introduce themselves—a moment unlike anything Esteban had witnessed before, he told me later.

His reaction confirmed for me that our approach was breaking down barriers and fostering collaboration, in part with the power of storytelling—thanks to patients and families like the Zabels, who contributed not only their words and passion but also the tissue removed during surgery. That night, the minidocumentary we watched showed cellular activity in tissue from Ken Zabel's tumor. With sped-up film technology, we saw dramatic movement on a slide of tissue that demonstrated the proliferation of the cancer cells. This research not only was promising, but it was happening at an accelerated pace—because there was a person on the team whom everyone now knew personally and whose life was on the line.

.   .   .

The story of Ken Zabel's battle was not over. While I'm not sure that I agree with him that everything happens for a reason, I can accept that if we study the mysteries of our lives, the answers will help direct us to our life's purpose. The direction of the work and the spirit at the lab certainly make me feel that way. I remember getting chills when one of our neuroscience postdocs, Hugo Guerrero-Cázares ("Guerrero," fittingly, means "warrior"), presented his findings reminding us that these migrating cells could be "the missing link" in unraveling the murder mystery of brain cancer, eventually showing us how to stop the most lethal tumors in their tracks and one day even revealing how to prevent them from growing at all.

I have not only been called crazy for believing such solutions are within our reach, I have also been called naive. But I see nothing naive or unrealistic about embracing hope. Many of the lifesaving therapies in medicine that we now take for granted came from individuals and teams who were similarly idealistic. Every day I see patients who know they are going to die, yet they choose hope over despair. Many do so because they want to savor every second of time they have left. Others find hope in contributing to science and playing a small role in making history.

They find comfort in the fact that what we learn from their suffering will help prevent and cure diseases in others.

As the main conductor of the orchestra that is Dr. Q's Lab, I not only have the opportunity to organize, motivate, and coordinate experiments but to be an instrumentalist as well—a researcher alongside the members of smaller, two- to four-person teams. After only three and a half years in existence, the lab today is terra firma where bright minds can feel safety and empowerment in their work, with my encouragement and trust that they are about to find something important.

For instance, one team of four researchers is looking at a promising new approach for treating GBMs that uses adipose-derived (yes, fat!) mesenchymal stem cells, which have been shown to migrate to tumors. With genetic modifications, these stem cells can be encouraged to secrete antitumor genes or proteins. The lab has created a cancer tumor model that replicates glioblastoma's deadly traits as well as cutting-edge technology for tracking cellular migration in real time that can be captured on MRIs. We are so impressed with the results in controlled studies that our next step will be to translate this therapy to patients with brain and other cancers.

Another team is launching work on what we call the "recruitment hypothesis." Because we know that removal of a GBM does not eradicate cancer—and leaves behind micrometastases that have migrated from the tumor—this team will study how normal neural stem cells migrate and what happens to them when they undergo change that makes them resistant to therapies. If the everyday parallel is the ability of one bad apple to spoil the whole bunch, then we hope to identify the signaling system between the cancer stem cells and normal neural stem cells and develop ways to interrupt their communication systems. These bad cells are very smart, and our challenge is to outsmart them.

Wearing many hats at the Friday meetings, I play cheerleader, teacher, student, and devil's advocate, poking holes in ideas or encouraging healthy debate and collaboration. Even if a presenter describes a scientific notion that sounds excellent in theory, I have the responsibility to ask questions about why current therapies aren't effective in banishing brain cancer. Such challenges can create "aha" moments or help a researcher spot areas that require more legwork. One promising study at the lab is tracking how radiation affects stem cells attempting to migrate from the main area in the brain where they live. In gaining a greater understanding of both progenitor cells and stem cells, the experiment also seeks to show how radiation may alter progenitor cells to participate in the promotion of healthy stem cells. We hope that clinical trials will soon follow. This work will help clinicians target radiation doses appropriately and determine effective dose levels; ideally, it will identify molecular and pharmaceutical agents for treatments that will promote progenitor cell survival and improve these cells' migration abilities.

With all these smart weapons, a hot topic of concern at our meetings is how to stay a few steps ahead of our killer. Since we have established that GBMs thrive in a state of low oxygen and where there is increased glycolic activity, we're also asking whether adjusting oxygen levels and limiting glucose metabolism can inhibit tumor growth.

In an experiment investigating Robo receptor cells and Slit proteins (a family of chemo-resistant proteins), our miniteam of researchers has used the tumor model from donated tissue to simulate tumor growth. This important work is equivalent to decoding the killer's language that directs the tumor stem cells to invade the brain.

When answers aren't forthcoming, time and again I return to the power of simplicity. By this, I don't mean that I search for a simple explanation or for a silver-bullet solution. As we know, the causes of brain cancer are multifactorial, so the treatment and methods of arresting the disease should be too. But I also know, just as I learned from Tata Juan and from the fateful (or accidental) meeting I had with Professor Schmidek at Dartmouth, big things happen when you do the work, follow your instincts, and let your imagination challenge you.

If I needed any proof of that belief, I found it one Friday night, like any other Friday night, at our lab meeting. Shortly before arriving, I had finished up a second case in the OR and had collected tissue to bring to the lab with me, appreciating as always our ability to immortalize our patients and make them part of our team.

After enjoying a buffet of delicious Middle Eastern food, we settled down to work, and the social atmosphere instantly changed to a serious one.

This day, one of our research fellows, Tomás Garzón-Muvdi, MD, MS, was going to present studies that he had been working on intensively. As Tomás began, our discussion went something like this:

ME: We believe that we can cure brain cancer, yet we know the cells responsible for making the cancer are migratory and invasive, which render them incurable due to recurrence and ultimately lethal in virtually all cases. What will you show me today, Tomás, that will change my statement? What progress have we made these past weeks?

TOMÁS: Professor, I think the data I will present today on ion transporters has been implicated in the migration of other cells by simply regulating intracellular volume locally during migration. And I think the findings I am about to show you will make you say "Holy guacamole!"

RESEARCH FELLOW HUGO GUERRERO-CÁZARES, MD, PHD (impressed): This could have high clinical relevance for understanding the mechanisms that these cells use to migrate, as a means to provide possible therapeutic targets.

ME: This is great, Tomás, and, yes, Hugo, I agree. My concern, however, is that many other groups have studied the role of many other ion channels in the past, and we still have no better understanding or, most importantly, a cure. What will you show me today that will make me change my mind?

TOMÁS: In our experiment, we observed that pharmacological inhibition and decreased expression of a sodium/potassium/chloride channel lead to decreased migration and invasion in a nanoplatform. Most impressive was that in our animal studies, when we studied these cells, we were surprised to see that these tumors were smaller!

HUGO (very impressed): Wow! This suggests that this simple ion channel may be largely responsible for the migration of brain cancer cells!

ME: Holy guacamole! (after a beat) Maybe, of course. We can't get ahead of ourselves yet, and we need to understand if it is by volume regulation or because of the ability of the cell to firmly adhere to its surroundings and travel through space and tissue.

TOMÁS: Maybe, Professor, we have an answer for that too! *(Cueing up his DVD and pointing to the screen)* Look at the movies of these cells. See how the cells move? Their little feet are not only attaching firmly to the surface of a nanostructure but also making it move very swiftly like a fish in the sea.

Well, the conversation might have gone slightly differently. But, yes, Tomás was right. We all saw the light and recognized that a transformational clue had been found, one we had been seeking for three years, this breakthrough coming only after a series of experiments that followed one after another. Big things were happening!

.   .   .

There are numerous reasons why I love what I do, but right at the top of the list is the opportunity to gain "perspective on life's values," as one of my patients, Adrian Robson, described it to me.

Adrian, a journalist, published a wonderfully written and humorous account of the "headache" that having a brain tumor can bring. Happily, his oligodendroglioma, a low-grade tumor that responds well to surgery, is not growing. He is now writing a book to chronicle his journey as a patient. Even with the ongoing uncertainty caused by his tumor, he has been able to discover blessings that had gone uncounted. As he wrote in his published piece, he was surprisingly grateful to reach a level of enlightenment that could have come only in facing his own mortality. In this manner, he wrote, he had reached a "different perspective on life's values." That ability to see the light, to recognize what matters, can be a gift. Perspective on life's values is what my patients give me every day.

I will never forget walking into an exam room with devastating news for my patient Sharon, a young mother in her early twenties who had traveled to Baltimore from out of state with her husband, a soldier just returned from an overseas tour of duty. When the couple arrived at the clinic, we first talked about their two children—a toddler and a baby—and the joys and challenges of parenting. Sharon was bright-eyed, thoughtful, and stoic when I described the surgery and the follow-up treatment for what I suspected was a high-grade, malignant tumor. We were able to reach her primary care doctor back home, put him on the speaker phone, and coordinate a plan of action for when she returned.

Everything went perfectly in the OR from a technical standpoint. But when I removed the tumor and sent it for an interoperative test, it looked as dangerous as I had anticipated. A senior pathologist came to the OR to confirm that the initial flash-freeze read showed it to be a high-grade, malignant tumor. The final biopsy in turn revealed it to be one of the faster-growing, higher-grade GBM tumors.

In my post-op meeting with Sharon and her husband, I first commented on her courage. "And, by the way, as you sit here today, you look great. What's your secret?"

With a nervous smile, she said, "Brain surgery?"

I then had to tell them that my worst fears had been confirmed about the nature of the tumor and describe the best- and worst-case scenarios for life expectancy. Of course, we had treatment options and would be vigilant in applying them. Sometimes in such meetings with patients, I explain that numbers mean little and that it's not helpful to put a finite limit on time left. But Sharon and her husband insisted on knowing the general expectations so that they could plan. I told them that we would try to buy more time and stave off an immediate progression; another year would be a blessing, but we would try for two more years.

At that moment, they realized with sudden certainty that she was really going to die. Sharon then did something that I will remember for the rest of my life. She turned to her husband, put her hand on his knee, and as both of them gave in to tears, she looked into his eyes, saying softly but powerfully, "I love you." With those three words, she said everything—that she knew he would be left with two little children to raise without their mother, that he would live the rest of his life without his soul mate and partner. She was not thinking of herself at that moment—only of her loved ones.

Six months later, the couple returned. The tumor had progressed, and Sharon was in a wheelchair, no longer able to walk well. We spoke about practical concerns, made the necessary phone calls from the office to obtain an extended leave from military duty for her husband, and contacted local agencies to arrange for home health care and child care.

As my two physician's assistants, Raven and Jill, and I said good-bye to Sharon and her husband, knowing that this was probably the last time we would see her, we had to help each other keep it together.

"Whatever you need, call us," I reminded them. "You have my number, anytime."

What else could I say? I didn't need to tell her to be strong—she was the teacher of that lesson.

Watching Sharon's husband bear the weight of his impending loss, still maintaining his military bearing as he pushed her wheelchair down the hall, I thought of the recurring image in my life of the light shining in the distance at the end of a dark tunnel or hallway or a high climb.

In the days and weeks to follow, I would be thinking of Sharon, reminding myself of the privilege I have of witnessing the journeys of patients, looking into their pasts, getting to know the members of their family, imagining what it was like when their kids were born and what it will be like when their loved one wakes in the bed or stirs at their bedside and sees them take their last breath. This is the gift—to feel with them, even in their pain, and to remember them always.

FOURTEEN

Finding the Steel in Your Soul

As 2010 got under way, the week ending January 17 hit with brute force, illustrating my long-standing belief that there are times when we simply can't fight nature and have to accept our human limitations. But the events of this week also reminded me of the important role that patients can play in their own healing, as well as the powerful contribution they can make to the effort to understand brain cancer. To be sure, we were enjoying a break between the monster blizzards that were bearing down on most parts of the country that January. But if any of us in emergency services thought that the few days of better weather were going to allow us to catch our breath, we were mistaken.

On Thursday afternoon, after two scheduled brain tumor surgeries, I had arranged for the evening off so that Anna and I could drive to Washington, D.C., to attend a special event honoring President Barack Obama. I had planned my time to the last minute so that I could complete the most pressing work of the day and then, at the scheduled moment, jump out of my scrubs, throw on a tux, and sprint out to the parking lot where Anna—dressed in a gown for this festive occasion—would be waiting in the car. As long as the weather held up, we would arrive at the capital with time to spare.

The day had gone like clockwork. My second patient, an older, wonderfully wise gentleman who had a tumor that we deemed more dangerous than the one that killed Senator Edward Kennedy, cemented the day in my memory by saying an extraordinary thing to me before surgery. Just before the anesthesia took effect, he called me over and said in a low voice, "I want to tell you something. I want you to dig deep, and you will find the steel in your soul." There was something mystical about the way he said it, something romantic about how he connected the brain to the soul. With every reason to be scared, not knowing whether he would wake up, he had to put his trust and his life into someone else's hands. He wanted me to search myself, my brain, to find the steel, to dig into the parts that we all have, that make us what we are, who we are, that allow us to battle the odds. He wanted me not to falter in this very tough case. He was giving me a pep talk!

His case was indeed challenging, but as I often tell people who ask me to describe my toughest case, every case is the toughest one I've ever handled at the moment I'm in the OR. The familiar joke applies: it may not be rocket science, but it is brain surgery. No matter how simple or straightforward the case, I am aware that I hold a human life in my hands and that the outcome is never one hundred percent certain.

Earlier in the week, another patient had compared my job as a brain surgeon to his line of work defusing improvised explosive devices and training Special Forces units to locate homemade bombs, grenades, and land mines in seconds without losing their cool. When he woke up from his surgery, with no deficits and rid of a nasty tumor that turned out not to be cancerous, he pointed out, "You can do everything perfectly, perform in record time, make no errors, and still have it blow up in your face." He added, "We have to be a little crazy to do it, you know? We must like the adrenaline rush or something!"

While we brain surgeons have other reasons for what we do (like preventing loss of life and injury), perhaps we too get an adrenaline rush, in our case from preventing another kind of bomb from exploding in the OR.

On that Thursday, my first patient had taken longer to wake up than I was comfortable with but then had roused and even made a joke, telling me after the removal of a huge 10-centimeter tumor, "I feel light-headed." But the gentleman who had asked me to find the steel in my soul appeared not to be waking up. Finally, he opened his eyes. But before I could exhale in relief, we realized that he had awakened unable to speak or move his right side, and we were in a state of emergency. With my heart plummeting, we determined that he had suffered a serious seizure and, according to a scan, a small blood clot in his brain was the possible culprit. After rushing back to the OR to address the clot, we were relieved that he woke up this second time and was able to speak and move his right side. In fact, the following morning, he was on his way to walking and talking as he had before the surgery. But in the meantime, we had no sooner taken him out of the OR than I was referred an emergency case that had to be handled that evening.

In the midst of this madness, Anna called from the parking lot to see how much longer I was going to be, and, of course, I was nowhere near ready. I was deeply remorseful and apologized to her. When my second surgery of the day had hit a crisis point, I had lost track of the day and hadn't thought to call her and say that our date night to the capital wasn't going to work out. Now she had driven an hour in messy weather, and I was going to be a no-show.

My devotion to my patients was great for them, but no matter how philosophical Anna and I tried to be about the situation, it was no fun for Anna. Too often, she paid the price of my triumphs in the OR. I encouraged her to go to the dinner without me, knowing it would be a memorable experience, but Anna decided to wait for another such occasion. So ended our excitement about having a date on a weeknight.

Working through into the early hours of the morning, I hoped that we had paid our dues with the day's earlier difficult cases and that the next case would be more straightforward. Not so. Our new patient was a young family man, a top-level executive at a major software company, who had suddenly been stricken by a massive tumor that had a will of its own when we went into surgery. Behaving like an alien creature, the tumor refused to come out, causing blood to spurt and flow all over the operating table, while my senior resident, Dr. Shaan Raza, and I bobbed and weaved to try to avoid the hits that kept on coming. When my patient stabilized, he did remarkably well, postoperatively and later on. Considering the perils he had survived, this was a miracle by any measure.

The following morning, a Saturday, after doing rounds a little early, I was once again preparing to head home, having set time aside that afternoon to work on a review of *Schmidek and Sweet's Operative Neurosurgical Techniques,* when I was alerted that a helicopter was on its way carrying a patient in critical condition from a massive hemorrhage in the brain.

In seconds, one of my fourth-year residents and I were flying down the hallway of the Johns Hopkins Bayview Medical Center with two other members of the Q Team following close behind. Just ahead of us, paramedics stormed out the hospital's exit doors into the freezing January morning to greet the arriving helicopter and transfer my patient to a gurney.

Waiting just inside, I studied the images of the CT scan that were registering on my laptop computer, mentally mapping a surgical plan for the patient, a fifty-two-year-old, developmentally disabled man who had suffered a mild head injury. The large blood clot that had resulted was causing his brain to swell up like a balloon, and it threatened to push out his brain stem, which would kill him at once.

We met the gurney as the paramedics brought the unconscious, already-intubated patient inside the hospital. My team and I took over, hurrying down the hallway and into the OR, with hospital staff stationed to hold back all other traffic. Once the patient was prepped for surgery, we needed to move full speed ahead—first to remove a large bone flap, then to suction the blood clot, evacuate fluids, weld shut the no-longer-clotted vessel, and secure other vessels in the vicinity, all the while making sure that the rest of his body's functions kept working. Finishing up, literally in the nick of time, I heard almost an audible exhalation from everyone in the OR when we saw that we were in the clear. Happily, my patient was soon awake, eyes wide open!

I had to agree with my bomb-defusing patient that sometimes you do have to be a little crazy to be in our lines of work. There is, however, a method to the madness. In fact, so as not to become really crazy, I had recently come up with some creative ways to use humor and competition to keep up people's spirits on more challenging days. One of my favorites was an ongoing arm-wrestling contest among the ranks of the Q Team, as contender after contender came forward to try to defeat me.

The battle for the championship started one day when one of the very fit young residents suggested that I might be past my prime.

"Are you sure you want a piece of me?" I warned him, as I prepared for the match. "I may be forty-two years old, but under these scrubs, I'm rippling with muscles of steel!"

My resident told me that perhaps what I had under my scrubs was "not fully mature stem cells—waiting to be developed." But I had a couple of Kaliman tricks up my sleeve. I knew that the secret is to lean your body into the job. Bingo! I won, much to everyone's surprise, including mine.

There followed a series of challenges by some of the buff young bucks on staff, with the events drawing large audiences of surgical staff, students, lab personnel, and nurses. As I faced increasingly muscle-bound challengers—and after Anna pointedly asked what would happen if I broke my arm or my hand—I soon had to resort to mental gymnastics to keep from getting crushed.

I was able to employ one of my more effective techniques at a match in the cafeteria lobby with a very muscular medical student. Acting completely confident, right before we started, I whispered so only he could hear, "Let me win!" Fortunately, he acquiesced. But I wasn't so sure other opponents would be as gracious, so I resorted to the stalling method, telling anyone who challenged me, "You aren't in good enough shape yet," and then adding, "Let me know when you're ready."

·   ·   ·

Nothing gives me a greater sense of urgency about the need for advances in our research than seeing young patients, who should have their whole lives in front of them, suddenly have their time cut short. Aaron Watson was one such patient.

Aaron and his sister, Ava, were raised by their father, Paul Watson, and all three became close members of my extended family. Aaron was the classic golden boy—a young African-American Adonis and music prodigy, whose trumpet playing at age twelve had brought him to the attention of Wynton Marsalis. During his first year of college, Aaron's prowess on the football field had earned him a statewide Unsung Hero award for his efforts with his team. He was, above all, a sunny, hopeful human being, with a future full of possibilities.

Then, when Aaron was eighteen years old, he experienced a flare-up of health issues that appeared to be related to football injuries. In July 2005, the month I arrived at Hopkins, Aaron saw a pediatric surgeon for bilateral shoulder instability and underwent surgery on the right side. Everything returned to normal, but in early November, he reported having headaches and double vision. As he had a history of migraines going back to the age of twelve or so, no one saw cause for alarm. But a few months later, he developed pain in his left shoulder that radiated through his left side, along with severe, constant headaches that woke him up at night. By the next summer, the headaches didn't feel like migraines, and he not only was losing his appetite but was having episodes of vomiting. In November 2006, he was found to have lost thirty pounds in five months, and his double vision returned. A facial X-ray at an emergency room at another hospital came back normal, and he was given pain medication. But when the medicine didn't alleviate his double vision, he went to a pediatrician—even though he was nineteen years old—who began to connect the dots when he reviewed Aaron's symptoms.

On November 15, 2006, an MRI revealed a large tumor behind his eye. We met for the first time two days later, at which time I determined that Aaron's brain was in danger of herniating and rushed him to the OR. Not willing to speculate about what I was seeing in the films, I nonetheless let him and his father and sister know that because of the tumor's location, the surgery would be dangerous and complicated. Aaron went in ready to fight. Though the tumor was heavily infiltrated in his brain, we tried to remove as much of it as we could without leaving him with deficits; on that score, I was confident that he would feel much better when he woke up.

Sure enough, Aaron came out of the OR and woke up like a champion, enjoying an immediate reduction of his headaches. But when I viewed the tumor tissue under the microscope and saw a GBM, I knew that this surgery had only been the first round.

During the post-op visit, Aaron, his sister, and his father had different reactions to the news about the type of tumor and the subsequent battle plan, which called for chemo and radiation. Aaron was mostly in denial, asking, "But I feel so much better. Why?" Ava had raised her little brother, acting almost as a surrogate mother, and was devastated, probably aware of the hard, hard road that lay ahead. And Paul was stoic, suggesting that though he also knew what was coming, he had to keep his emotions together and conserve his energy.

If we were lucky, we would get six good months for Aaron. Instead, we got three months, during which he felt somewhat better, followed by the discovery that the tumor was not only still growing but a cyst had developed in his brain. During this time, Paul and Ava had become distraught about the radical changes in Aaron's personality caused by the pressure in his frontal lobe. The sweet, sunny, mellow person disappeared, and Aaron became aggressive, defiant, and distant, often not showing up or caring about follow-up appointments and partying to excess, either as a way to avoid pain or because of lowered inhibitions. In October 2007, I took Aaron back to the OR to deal with the cyst and to find out what the tumor was doing inside his brain.

Paul's eyes reflected pure agony when he wheeled his son into the OR for the second surgery, as if he didn't want to let go. But once again, the life force in Aaron was so strong that he woke up and felt like his old self again, at least for the next month or so. Then, bit by bit, the slide toward the end began.

Paul had been riding a roller coaster of his own throughout this time. After having had success as a financial investment analyst, he made the decision, right when he was at the top of his game and his children had grown up and moved out of the house, to devote all his energies to caring for Aaron. Paul moved his son back in with him and stayed by his side until his last dark days, depleting his savings in the process. When Paul buried his son in March 2008, he was effectively homeless.

Paul wrote me after Aaron passed away: "I don't really know how to begin so I'll just start. As you can imagine, this has been one of the roughest times in my life. I really do miss my son. In his last week on this earth with us, I would lie beside him and talk. Sometimes not knowing what to say other than I love you and I will see you again. It was an honor and a gift from God to be his father."

As Paul and Ava were grieving, I was frankly angry. We weren't doing enough in our field to move at the pace necessary to save lives. When I saw Paul, after he made an appointment to see me that summer, the first thing I said was, "Your son didn't have to die."

A wise, deeply intelligent, and stylishly dressed African-American man who looked to be younger than his middle age, Paul was deep into his own struggle to make sense of a world turned upside down. But he had made a promise to Aaron that his death would not be in vain. Paul told me, "In Aaron's last days with us, I would say that I didn't understand why this was happening to him. The only rationale I could give was that through his death, others would live."

A short time after we spoke, Paul Watson came to see me again to present his plan to keep his promise to his son. He and Ava had drawn up the papers to create the Brain Cancer Research for a Cure Foundation. The moment that word had gotten out about the idea, he told me, his phone had begun to ring with offers of help. He was back at work too, doing better financially. "I feel Aaron looking over this effort and blessing it in surprising ways every day."

At the top of the flyer for the foundation's dedication ceremony, he and Ava had written, "Remembering a life taken by brain cancer by creating hope for those living with it." In the foundation's mission statement, the Watsons laid out their hope to "create a better quality of life for brain cancer patients by increasing public awareness and making quantum leaps in scientific research" and "to one day be able to give a brain cancer patient the news that they have a condition that will not control them but can be controlled." I was moved by their determination to turn Aaron's death into a force for good, no more so than the members of my team were when Paul and Ava came to the Friday night meeting to tell their story and outline their plans.

.   .   .

Every patient's story, whether tragic or triumphant, is different. And yet, the more we learn, the more we know that brain tumors, whether benign or malignant, low or high grade, are equal-opportunity offenders and know no boundaries—striking at victims of all ages, cultural and socioeconomic backgrounds, and nationalities. In our work at the lab, the greater the number and diversity of the patients and their families who participate, whether by attending our Friday meetings, speaking in public arenas, or donating tissue and brain fluid samples, the more empowered we all are.

My patient and dear friend Don Rottman is a testament to the power of patient involvement in battling brain cancer. Don has also said that in spite of the devastation of his diagnosis, he wouldn't give away the lessons about himself, love, and life that his journey has taught him. During our four years of getting to know one another, I have often thought of how much alike we are in temperament and energy. An outdoorsman, fisherman, and student of literature and philosophy, Don and I are both in our early forties, both driven—although in different fields. Baltimore born and bred, from a blue-collar background, Don wanted to go to college, but without family resources, he ended up in the military. In the army, he rose in the ranks, at the same time cobbling together an education part-time and working his way through many libraries. When he left the military, which had taken him to countries like Panama and Costa Rica, he spoke excellent Spanish and went to work for an international organization training teams in developing and sometimes war-torn countries.

When I first saw Don in June 2007, he was divorced and the father of a fourteen-year-old daughter and a self-avowed workaholic. Very successful in his career, Don had gotten the first inkling that something wasn't right when he was out of town giving a presentation at a conference. As he told me, "I kept hitching my words."

"Hitching?"

"I'd open my mouth and the words wouldn't come out. I wondered if something was wrong but hoped nobody else would notice. I thought I was hiding it very well." However, when he went to dinner with friends, he had another incident of being unable to speak. Again, he could hear the words in his head, taste the words in his mouth, but nothing came out. He recovered and moved on while his companions politely ignored his problem. "When I got my faculties back," Don continued, "I said that I was going to go to the gym to work out." When a couple of his colleagues went to meet him at the gym and he didn't show up, one of the women in the group, having sensed a problem earlier, became concerned, announcing, "Don Rottman is never late." In the meantime, neighbors in hotel rooms adjacent to Don's heard strange noises and summoned hotel security when he didn't answer their knock on the door. The security personnel found Don in his gym clothes, convulsing on the floor, in full seizure, about which he later remembered nothing.

Don woke up a day and a half later in a nearby small regional hospital, after having five seizures. The emergency room physicians weren't specialists but could see from his MRI that he had a tumor and advised him to see a neurosurgeon as soon as possible.

Back in Baltimore a few days later, Don's regular doctor became very concerned when he saw the MRI and referred him to Dr. Cliff Solomon in Annapolis, a highly respected, prominent surgeon and a good friend of mine. After looking at the films, Dr. Solomon told Don, "There are few people in the world who could even touch you. . . . You're very lucky because one of the few brain surgeons who could do this is in our backyard at Hopkins."

And this is where Don's and my journeys intertwined. From the beginning, he was both determined to overcome the odds and eager to be part of the bigger war. At first, I hoped that the tumor would prove to be benign. But before undertaking the necessary surgery, we required several MRIs over a couple of months to give us a map of where the speech and motor functions resided in his brain. Once the operation was scheduled, with Dr. Solomon assisting, I asked Don for a favor.

The producers of PBS's *NOVA* series were interested in doing a feature about my work as a surgeon/scientist and particularly wanted to include footage of an awake craniotomy, which is the procedure I would be doing on Don. When I asked if he would consider having his surgery filmed, he could easily have declined or taken a few days to mull over his decision, given the level of fear that any patient has before surgery, let alone how he might feel about having his brain shown to the world. Instead, Don immediately said, "Absolutely, I'm in." From the beginning, he understood that the decision to embrace his journey wasn't only for himself but for others, many of whom are as much in the dark as he had once been about what goes on inside their heads. Don proved to be the star of the show. In the operating room, we stimulated his brain, employing a map showing us the locations that controlled his mouth movement, hand movement, and speech functions. With him awake and able to speak, we could establish where he produced words and where he perceived images and see which parts of his brain were activated by certain questions. With Don as our navigator, I felt confident we could manage this difficult surgery and bring him out without any deficits.

At one point during the surgery, I thanked Don again for agreeing to donate some of his tissue and brain fluids to our lab for research.

Not missing a beat, Don replied in all sincerity, "Take as much as you need," causing the entire film crew to crack up.

Don's only complaints were about the discomfort of being bolted to the table for that many hours and the need to go without coffee. Finally, we finished, but as he began drumming his fingers waiting to be unbolted, he suddenly found that he couldn't move them anymore, and shortly thereafter he couldn't move his arm—all of this developing in front of our eyes so quickly that we couldn't prevent the setback. We rushed him to the neurosurgery intensive care unit to have a neurology team assess what had happened. The verdict was that the impairment of his arm was likely temporary and that he would recover much of its function once his brain adjusted and rewired itself.

A little later, during a coffee break, I checked in to see how he was.

"Fine," Don insisted. "But I really need some coffee!"

"Here," I said, "have mine. It's the least I can offer you."

The biopsy that should have taken no more than five days confounded the pathology lab and took three weeks instead. When I finally received the results, I was miserable to see that we were dealing with an anaplastic astrocytoma—a cancer that is a grade below a glioblastoma and not the news Don or I wanted to hear. The tumor was star shaped, with tentacles that bridged different parts of the brain, and it was composed of many types of cells, which explained why it had been so difficult to analyze. We went after it aggressively, and Don was Muhammad Ali to my Dr. Ferdie Pacheco. Even throughout combined radiation and chemo treatments, Don never missed a day of work. The toughest discussion we had was when we met in my office, along with his sister, Amy, to evaluate his state after six months of treatment—almost a year after detecting the tumor. We were still dealing with an unknown, but so far there was no regrowth of his tumor. Don wanted to get a measure of his life expectancy.

"You know, numbers don't tell us everything," I said. "Everybody is different, and we have no idea how you'll fare in the big picture." When Don and Amy indicated that they would still like to get a sense of the odds, I told them that 50 percent of patients survive between two to five years, but I quickly added, "The reality is that you are not a number. You are a human being."

Amy broke down sobbing. Don was emotional too but appeared to be more in shock than anything else. For as long as he was healthy and things were looking as positive as they were, I suggested that we focus on that. I reminded Don of what he and other patients had taught me—to approach life not by preparing to die but by choosing how to live the rest of your life. Don Rottman soon set down a path to exemplify that attitude.

Before long, he became an impassioned, tireless spokesperson for the work of the lab, deploying his considerable writing and speaking skills to tell people what he had learned when his disease forced him to be vulnerable—not his strong suit before being T-boned by brain cancer, a metaphor that I have used often since he introduced it. He also wrote eloquently about the impact of his diagnosis on his relationship with his teenage daughter, the light of his life: "Tori's first question to me after I discussed my disease with her was, 'How long did they tell you that you had to live, Dad?' And my response was probably the most inappropriate and the most wrong answer that I could have given her; I simply burst into tears, not because of my fear or my own sadness for myself but what I felt I was doing to her. She took my response better than any adult could have. She came over to me and hugged me and told me she would be all right."

Anna and I have never tried to separate our social networks from our extended Hopkins family, and she has become as fond of Don as I am. A kindred spirit and not one to back down from a challenge, he would likely have become a friend no matter how I met him. Three years after his diagnosis, Don Rottman hasn't given up the fight. With all his work in the trenches, he could probably earn a medical degree. He has also been an extraordinary resource for newly diagnosed patients and has recruited many of them to get involved with the lab, either through fund-raising or helping to raise public awareness about brain tumors.

Don, Paul Watson and his daughter, Ava, along with many of my patients and their loved ones who contribute to our lab and its work, make me feel like I'm not doing enough. When I see how far the lab has come in a relatively short amount of time, it's proof that we can accomplish so much more if we set our sights higher and find the steel in our souls to pursue them. One of my pet "spare-time" projects is to use the fantastic National Institutes of Health databases, which cost nothing to access yet get little use, to study morbidity rates in different populations. We need to start studying families in which cancer occurs across generations and look for possible genetic links or environmental causes. What allows one patient to defy the odds and leaves another patient without the resources to avoid or triumph over a disease?

In my opinion, though we have yet to prove this notion scientifically, patients who participate actively in finding a cure for brain cancer seem to be more hopeful and have better all-around health. Similarly, scientists and physicians who are hopeful are motivated to go the distance in their search for answers.

On this point, I have great news to report about the character of the current and next generation of students that I teach—whether in the lecture hall, during clinic hours, in the OR, in the laboratory, or in the many settings that I've been fortunate to visit as a professor. Teaching is coming full circle for me. For one thing, the dream of becoming a teacher was my focus during my studies in Mexico, a dream that I wasn't able to attain. For another, teaching allows me to champion the next generation of physicians and scientists in the same tradition of the many mentors who contributed to my development—some who barely knew me but opened doors for me that wouldn't have budged otherwise.

Not long after I arrived at Hopkins, Dr. Joe L. Martinez invited me to teach a weeklong course in human brain anatomy at the Summer Program in Neuroscience, Ethics, and Survival (SPINES) at the Marine Biological Laboratory in Woods Hole, Massachusetts—where he is the director.

What do you say when your mentor, one of the great minds now leading the way in the study of the neurobiology of learning and memory, presents you with such an honor? Well, if you're me, it's, "When do I start? Let's rock 'n' roll!"

In addition to wanting to work with Joe, I wasn't about to turn down the chance to include a glorious family vacation in Woods Hole, right on the ocean, across from Nantucket and Martha's Vineyard—a place that would become a home away from home for one week every summer at the historic Marine Biological Lab, built in the 1800s.

When discussing the curriculum for the course, I told Professor Martinez that I was eager to take an unconventional approach and make the week a memorable experience for the many science undergraduates who attended the program. In his typically terse fashion, Joe listened to my proposal without reacting until I explained, in short, that I wanted to go the extra effort to bring in cadavers and human brains.

Joe erupted with laughter. "You've come a long way!" he said, and then reminded me how squeamish I had been at Stanford's Día de los Muertos the first time I dissected a body. Well, I was living proof of the power of education.

As I had hoped, my students at Woods Hole were enthralled by our use of cadavers and the experience of handling brains, dissecting them, and looking at tissue under the microscope. And for those who were hesitant, in 2009 I hired a very helpful chief lab assistant who told them that if she could overcome trepidation about this work, anyone could. Who was this persuasive assistant? Ten-year-old Gabriella Quiñones, who, I might add, stole the show.

The week in Woods Hole is also as close to a honeymoon as Anna and I may have for a while—even with our kids along and the company of the students and the rest of the faculty of SPINES. Time slows down, and for once, I am not in a hurry. Anna and I manage to get in some romantic walks along the water and, with the help of qualified babysitters, are able to fit in dinner and a glass of wine too. As I gaze into Anna's green eyes and tell her of my latest brainstorm, perhaps it's just the wine and the food, but Anna always seems to say that I'm onto something!

.   .   .

Of course, I have my share of discouraging days, when I can't easily find the steel in my soul. But invariably I come back to the fact that I have survived a few close calls and am alive to tell the tale and to do my work, and this thought provides incentive for me to stay on my path.

In recent years, I have come to realize that there is something, in addition to a desire to find the cure for brain cancer, that drives me— something even bigger: the quest to understand through this work how we can use our abilities to do a better job at being good to each other, as my father admonished me years earlier. Maybe the steps for each of us to improve the world for humanity and to learn to treat each other with more care are not so different from those we must take to arrest brain cancer. Certainly, we need to raise awareness about the social diseases that separate and divide us, that fuel hatred and stigmatize those who are different and underrepresented. Certainly, equal access to quality care is a value we can all agree on, even if we can't agree on the means to get there. Certainly, we all thrive when we don't limit opportunities for anyone willing to go after his or her dreams.

These thoughts lead me to wonder, in spiritual terms, how our understanding of the brain can help us better understand the grand order of the universe—and the moral lessons that God may be trying to teach us. For me, it's impossible not to believe in God—or whatever name one chooses—after studying the miracle that is the brain. It's impossible not to feel that a higher force guides me every day, keeping me humble and grounded in the belief that what we do here on earth has purpose. My faith is also a reminder that there are matters of life and death that I don't control, just as it helps me accept that the terra firma I have sought throughout my life is not a real place at all.

Granted, if we ever stopped crossing borders and hopping fences in our search for more solid ground—personally, scientifically, and spiritually—the human race would cease to exist. But unraveling the mysteries of the journey requires us to continue in our migration through life, in pursuit of the light of answers that may sometimes be beyond our reach.

One mystery I may never answer is how we manage to forge ahead when all seems dark. What spark fired up the fighter in me during those moments when death was pressing in? And what allows my patients to move forward and find joy despite the grimmest prognoses? I return to Ken Zabel's unswerving faith that each of us is part of a plan.

After the Zabels first spoke at our lab meeting, I saw Ken again for a third and final surgery—"our last round," as he put it. Ken was not worried. "God has a plan," he continued to tell me.

On the morning of Ken's third surgery, Raven Morris went to meet him and Betty in pre-op to review Ken's recognition of the same list of words and images that we had used during his first operation about a year earlier. Halfway through the test, Raven realized that Ken couldn't identify common images and was having trouble reading some of the simple words. Not wanting to show him her concern, she stepped into the hall and called me, saying, "He missed eighty-five percent of the time. What do you want to do?"

I ran a partial review myself. Ken's speech was going fast. He was struggling to identify an "owl," calling it a "bird." Sometimes he said, "Oh, I know, it's a . . . " and then was stumped by a picture of an umbrella or a table.

"Ken," I told him. "We're going to put you to sleep for this surgery, if you don't mind. I wouldn't be doing the best job for you if I asked you to stay awake." He agreed and pulled through beautifully. We were able to take a lot of pressure off his brain, and days later, his speech was improving.

For a month following surgery, he returned to work and gave himself speech therapy on the job, using a blackboard and handmade flash cards.

But almost overnight his language and coordination started to go. Betty told him that she would oversee the office and he needed to rest. When she called to tell me about the change, I decided to try to find a way to visit him before too much more time passed. I'm not able to make many house calls, but with Ken no longer able to travel from Florida to Baltimore, I felt a need to visit him. Part of my decision to go had to do with our special connection and everything I had drawn from his positive attitude—his proud, courageous focus on battling the dragon; the sight of him brokering deals on his laptop in the ICU six hours after surgery; and the audacious way in which he had managed to become my patient in the first place. Another reason I was intent on visiting Ken was to reconnect to my earliest motivation to become a doctor, passed down in my heritage. This was what my Nana Maria used to do, after all, in making house calls. Something told me to go—another important rite of passage was at hand.

The truth was that at the point at which Betty called about Ken's deterioration, I was at a critical place in my life and career. As the underdog, a role I intentionally play so that I can remain humble and work harder every day, I could feel my spirits sagging after a series of patients had died from brain cancer. Though self-doubt remains a regular force in pumping myself up to intensify the fight, at that moment I was low enough even to question whether I should continue. Perhaps seeing my hero Ken Zabel would give me a needed jolt of energy—the inspiration to keep moving forward.

After clearing my schedule, I headed down to Florida and spent the day with the Zabels. Heartbroken though I was at the prospect of losing this great, noble patient and at the thought of the grief and loss his wife and children would suffer, the day proved to be a joyous one in many ways, and I was once again struck with Ken's spiritual presence.

Still the big muscular fellow he had been before his illness, he had not allowed the cancer to take away his infectious smile and easygoing manner. At one point, he was embarrassed to say that he had to go to the bathroom but didn't want to use the bedpan.

"Well, then, let's go pee," I suggested. "You don't have to be modest. I've seen your brain naked a few times."

Laughing, he let me walk him to the toilet, and as he stood there buck naked, with me trying to hold up all two hundred pounds of him, he was unable to urinate.

"Why don't we turn on the water?" I suggested. But all this did was make me feel like I had to go! "Ken, you'd better go, because if you don't, I'm going to wet my pants!"

Soon we were all laughing and enjoying ourselves. Ken was in such fine spirits, he wanted to sit in the living room for a while. Rather than get dressed, he draped a sheet over himself like a Roman toga. Sitting there as we conversed—with me carrying on the bulk of the conversation and him chiming in occasionally with funny comments—he reminded me of a noble Roman warrior, like Caesar toward the end of his rule, vulnerable and fading. When the time came for me to depart, Ken hugged me many times. Even though I was the one leaving his house, I sensed that he was already leaving this world, walking down a tunnel and looking back over his shoulder, not quite ready to go—as if he had more to say. He gestured for me to come closer to him. He told me that I was his hero, but I had to disagree and point out to him, "You're my hero."

With nothing more to say, I started off again, and he pulled me back toward him to say something I wasn't sure I understood at first.

"You are so rich."

When I arrived back in Baltimore late at night and drove from the airport home to our neighborhood, out near a rural part of the suburbs with few streetlamps, the sky was pitch black and starless. Even so, I thought about being on the roof in Palaco and feeling that the whole starry sky was mine. Yes, I was rich!

The quiet of the world gave me comfort as I thought about the loneliness of the passage from life over the border to the next place where we can only travel on our own.

As I drove on, the stillness of the night gave me time to think about the action-packed day that lay ahead. What new patients with exciting, inspiring journeys would I meet during clinic hours? What discoveries would my students and residents share with me? What might happen tomorrow in the laboratory and in the OR that would help us slay the dragon of brain cancer? Even having the opportunity to ask the questions made me feel like the luckiest man alive.

Then again, I was reminded of what Santiago Ramón y Cajal said about luck. Borrowing from a Spanish proverb, he pointed out that luck in scientific research, as in life, doesn't come to those who want it but to those who look for it. Thomas Jefferson, founding father of my adopted homeland, may have said it even better: "I'm a great believer in luck, and I find the harder I work, the more I have of it."

Epilogue

WHEN THE SUN COMES UP

A storm brews
and lightning strikes.
the tree falls
onto grassy spikes.
the clouds roll away,
and night turns to day,
then the sun shines on the tree.
the days go by,
the tree decays,
and all life withers away.
but when all hope is lost,
tiny leaves sprout out,
and soon sproutlings sprout.

"Sproutlings," Gabriella Quiñones, age eleven

Sunday mornings are my favorite part of the week—when I can work from home and spend more time with my family. I haven't found the perfect balance yet, but I'm greatly improving! Whenever I've been in the OR late at night and feel that the war is overwhelming, when things look bleak, lo and behold, night draws to an end and it's another day. Like clockwork, the sun's coming up and I'm safe and secure at home, ready to jump out of bed and have a new adventure.

I can recall many such mornings—in Palaco as a child, in the fields of

Mendota, in Stockton at the port when I was scraping fish lard and shoveling sulfur, out on the tracks welding and refurbishing the train cars, in school, and during my training, when my nights and mornings blurred into each other. I vividly remember the long night's drive the first time I decided to return to Mexico for a visit—how, when the world seemed its darkest as I came down the freeway, my spirits lifted the moment I turned east to see the sunrise over the valley—with the light illuminating spots here and there before the sun had fully risen.

But the best mornings are when Anna and the kids and I get up and have a full day of fun ahead. What excitement awaits, what lessons are to be learned? At home with Family Q, Sunday breakfast is a buffet of choices and an informal celebration that may involve a few courses. Why not? We might follow breakfast with a family run outside or, when the kids are competing in a swim meet, we load up in the midnight blue SUV and go off together to the event. Afterward, when there is time, a Sunday afternoon trip to the mall is a good opportunity to buy clothes or school supplies and presents for friends. And no trip to the mall is complete without stopping for ice cream before heading home. After having dinner together, the conclusion to any perfect Sunday is having the kids pick a movie we can watch on TV as a family. The power of stories told on film never ceases to delight me.

Anna and I marvel at our children—how different they are from one another and what interesting individuals they are: Gabbie at eleven; David, at nine; and Olivia, at five. And the most recent arrivals to the family, Leo and Luna, are also growing into fine young cats.

Like all parents, Anna and I know how fast time flies and that our children will soon go off and hop their own fences. In the meantime, we're eager to learn everything we can from each of them. From Olivia, we are continually learning the art of readiness, knowing that we can never be sure what new activity she will decide to undertake or what fascinating observation will come out of her mouth. We also know that sometimes when she isn't saying a word, she is watching and listening with acute superpowers—not missing a beat.

One of my favorite exchanges with David came when he was only four years old, shortly after we arrived in Baltimore. That day, he and

I woke early on a beautiful Sunday morning and went for a walk to a nearby park.

Looking at him proudly, I said, "David, you are the man!"

David was quiet for a few seconds and then replied, "No, Dad, I am not the man."

I pondered this statement for a few seconds and then, thinking that I was going to tell him something he didn't know, said, "I just want you to believe in yourself."

David looked me in the eye and said, "Dad, I do believe in myself. But I know I am not the man."

At four years old, he already knew a few things about humility and self-awareness that I was still trying to learn.

A couple of birthdays later, the kids presented me with a T-shirt bearing the words, "Proud to be awesome," which I indeed wore proudly because they had given it to me. Then, the next year, they gave me a T-shirt that said, "Dad, you're the man!"

When I held it up to admire their handiwork, I told them, "I know I'm not the man, but I do believe in myself."

We all laughed at this running bit between me and David, but ultimately I do not take the statement lightly. I know that my journey would not have taken me to where I am today if I hadn't been led by countless mentors or inspired by heroes like Kaliman to believe in myself, to imagine leaping fences in a single bound and defeating challenges with gravity-defying maneuvers. At the same time, I have further to go in my ongoing struggle to be "the man"—to live up to my own expectations to be good to others, to restore people to health or ease their suffering, to probe the brain's mysteries and find new ways to heal its diseases, and to inspire others in their journeys. Thanks to the opportunities I have had, my children will not have to fight the same battles I did to find their places in the world, but they will have new and different challenges. Anna and I only hope that they will take the lessons we have learned to heart. Not too long ago, Gabbie, at age eleven, brought Anna and me a poem she had written for my patients—wanting in some way to give them hope. Her effort to reach out in this way touched us, and we assured her that the poem would lift the spirits of anyone who read it. In turn, I was struck by the fact that her images roused the migrant farmworker in me, linking my past with Gabbie's hopes for the future.

Each generation asks itself how it can survive the challenges of the day, which always seem bigger and more confounding than those faced by any previous generation. Some people even wonder if our troubles and the threats to our future will bring our journey as human beings to an untimely end. Gabbie's poem and my convictions say otherwise. My hope is that my unlikely story may light a spark in a boy or girl who currently faces bleak prospects to embrace the power of his or her imagination and special magic. Or spur on an exhausted medical resident to know that there *is* a light at the end of the tunnel—in the best meaning of the phrase! Or challenge a scientific sleuth who is about to give up to try one more experiment. Or cause any busy, overworked health care provider to stop for a moment and have a personal chat with a patient. Or, especially, to encourage any of us who allow ourselves to judge others by their ethnicity or socioeconomic background to open our eyes to all that we have in common. If telling this tale does any one of these things, then I have indeed pulled off a Kaliman maneuver!

And if such is the case, then I can forgo being "the man" and simply celebrate the journey of becoming Dr. Q.

Acknowledgments

In early 2008, a short time after I appeared on the ABC documentary series *Hopkins,* I received several phone calls from people in the publishing and film worlds. Though I was flattered by their exciting offers to turn my story into a book or movie, I had some concerns. For one thing, I assumed that writing a memoir was a journey to be reserved for my sunset years, when I would have an abundance of time for introspection and remembrance of those who had helped light my path. When these calls came in, I had just turned forty and had been at Johns Hopkins only a little over two years. Not only was the timing bad, but I was dismayed that most of the book and movie people who called envisioned projects about a medical miracle worker—starring someone like George Clooney (in his *ER* days) with an instant accent. Although such stories, told well, can be inspirational, the offers I received seemed too "Hollywood" for my less-than-conventional journey, the story of a little boy from Mexico who had been encouraged to be the architect of his own destiny.

But my misgivings vanished after I received a phone call from the person who became the driving force for *Becoming Dr. Q.* A producer who specializes in bringing true stories to life in books and films, Mary Martin is also a champion of underdogs from all backgrounds—a fellow believer in the value of going against the grain. She convinced me that together we could find the right publishing home for the story of hope and imagination that was in my heart to write. Toward that end, she helped assemble a stellar team, including the indefatigable Mel Berger, my literary agent at William Morris Endeavor. My lasting appreciation goes to you, Mel, for your devotion to this project, for your friendship, and for your careful reading of multiple drafts and endless supply of words of encouragement. And, Mary Martin, I thank you with all my heart for your passion, belief, and unrelenting determination to see the journey through. Without you, *Becoming Dr. Q* would not have become a realized written work—certainly not this one, of which I am so proud.

My profound gratitude goes to everyone at the University of California Press, Berkeley, the perfect publishing home, which has taken me back to my roots as an undergrad in the vicinity and has made me feel like family. Executive editor Naomi Schneider, *mil gracias* for honoring my story with your commitment to shining a light on the experiences of marginalized communities and promoting unconventional thinking about contemporary issues. You are this book's angel! Principal editor Dore Brown, I can't thank you enough for your meticulous work as head of production for *Becoming Dr. Q.* And I thought doing brain surgery required exacting attention to detail! Additional thanks belong to our indomitable, gifted copyeditor, Adrienne Harris. Thank you to our very talented designer, Claudia Smelser, and to publicist Alex Dahne for your wonderful work.

Though I had anticipated that writing my story wasn't going to be as simple as dictating my notes into a tape recorder, I did not realize until I began the process how difficult it would be to recall and describe myriad events of the past with accuracy and authenticity. Holy guacamole! Fortunately, I had a coauthor willing to come along for the ride—Mim Eichler Rivas. Words cannot properly express how blessed I feel to have the incredible Mim as my colleague and friend. My gratitude also goes to her lovely husband and my friend, Victor Rivas Rivers, and to their son, Eli. Mim never gave up on me and worked tirelessly to find my voice through our writing. Throughout the several years of this project, often under considerable pressure, she kept a positive attitude that was not only contagious but inspirational. She was available any time I needed her, which too often was very early in the morning, late at night when I got out of surgery or the laboratory, and on weekends. Mim's ability to bring out my childhood, adolescent, and adult memories made this journey both enjoyable and fulfilling. I not only learned more about myself during our work together but also was able to embrace *Becoming Dr. Q* as a journey of hope, love, imagination, determination, resilience, and strength. Thank you, Mim!

Many people contributed mightily to the storytelling in this book by sitting down for interviews at different stages of the writing. For their insights on my early years, thank you to everyone in my family—my mother, father, and siblings, and especially my brother Gabriel, my brother-in-law Ramón, and my cousin Fausto.

I am deeply grateful to the professors, mentors, and colleagues who offered their recollections of my days as a student and my years of medical training, whether on the phone, on tape, in person, or in passing: Drs. Joe Martinez, Esteban González Burchard, Ed Kravitz, Michael Lawton, Nick Barbaro, Michael McDermott, Wells Messersmith, Reuben Gobezie, Geoff Manley, Ed Vates, Frank Acosta, and Nader Sanai. I used to define a true friend as someone who helps you load the van on moving day. Now I know that an even truer friend is one who agrees to review your manuscript. I am grateful to my dear friend and neighbor Pam Rutherford for your insightful input. A million thanks as well to those of you who were willing to read not one but a couple of versions! And more thanks to the colleagues, mentors, and media figures who generously read the last draft and contributed blurbs to publicity materials. You're all on the payroll now!

I can scarcely find the words to express my deep thanks to all my patients for inspiring me every day. Thank you to all of you, some of whose identities I have kept private and some of whom have granted permission for your names to be used. I am honored by your trust and your generosity in sharing your stories with readers. I offer special acknowledgments to those of you, and your family members, who shared your writing and your time during interviews with me: Don Rottman, Paul Watson, Ava Dorsey, Ken and Betty Zabel, and Adrian Robson.

I am eternally thankful to the faculty and students at San Joaquin Delta College, UC Berkeley, Harvard Medical School, UCSF, and Hopkins for giving me an opportunity and for believing in me. So many people have helped me during the years (some of whom appear in the book), including Drs. Chris Ogilvy, Ken Maynard, Del Ames, Bill Silen, Al Poussaint, Grant Gauger, Sandeep Kunwar, Paul Larson, Phill Starr, Praveen V. Mummaneni, Warwick J. Peacock, Philip R. Weinstein, and David Hellmann. Special thanks belong to many nurses on the floor and in the operating room, dating back to my time at UCSF, including April Sabangan and Julie Broderson, and at Hopkins, including Allison Godsey, Brigida Walston, Sara Brooks, Lilita Douglass, Ricardo Cosme, Monique Bruton, Khywanda Coleman, Jackie Brooks, Gerald Agbayani, Cyril Bangud, Leticia Benitado, Angela Cascio, Marites David, Terry Emerson, Lugel Gaid, William Isabelle, Jamelia Maher, Elmer Medina, Kelly Menon, Kendra Meyers, Mark Nicholson, Sherry Quion, Cecilia Reyes, Timothy Smith, Raniel Tagaytayan, Anna Ty, Keith Wiley, and Stephanie Dilegge.

I owe much gratitude to a long list of individuals who are with me every day in the trenches at Hopkins—in the operating room, the clinic, and the lab—without whom I could not have carved out enough time to write this book. I also thank the other faculty members in the department of neurosurgery at Johns Hopkins University for being so patient with me and for allowing me to be who I am and to pursue my dreams. My dear colleagues and friends Drs. Henry Brem, Alessandro Olivi, Ziya Gokaslan, George Jallo, and Ben Carson have been incredible supporters and have encouraged me to pursue my dreams since I first came to Hopkins in 1998 to interview for a residency in neurosurgery.

Thank you to Drs. Judy Huang, John Laterra, Michael Lim, Jon Weingart, Rafael Tamargo, Justin McArthur, Daniele Rigamonti, Richard O'Brien, Kofi Boahene, Gary Wand, Roberto Salvatori, Edward Miller, Levi Watkins, Ali Bydon, Tim Witham, Hongjun Song, Curt Civin, Richard Bennett, Neil deGrasse Tyson, Katrina Firlik, Sanjay Gupta,

Mark Duncan, Dalal Haldeman; and to Maria Hinojosa, Kelly Carter, Carla Denly, Venus Williams, Rosa DaSilva, Jimmy Santiago Baca, Jason McElwain, Ron Peterson, James Dresher, Kim Metzger, Emily Ehehalt, Charles Reuland, Steve Hartmann, and Jorge Ramos. And the list is not complete without a thank you for my team of residents—in particular, Drs. Shaan Raza and Kaisorn Chaichana, physician assistants Raven Morris and Jill Anderson, and academic assistants Anita Krausman and Colleen Hickson.

In the laboratory, I have been surrounded by an incredible group of young investigators who keep challenging the boundaries of neuroscience and in the process challenge my knowledge and abilities to lead by example. They have kept me grounded in my pursuit of cures for brain cancer. I could not have done it without all my collaborators, postdocs, graduate students, fellows, medical students, and undergraduate students: Pragathi Achanta, David Chesler, Tomas Garzon, Nes Mathioudakis, Ahmed Mohyeldin, Candice Shaifer, Liron Noiman, William Ruff, Linda Chen, Tom Kosztowski, Eric Momin, Kat Sperle, Kristy Yuan, Hasan Zaidi, Sara Abbadi, Sagar Shah, Chris Smith, Hadie Adams, Alex Liu, Brian Liu, Chris Mancuso, Nate Tippens, Guillermo Vela, Debraj Mukherjee, David Chang, Andre Levchenko, Deepak Atri, Lyonell Kone, Sooji Lee, Jose Manuel Garcia-Verdugo, Steven Goldman, Oscar Gonzalez-Perez, Samson Jarso, Andre Levchenko, Honjun Song, John Laterra, Andrew Feinberg, Jef Boeke—thank you all! In particular, I want to thank a superb Hopkins medical student, Courtney Pendleton, a gifted writer who took the time to read this book and give me valuable insight. I also thank Hugo Guerrero-Cazares, who has been an unsung hero in my laboratory, supporting the effort to build the best team possible in the fight against brain cancer.

Outside my work realm, I owe thanks to the print and broadcast journalists who have championed my story over the years and addressed the issue of undocumented migrant workers with thought and respect. With more like you, I hope we can have a serious, productive conversation about immigration reform, which I believe will strengthen all sectors of our nation's economy and society. I am also grateful to media outlets like National Public Radio and the *New York Times* and programs like PBS's

NOVA and the *Hopkins* documentary series for helping to raise awareness about the high stakes in the battle against brain cancer.

Finally, I remove my hat and make a sweeping bow to my three children, Gabriella, David, and Olivia, for your contribution to the book. I share the sentiments of journalist Anna Quindlen, who wrote in an article on parenting that she had "wound up with the three people I like best in the world, who have done more than anyone to excavate my essential humanity." How can I thank my wife? Anna, you are the best in-house editor, fellow traveler, life partner, friend, mother, and role model I could have imagined in the journey of writing this book. Thank you for everything. I love you.

Text: 10/14 Palatino
Display: Univers Condensed Light 47 and Bauer Bodoni
Compositor: BookMatters, Berkeley
Printer and binder: Sheridan Books, Inc.